# Tolerance and Modern Liberalism

# Tolerance and Modern Liberalism

## *From Paradox to Aretaic Moral Ideal*

### René González de la Vega

LEXINGTON BOOKS
Lanham • Boulder • New York • London

Published by Lexington Books
An imprint of The Rowman & Littlefield Publishing Group, Inc.
4501 Forbes Boulevard, Suite 200, Lanham, Maryland 20706
www.rowman.com

Unit A, Whitacre Mews, 26-34 Stannary Street, London SE11 4AB

British Library Cataloguing in Publication Information Available

**Library of Congress Cataloging-in-Publication Data**

Names: González de la Vega, René, author.
Title: Tolerance and modern liberalism : from paradox to aretaic moral ideal / René González de la
    Vega.
Description: Lanham : Lexington Books, 2016. | Includes bibliographical references and index.
Identifiers: LCCN 2016032881 | ISBN 9781498529068 (cloth : alk. paper) | ISBN 9781498529075
    (electronic)
Subjects: LCSH: Toleration. | Liberalism. | Ethics.
Classification: LCC BJ1431 .G66 2016 | DDC 172--dc23
LC record available at https://lccn.loc.gov/2016032881

Printed in the United States of America

To Mila and Juan
For making my reality a dream

# Contents

*Contents*

# Acknowledgments

I have generously benefitted from many colleagues, professors and friends for along many years in the realization of this book. Suffice to mention their names with the ample hope that they will recognize their thoughts in some of the arguments and critiques that they will find all along these pages.

These persons are Edgar Aguilera, Macario Alemany, Amalia Amaya, Juan Federico Arriola, Manuel Atienza, Melike Akkaraca, Myriam Bayet, José Luis Caballero, Rafael Caballero, Enrique Cáceres, Jorge Cerdio, Kira Ciofalo, Mircea Cojanu, Valérie Couillard, Mariana Cortina, Javier Couso, Juan Antonio Cruz Parcero, Wojciech Cyrul, Edgar Elías, Frank Fleerackers, Imer B. Flores, Marie-Claire Foblets, Raymundo Gama, Leopoldo Gama, John Gardener, Mauricio García Villegas, Leonardo García Jaramillo, Ernesto Garzón Valdés, Raf Geenens, Philippe Gérard, Mónica González Contró, Daniel González Lagier, Tim Heysse, Carla Huerta, Marc van Hoecke, Jesús Ibarra, Marianne Kennis, Guillermo Lariguet, Pablo Larrañaga, Isabel Lifante, Kathleen Monsieur, Martonio Mont'Alverne, Félix Morales, Francois Ost, Juliane Ottmann, Alberto Puppo, Miguel Rábago, Victoria Roca, Ángeles Rodenas, Victor Rojas, Pedro Salazar, Andrea Slemian, Germán Sucar, Marc Swyngedouw, Szilard Tattay, Philippe Thion, Rodrigo Uprimny, Diego Valades, Rodolfo Vázquez, Juan Vega, Oscar Vilhena and Luc J. Wintgens (who deserves a special mention and recognition).

I am also very grateful for the support provided by several academic institutions, namely the Universidad Nacional Autónoma de México (UNAM), the Consejo Nacional de Ciencia y Tecnología (CONACYT, México), The Instituto Tecnológico Autónomo de México (ITAM), and with the Universtity of Leuven (KUL) and Brussels University (KUB).

# Introduction

At the very beginning of his *Law and Disagreement*, Jeremy Waldron gives us quite an accurate description of the world we live in:

> There are many of us, and we disagree about justice. That is, we not only disagree about the existence of God and the meaning of life; we disagree also about what counts as fair terms of co-operation among people who disagree about the existence of God and the meaning of life. We disagree about what we owe each other in the way of tolerance, forbearance, respect, co-operation, and mutual aid. Liberals disagree with conservatives; socialists disagree with market economists; the party of freedom disagrees with the party of community and both disagree with the party of equality; feminists disagree with those who want the government to stand up for "family values"; last-ditch defenders of the welfare state disagree with triumphant opponents of taxation; and pragmatists and utilitarians disagree with those who think that the task of law is to vindicate the claims or order, retribution, and desert. [1]

As Waldron puts it, one characteristic of modern liberal societies is that they are submerged in conflict and disagreement. We disagree about almost everything, not only about matters of justice, but also about issues that concern us in a more private way. There is no doubt that liberals and conservatives disagree on how we should interpret freedom and equality. They disagree on matters related to markets and commerce. They also disagree on migration policies. We can say that they disagree about core concepts related to the construction of general public policy. However, in modern liberal societies these are not the only issues people disagree about. We also find ourselves in disagreement and even conflicts when we discuss the use of veil, or when we talk about children wearing crucifixes in public spaces or when we discuss whether religious symbols should be present in public schools. Likewise we enter into conflict and disagreement when we talk about issues such as homosexuality, extramarital sex, drugs, euthanasia, abortion, suicide, smoking, and experimentation on animals. All these problems can be understood as moral problems. But we do not only disagree about moral matters. We also disagree about aesthetics, fashion and other topics which are not related to moral issues at all.

Modern liberals have declared themselves victorious regarding the established possibility (at least in some societies) of people expressing themselves in a free and equal way and also having the right to disagree.

This fact is indeed one of the biggest triumphs in the history of modern liberalism: the fact that many societies have come to be constituted by autonomous and free individuals that have the capacity to choose the course of their lives and the values that guide them. However, we have also been seeing that people do not necessarily make their life and value choices peacefully and that often their choices contradict with those made by others. Humans often disagree over the way other people live and with others peoples' values: it is not uncommon that these are also found to be immoral, distasteful or sinful. Nevertheless, liberals think that this diversity of opinions and points of view offer possibilities that we should embrace in modern democratic and liberal societies. Liberals claim that conflict and disagreement, diversity and pluralism are only possible if societies provide individuals with the capacity to become autonomous. Autonomous individuals have the possibility to choose the kind of people they want to be, the life that they want to live, and the values they want to embrace. This means that an autonomous being seeks to be the author of his or her own life.

In the middle of this panorama in which people are autonomous, free and capable of exercising their right to disagree with one another, tolerance plays an extremely important role for liberal thinking. Without tolerance, disagreements and conflicts will hardly coexist or be resolved in a peaceful manner. Liberals say that despite the fact that there is a plurality of values and diversity within the different lifestyles, we should tolerate all those who do not agree with us. In this context, tolerance becomes a key element for the flourishing and progression of our moral life.

This book is about "tolerance." Tolerance is mainly understood here as a moral ideal, just in the same way as deontological moral philosophers understand it. The main object of my work is to address and analyze the concept of the moral ideal of tolerance including the types of problems arising from such an understanding of tolerance and its relation with the deontological structure of practical reason. I am specifically interested in the controversies that tolerance has opened up in this version of the liberal thinking that have emerged since the second half of the twentieth century. The main question that this book addresses is: Is deontological liberalism's structure of practical reason compatible with the moral ideal of tolerance? My conclusions will be negative. I will argue that moral deontological theories cannot give proper answers to the main problems raised by the moral ideal of tolerance.

Tolerance as a moral ideal represents two basic problems that, in various ways, are related to each other: (1) the problem of the limits of tolerance, and (2) the problem of the so called 'moral paradox of tolerance.' The first one represents one of the main moral concerns: if tolerance is not surrounded by a fence of 'intolerances,' it losses all of its meaning. Tolerance cannot be understood as the philosophy of 'everything goes,' or 'every action or every conduct are valid.' To be reasonable tolerance needs a further distinction between what is tolerable and what is not tolerable. The second problem mentioned above arises from the very conceptual nature of tolerance understood as a moral ideal: if tolerance is the practice of accepting something that is strongly disapproved of, then, it appears that tolerance requires individuals to accept things that they consider to be morally or ethically wrong. Then, how is it possible to conceive tolerance as a value?

In the next pages I will defend the idea that deontological liberalism cannot face plausibly any of these two problems, or others that derive from them. My arguments to support such a negative conclusion will be guided by the following assumptions:

The *first* refers to the kinds of conflicts that tolerance as a moral ideal incarnates. Tolerance so understood raises two types conflicts: one between moral values and other kinds of values (ethical, aesthetic, social, etc.), and another between moral values themselves. Due to the difference that deontological liberalism makes between *moral norms* and *ethical values* and the priority that it gives to the *right* over the *good*, it will be argued that moral deontologism cannot give a plausible answer to any of them. In the first case, this is mainly because moral deontologism neglects the value that ethical beliefs and other kind of values have in the life of individuals. In the second case, it is because deontological moral theory either does not accept the existence of these kinds of dilemmatic problems arguing that they must be conceived as epistemic deficiencies, or obviates the ontological side of dilemmatic conflicts.

The *second* is guided by the way deontological philosophers such as John Rawls, Rainer Forst and Ernesto Garzón understand the nature of a tolerant individual. According to these authors tolerance must be understood as a dispositional property adopted by any reasonable agent that is reiteratively tested. It will be argued that tolerance, under the deontological structure of practical reason, cannot be understood as such. Furthermore, it will be argued that under this scheme tolerance becomes a victim of another kind of paradox, a conceptual paradox, which consists in the idea that every act of tolerance strengthens up the realm of intolerances, making out of tolerance a 'suicidal ideal.'

This book is only concerned with the concept and the justification of tolerance within deontological liberalism. It is neither about the history of tolerance nor about what philosophers of other centuries and times have said about the topic. The question that it will address does not try to answer the practical question: *What is tolerable and what is not?* It will neither propose a different way of understanding tolerance besides the one accepted by deontological liberalism nor propose a new conceptualization. Although these questions and topics are interesting by themselves, this book is concerned with other kind of problems; problems that can be qualified as an internal problem of *philosophical coherence*.

The book is divided into five parts. The first three are descriptive and the remaining two delve into the abovementioned arguments and the critical assessments of deontological liberalism.

In the case of the last seven chapters, chapters 11 to 14, I focus on the internal problems of consistency and coherence introduced in the first three parts. Chapters 15 to 17, provide an external criticism to the deontological moral system and an answer to the problems of tolerance based on a perspective related to virtue ethics.

Chapter 1 in particular, aims to discuss three ideas that are nuclear for distinguishing deontological liberalism from other kind of liberalisms. These ideas are: (1) the distinction between the *right* and the *good* and the priority of the former over the latter, (2) the difference between the *public* and the *private* realms of normativity, and (3) the idea of a neutral State. Although this chapter is guided mainly by the work of John Rawls, some other philosophers' ideas and theses are also considered. In the first and second part of chapter 1, the distinctions between the 'right' and the 'good' and the 'private' and the 'public' will be addressed. In this context, the criticisms of authors such as Michael Sandel are taken into account. The idea of including the critics of communitarian authors is to make a contrast between the ideas hold by these two radically different theories and to highlight, the main thesis defended by deontological liberalism.

In the last part of chapter 1 I discuss different arguments that defend the neutrality of the state principle, being this one of the main philosophical claims of all deontological accounts of liberalism. These arguments are: *the moral argument* (defended by John Rawls and Ronald Dworkin), *the argument of fear* (defended by Judith Shklar), and *the dialogical argument* (defended by Bruce Ackerman and Charles Larmore).

The main reason for presenting these three nuclear ideas of deontological liberalism is to introduce some of the basic premises that will be used into further discussions. The priority of the 'right' over the 'good' thesis, for example, will be a main source of my critics of the deontological structure of practical reason. This, mainly, in reference to the two conflicts of values mentioned above. So is the case of the distinction between 'private' and 'public' as two separate realms of normativity which will play an important role in the general construction of my arguments.

Chapter 2 is dedicated to John Rawls's conception of practical reason that holds his entire theory of justice. It is important to keep in mind that my aim in the first three chapters is descriptive. Thus my central point for discussion in chapter 2 is the relationship that Rawls proposes between the 'reasonable' and the 'rational' and the 'relevant' as central ideas of his theory.

Chapter 3, entitled "The Moral System" makes specific reference to Bernard Williams's skeptical stand towards certain conceptions of morality (particularly deontologism and utilitarianism). Although Williams's idea of 'moral system' will not be explicitly defined until chapter 15, the chapter begins with an explanation of what will be understood as *Deonto-logical Moral System* (DMS) as an advance of Williams's idea of 'moral systems.'

Part II will dwell into the way tolerance has been conceptualized within deontological liberal theories. The central aim of this part is to discuss the way in which deontological authors have interpreted the three 'circumstances of tolerance,' namely: *the injure of a relevant conviction, the 'power' and 'competence' to act against an act or a conduct that injures one of our relevant convictions* and *the balance between the value of the relevant conviction and the reasons for not-intervention.*

In the case of the first 'circumstance of tolerance,' discussed in chapter 5, I will argue that deontological authors defend the idea that only 'rational and relevant' convictions can be candidates for tolerance. Hence, convictions that are based on prejudices, false beliefs, or merely passions or desires cannot raise questions of tolerance.

In chapter 6 I will discuss the second circumstance of tolerance. In that case I will defend two points. The first is that deontologism does not only recognize 'power,' understood as the physical strength or the number of individuals included in a social group, as a resource to act against a conduct or an idea that injures one of our relevant convictions, but it also includes 'competence' understood as a moral capacity or authority based on justified moral principles to act against conducts or practices which are considered to be morally wrong.

Taking into consideration both resources as constituents of the second circumstance of tolerance, there is an idea introduced in chapter 6 that later will help us to sustain the contextual dependency argument proposed in chapters 11 and 16 mainly. This idea states that not all hierarchical relations are as neatly determined by rules as they are supposed to be, according to deontological authors (Robert Alexy and Ernesto Garzón Valdés among others). On the contrary, these ones also rely in what I call 'roles,' making reference to the type of psychological makeup that every individual uses in his or her everyday life by playing different roles: as a father/mother, a teacher, a director, a student, a priest, etc.

Accordingly, the second idea I advance argues against the thesis according to which tolerance can be displayed among equals. The latter thesis has been strongly defended by Ernesto Garzón Valdés. According to him it is not necessary that the tolerator finds himself/herself in a superior-hierarchical level (either based on *power* or on *moral competence*) than the tolerated to talk about tolerance. This idea will be challenged concluding that, conceptually speaking, in order to judge an act as a tolerant one, the tolerator must be in a situation that allows him/her the possibility (through physical or other source) to detain, stop, deter or dissuade the tolerated act.

Part III contains four chapters that are fully dedicated to analyzing the concept and the justificatory mechanism proposed by three authors who are representative of modern deontological liberalism—John Rawls (chapter 7), Ernesto Garzón Valdés (chapter 8) and Rainer Forst (chapter 9)—and sustain very similar ideas about the concept of tolerance and its means of justification. Considering these authors is important since they are representative of moral deontologism and have applied explicitly the *Deontological Moral System* to analyze the problems of tolerance and its justification.

In chapter 10, I make a description of the main theses of the *DMS* with the purpose to explain, on the one hand, the structure that deontological authors sustain in order to justify tolerance as a moral ideal and, on the other, to underline some of the basic premises that will be used in other chapters to criticize and object parts of it.

Despite the fact that parts IV and V are very similar in many aspects, they treat different problems. In both of them the general idea is guided by a critical assessment of modern deontological liberalism in its relation to the moral ideal of tolerance. These critics, as stated before, are made from the 'inside,' meaning, that they are directed to assess the philosophical and theoretical coherence and consistency of deontologism facing the major problems of tolerance (mainly part IV). Thus, the general idea is to denounce the tensions and contradictions found in this relationship.

With this in mind, both parts are guided by the concepts and the principles that build up the deontological moral theory. Later, in part V, I will advance another kind of criticism formulated from the 'outside' or from the structure of a different philosophical perspective than that of deontologism liberalism.

Chapter 11 will treat the problems of the limits of tolerance. In the first part of this chapter it will be argued, following Rainer Forst, that tolerance is a *normative dependent concept* which creates one of the main constraints to define in an abstract and general way the limits of tolerance without making any reference to a specific normative structure. Hence, the limits are to be drawn by each normative theory that embraces tolerance as a value. Accordingly some of the possible limitations that different moral theories would put into tolerance are advanced. In this case some of the most representative moral theories are considered, namely *moral relativism, moral consequentialism,* and *moral perfectionism.* Although these constrains created by the normative dependency thesis, I will argue that some of the limits of tolerance can be deduced from within the conceptual frame of tolerance itself. In this same part of chapter 11, I will advance the idea that tolerance is not only *normatively dependent* but also *contextually dependent.* Further, in chapters 16 and 17, the *contextual dependence thesis* will be defended.

The other three chapters of part IV (12, 13 and 14) will be dedicated completely to the limits of tolerance within deontological liberalism. As the problems of the limits of tolerance refer to the things that can or cannot be tolerated, this part will focus on the two problems mentioned above: first, the kinds of problems related to the conflicts that a tolerator will have to face if he/she adopts a deontological structure of practical reason to justify them. The conflicts I am interested in during these chapters are those faced by one single individual: the tolerator. As argued before, tolerance raises two different kinds of conflict of values: one, between the moral and other kind of values, and another between moral values themselves. In this part of the chapter I will conclude that under a deontologist structure of practical reason—mainly because of the priority principle, the universality principle and impartiality principle—tolerance is condemned to become either a suicidal concept or an irrational attitude.

In chapter 15, I will present another kind of critical objection against moral deontologism. Following the same kind of criticisms, this chapter is designed to present them from another philosophical stand. The basic idea defended here is the impossibility of deontological liberalism to defend and to justify within its structure the moral ideal of tolerance.

In the first part of chapter 15, I introduce the arguments of Bernard Williams. The presence of Williams in this chapter is indispensable for two reasons. Firstly, Williams is one of the first philosophers who argue the impossibility of deontological structures of practical reason to sustain tolerance as a moral ideal. Secondly the moral perspective of Williams will serve as a philosophical support for the rest of the arguments that will be presented in the rest of the chapters of this last part of the book.

These other arguments presented in chapters 15 and 16 are provided to support the *contextual dependence thesis* mentioned before. What I will claim is that if the moral ideal of tolerance is to be understood as a dispositional property of moral agents it needs to be supported by a structure of practical reason that, on one side, gives a significant place in our moral deliberations to contexts and circumstances (this goes with the idea that a tolerant agent must be able to tolerate an act $X$ of a person $A$ in a time $T1$, and not tolerate and act $X'$ of a person $B$ in a time $T2$), and on the other side, takes seriously the values and beliefs that individuals take as *important* for the achievement and pursue of their life plans and that does not put in jeopardy those values and beliefs that constitute what Williams call the *character* and the *personal integrity*.

The structure of practical reason I am referring to is a special kind of moral particularism. The sort of particularism that will be defended is a 'particularism of reasons' as something different from a 'particularism of rules' or a strong particularism, as the one Jonathan Dancy defends, which holds both a particularism of reasons and a particularism of rules. The benefits of taking this approach to the justification of tolerance are at least three: (1) The possibility to tolerate certain acts or practices without this implying that we must 'moralize' our ethical system of values or eliminating one of our most relevant convictions, (2) the possibility to solve the dilemma of tolerance without ignoring the idea of moral residues (as moral regret), and (3) the possibility of counting with a flexible idea about the limits of toleration without trying to impose a strict fence of intolerances as deontologists do.

## NOTE

1. Jeremy Waldron, *Law and Disagreement* (Oxford University Press, 1999), 1.

*I*

# The Premises of Modern Liberalism

# ONE

## Three Philosophical Claims

As previously stated in the introduction, the purposes of this book are to analyze how modern deontological liberalism conceptualizes and justifies tolerance and to show the theoretical tensions that tolerance generates within this particular philosophical structure.

In this chapter I will adopt the deontological liberalism of John Rawls as a paradigmatic example of modern liberalism. The importance of the work of J. Rawls on political and moral philosophy has an undeniable relevance in its field. It has raised an infinite number of discussions and debates not only within the field of philosophy, but also in economics, law, social sciences and many other related areas. Nevertheless, in this chapter we will focus exclusively in three topics that are defended by Rawls in particular and by modern deontological liberals in general. Although these three topics are strongly related and even sometimes tend to overlap, it is possible to make an analytical distinction between them. This will help us later on to underline some of the main theoretical characteristics of modern deontological liberalism in its relationship with tolerance.

The first one which has been of a fundamental value for contemporary philosophical discussions and specially for the discussions about tolerance, is the difference between the 'right' and the 'good,' 'morals' and 'ethics' or 'justice' and the 'conceptions of the good.' This distinction has been one of Rawls's philosophical cornerstones, which has helped him to differentiate between an 'ethical' and a 'moral' person and also to distinguish between a 'political' and an 'ethical' or 'comprehensive' liberalism.[1]

The second one refers to the distinction between the 'public' and the 'private' realm. One of the main outcomes of this distinction consists in the formulation of two ways of perceiving individuals: as citizens partici-

3

pating in public deliberations and exercising their rights, and as a source of self-regarding interest and desires, as architects of their own life within the privacy of their home, so to say. The difference claimed by these two perspectives is between the 'legal' or 'political' and the 'ethical' side of the self. This difference will help us later on to grasp the difference between cases of public and of private tolerance.

The third and last point that will be discussed refers to the neutrality principle. The distinction between the 'good' and the 'right' has a direct impact in how we perceive the function of the State's legal and political enforcement. It is important to consider that I use the term 'State' in broad terms in order to refer to all branches of public administration: administrative; legislative and judicial powers; including autonomous and decentralized public institutions.

## THE 'RIGHT' AND THE 'GOOD'

Michael J. Sandel in his *Public Philosophy* says that liberals often take pride in defending what they oppose—pornography, for example, or unpopular views. They say the state should not impose on its citizens a preferred way of life, but should leave them as free as possible to choose their own values and ends, consistent with a similar liberty for others. This commitment to freedom of choice constantly requires liberals to resort to conceptual distinctions. For example: the difference between 'permission' and 'praise.' One thing is 'allowing a practice' and another is 'approving a practice.' One thing is to allow the production of pornographic films and quite another to approve of the production of sexually explicit films. Still, how is it possible to permit a practice although we ethically disapprove of it? How can we do this without falling into contradiction or incoherence?

For modern liberalism this is possible thanks to the distinction between 'ethics' and 'morality' or between the 'good' and the 'right' or between 'justice' and 'comprehensive conceptions of the good.' Nowadays it is a common practice in political and moral philosophy to distinguish between these two realms: the realm of universally binding norms and the realm of individual specific values. In a genealogical perspective it has been said that this distinction can be traced back to the difference between the Kantian *Moralität* and the Hegelian *Sittlichkeit*. 'Justice' or what we consider to be the 'right,' is aligning with the Kantian *Moralität*, while 'ethics,' the different and individual 'conceptions of the good,' is related to Hegel's *Sittlichkeint*. Traditionally, it has been stated that the latter claim is about what people should do to live well: what they should aim to be and achieve in their own lives. The former is a claim about how people must treat other people. *Ethical* issues are personal or particular, while *moral* issues claim universal validity and acceptability.

Although this difference can be traced through the works of Kant and Hegel, it was John Rawls who popularized it in the contemporary political and moral philosophy debate. Since *A Theory of Justice* appeared, liberal authors have been discussing these two realms of normativity and consequently many other related distinctions have appeared. For example, one common and important distinction of contemporary liberalism that came from the work of John Rawls is the distinction between "political liberalism" and "comprehensive or ethical liberalism."[2] Nowadays it would be hard to understand the difference between these two ways of constructing a liberal political theory if we do not take into account the difference between the 'right' and the 'good' and its normative consequences.

Rawls's liberalism is the best example of the former while Joseph Raz and Ronald Dworkin offer the most remarkable contemporary examples of the latter. I do not pretend to claim any resemblance between the theories of Raz and Dworkin, on the contrary, the differences between them are remarkable (for instance, Raz favors a perfectionist liberal perspective that Dworkin does not). My only claim is that under Rawls's distinction both are considered as comprehensive or ethical liberalisms despite their differences. Political liberals claim that the principles of justice should not be ethically guided. This means that public institutions and individual rights should be neutral regarding any comprehensive conception of the good. In this sense, political liberalism is not only characterized by accepting this distinction but also (and mainly) by sustaining the independence of morality from ethics and the priority of morality over ethics. Contrary to this view we can find the perspective constructed by comprehensive liberals who normally defend two different views towards this distinction: One, according to which the 'right' consists in maximizing the 'good' (which is a perspective related to utilitarianism), another that considers the distinction and the priority but does not sustain the independence of morality from ethics (this will be the perspective defended by liberals such as Ronald Dworkin), and another one, which is skeptical about the distinction, and claims that the concept of 'morality,' as such, is an artificial and pernicious byproduct of contemporary moral philosophy (this could be attached to Bernard Williams's perspective).[3] Although most comprehensive versions of liberalism do not reject the distinction as the skeptical perspective does, they sustain that justice depends on the good and is not independent from it. Therefore the justification of public policies, principles and individual rights cannot be detached from a specific conception of the good life. Other examples of liberalism, which constitute a comprehensive moral doctrine, include the liberal visions of Kant and of John Stuart Mill.

According to Sandel the main reasons why deontological liberals, such as Rawls, defend the priority of the 'right' over the 'good' derive from two claims: "The first is the claim that certain individual rights are so important that even the general welfare cannot override them. The second is the claim that the principles of justice that specify our rights do not depend for their justification on any particular conception of the good life or, as Rawls has put it more recently, on any 'comprehensive' moral or religious conception."[4]

Thus, the priority of the right over the good thesis relies in two different "*musts*": one is the moral *must*, and the other is the epistemological *must*. Justice *must* be prior to the good in the moral sense because what makes individual rights so important, as for them not be overridden by any other consideration, is the type of justification that these kinds of rights have: the protection of the integrity and individuality of each and every person. According to the kind of deontological liberalism defended by Rawls, the justification of these rights is independent from any comprehensive conceptions of the good and they are the product of a collective choice in what Rawls has called the "original position."

At this point, we can find the epistemological argument which tends to give an answer to a very old, but still very puzzling dilemma: how to justify the principles of justices (morality) without letting our own interests, desires and beliefs get in the way and not falling into a realm of transcendence (as Kant's moral philosophy does). The answer that Rawls provides to this puzzle is to be found in the "original position" understood as an ideal situation in which individuals are not biased by their own conceptions of the good or those that have been individually chosen in the real world.[5]

The principles of right, respectively, are rooted in a particular conception of the self which understands justice as something that is not founded by its object but by its subject. This implies that the subjects are prior to their ends and desires and these ones are to be chosen by them. The epistemological argument, then, consists in the idea that the principles of 'right' assure individuals the right to choose their own conceptions of the 'good.' In this epistemological way, the 'right' is prior to the 'good' because it limits the conceptions of the 'good' that may be chosen by factual individuals. And here arises the moral argument again: if any of these conceptions of the 'good' enter into conflict with the principles of 'right,' the 'right' will always prevail.

In order to explain the priority of the 'right' thesis under these two different routes taken by Rawls—the normative and the epistemological—it is necessary to distinguish between three different levels of his argument: 1) the priority of the self argument, 2) the independence of the foundations of morality, and 3) the supreme importance of justice (justice is not one value more among others) argument. We will notice that the first one—the priority of the self—is in fact, the one that permits us to transit to the other two and that serves as a spinal cord for the construction of Rawls's entire theoretical structure.

The argument starts with one of Rawls's biggest contributions to the social contract theory and to the deontological liberal standing: the idea of locating individuals in an "original position" and under a "veil of ignorance" in order to decide which principles of justice are supposed to rule them in society.

Rawls characterized the so called "original position" and the "veil of ignorance" in the following way:

> Among the essential features of this situation is that no one knows his place in society, his class position or social status, nor does anyone know his fortune in the distribution of natural assets and abilities, his intelligence, strength, and the like. I shall even assume that the parties do not know their conceptions of the good or their special psychological propensities. The principles of justice are chosen behind a veil of ignorance. This ensures that no one is advantaged or disadvantaged in the choice of principles by the outcome of natural chance or the contingency of social circumstances. Since all are similarly situated and no one is able to design principles to favor his particular condition, the principles of justice are the result of a fair agreement or bargain.[6]

The idea of Rawls rests on detaching individuals from almost any knowledge about themselves (ethical, philosophical, religious, physical, and so on) so they can be able to choose *impartially* the principles that will rule them in society. This is, without the burdens that bargaining can put upon them while trying to agree, in reasonable terms, on converging their diverse conceptions of the good that can be—and as they usually are—radically different. Definitely, this is one of the most relevant maneuvers made by deontological liberalism so far. With the "original position" Rawls wanted to guarantee the two main elements of his theory, namely those that he perceives other political philosophies—mainly the utilitarianism, moral perfectionism and dogmatic political traditions—are lacking:

> (1) To construct a way to justify the principles of justice that is independent from any contingent philosophical, religious or ideological conceptions of the good life neither that is part of an external set of values such as perfectionist or theological values about human nature.
> (2) To preserve the idea of individual agents who are capable of choosing freely and rationally their plans of life.

With the first one he manages to keep the principles of justice away from arbitrary and contingent sources, while with the second, he guarantees that individuals would not be conditioned by their surroundings, considering them as subjects that are prior to any values or ends. Thus for Rawls, "the self is prior to the ends which are affirmed by it."[7] As Rainer Forst has explained: "Rawls's self is a "subject of possession" that "has" ends, values, and conceptions of the good and "is" not identical with these; it is an antecedently individuated self whose identity is not connected in a constitutive way with its surrounding world, in particular with other subjects. The good is simply a pure preference of an independently defined subject."[8]

This formulation of the self—as free, rational and prior to its ends—tends to achieve an 'Archimedean point' that is considered capable of providing an answer to the dilemma mentioned previously. Participants in the original position ignore sufficiently so as not to be biased in their choice and know sufficiently so as to act rationally in their best interests. What they do not know is their place in society, their race, sex, or class, their wealth or fortune, their intelligence, strength or abilities, what they know is that they do in fact possess such conceptions and deem them worthy of advancement.

We can say that Rawls's 'Archimedean point' locates the participants in the original position in two different levels: a more abstract and detached perspective from which they choose impartially the principles of justice and, another, from where they face, from a more concrete perspective, the social structures that will deal with such principles. In this way, Rawls presupposes an ideal participant who has full rational capacities and who is capable of adopting an impartial perspective towards the principles of justice. Thus, morality's content does not depend on any transcendental criterion neither on ethical, natural, traditional or theological believes, it relies exclusively on the autonomous-rational choice of individuals who are free and equal.

Putting things in this perspective makes clear the modifications that Rawls has made to its original source: the Kantian categorical imperative. With these changes, Rawls manages to bereave the Kantian formulation from the metaphysical cloud that used to surround it.

Rainer Forst agrees on this view when he says that Rawl's ideal of the person provides a *procedural interpretation* of Kant's conception of autonomy which is detached from the "metaphysical surroundings" of Kant's theory.[9]

Hence, the priority of the right over the good works on the terms of a particular conception of the self which is a choosing self; independent of the desires and ends it may have at any moment. Under this construction, the foundations of morality become independent from any contingent or arbitrary sources of justification. Its aims tend to construct a conception of justice considered to be supreme among other values. Justice seen in this way is not one value more among many other, it becomes the metric to weight and assess the universe of values. "This priority means that admissible ideas of the good must respect the limits of, and serve a role within, the political conception of justice."[10]

With the priority of the right over the good thesis in mind there are two issues that should be of our concern now. The first one refers to the conception of a moral person which is not a conception of the ethical self. Rather, the emphasis is placed on an abstract political-moral level which apparently leaves aside the ethical self-identification level. Thus, we should ask ourselves, where does this conception of the self leave the problem of the ethical identity of a person? How and when is this other side of the self taken into consideration? The second concern is the following: if liberals sustain, as they do, that principles of justice upon which individual rights are based are prior to any conception of the good life, then, which is the scheme that the State should adopt to act onwards? In what follows I will address both problems. This descriptive part of the book has the purpose of settling the bases that will lead me to further discussions and criticisms about the compatibility between this philosophical structure and the claims of tolerance as a moral ideal. It that sense I deem them worthy of attention.

## THE 'PUBLIC' AND THE 'PRIVATE'

Throughout the years, Sandel has strongly criticized Rawls's conception of the self. According to him, Rawls visualizes individuals as 'unencumbered selves,' detached from their circumstances and foreign to the values and ends that they hold.[11] Sandel has expressed this critique in several places, but in all of them he advances, in more or less the same fashion, the following objection: Cannot deontological liberalism's account of the self give a full qualitative version of self-identification, taking in consideration the persons ends, desires and personal attachments? Is it not important to take into consideration the relation that individuals hold with their own conceptions of the good? If it cannot and if it is not important, does this mean that this side of the individual's life is brutally neglected by the deontological version of liberalism?

For Sandel (among other philosophers such as Charles Taylor),[12] this particular liberal conception of the self is so limited that it cannot give an account of a very important part of the moral life lived by human beings as they are in everyday life. In sum, this conception does not correspond to our ethical experiences. In addition to this, he also objects to Rawls's conception of individual obligations saying that it is a very narrow conception. According to this critique there are many other kinds of obligations than those recognized by Rawls's conception. For instance, let us remember that for Rawls "obligations can arise in only one of two ways: as "natural duties" we owe to human beings as such or as voluntary obligations we incur by consent."[13] Under Sandel's view this constitutes a very "thin account for the full range of moral and political obligations we commonly recognize, such as obligations of solidarity" and obligations that we have towards our own communities.[14]

Rainer Forst has argued that Sandel's objections are misdirected in two senses: the first is that Sandel foresees the treatment that in his theory Rawls gives to the relation between individuals and their conceptions of the good and, the second is that he is not considering the idea of the "unity of the self" which is considered by deontological liberalism as a strong and tight interconnection between the *ethical* person and the *moral* one.[15]

Forst is right in one aspect but wrong in another. Certainly, Sandel's objection does not pay attention to the many ways in which Rawls treats the *ethical* side of the self, but this does not discard Sandel's objection entirely. In the following chapters I will discuss that the obligations derived by the *Kantian Moralität* have a great impact in the practical deliberations of an *ethical* self. The priority of the right, as it has been formulated by deontological liberalism, stressed that moral norms should—in terms of justification—be above all other kinds of practical considerations. This way of putting things has a remarkable impact in the practical deliberations of common and regular individuals who, like Sandel presumes, have other kinds of obligations (that are important for their life plans, interests and personal attachments) that do not necessarily belong to those considered by Rawls's formulation of moral duties. In this way, Sandel's critiques to deontological liberalism, as formulated by Kant and Rawls, can be taken as a starting point for these other kind of considerations that are best formulated by philosophers à la Bernard Williams.

Leaving these other issues aside, which will be addressed in more detail in further chapters, now we should pay attention to Forst's vindication of John Rawls's conception of the self, which I believe will bring clarity to further discussions.

The main arguments of Forst are directed to demonstrate that Sandel's critiques are on some occasions implausible, and in others just weak. In response to Sandel's critique about the "unencumbered self," Forst reminds him two things: "First, though he does not call into question that a particular conception of the "moral person" is at the center of [Rawls's] theory, he does however dispute that this can be read off the description of the parties of the original position [. . .] second, this conception of a moral person is not synonymous with a theory of personal identity; instead, it is a "political" conception inasmuch as it refers solely to the more abstract level and not that of the constitution of the self."[16]

Both of Forst's appreciations about the theory of Rawls are extremely clarifying in two ways: (1) Deontological liberalism does not neglect the idea of a "moral person" as something that unites both the moral and the ethical identities altogether, and (2) that political liberalism, by paying more attention to the "political" side of the self, is able to distinguish, in an analytical way, between two sides of the self: one, that is more abstract and formal, which is the "political side," and the other, which is more concrete and substantial, and refers to the "ethical side." It is important not to lose sight that in both cases, in fact, they are not formulations that Rawls considers in his later papers. On the contrary, these formulations can be found, as Rawls in fact denounces it, in his *A Theory of Justice*.[17]

Under the title "The unity of the self," Rawls clarified what he has understood as a "moral person." In those pages, Rawls defends the idea that a moral personality is characterized by two capacities: one, for a conception of the good and the other for a sense of justice.[18]

In this sense, Rawls understands a "moral person" as the one who has rationally chosen a conception of the good and is capable to adjust it to the principles of justice. The unity of the self is understood, precisely, as the rational capacity that individuals have of putting their conception of the good under the constraints of the right. The principles of justice, in this sense, constitute a framework for the good. But in any sense the right discards the existence or the importance of the good. It is enough to consider the next words of Rawls:

> First, the citizen affirm the same political conception of themselves as free and equal persons; and second, that their (permissible) comprehensive conceptions of the good, however distinct their content and their related religious and philosophical doctrines, require for their advancement roughly the same primary goods, that is, the same basic rights, liberties, and opportunities, as well as the same all-purpose means such as income and wealth, all of which are secured by the same social basis of self-respect.[19]

Following these remarks made by Rawls, it is easy to understand why Rainer Forst defends, against Sandel, that Rawls indeed considered this other side of the self: the ethical side. More importantly, nor did Rawls neglect the obligations that can be imposed by a determined conception of the good that is freely and autonomously chosen. The problem is that Sandel is not willing to recognize this, as Forst notices, because his standing point is from a conception of the self that is "radically situated."[20] Sandel thinks of the self as of someone who does not "choose" but rather "finds" his or her identity.[21] This arbitrary and contingent source of normativity is exactly the point that deontological liberalism is trying to avoid in favor of securing free and rational choices. Is not that Rawls neglects the kind of obligations that Sandel considers but rather that he does not consider them valid if they have not been voluntarily and rationally chosen, and if they are not reasonable enough.

The difference between "rational" and "reasonable" is fundamental to the understanding of deontological liberalism's distinction between ethical conceptions and a sense of justice; between a "public" and a "nonpublic" side of the self. Although this will be discussed in the next chapter, for the sake of the argument it is important to consider some of Rawls's formulations. For Rawls, the "rational" corresponds to the first "moral power" of the person, namely, the capacity to form, revise and pursue a conception of the good, whereas the concept of the "reasonable" corresponds to the second moral power, to the capacity to have an effective sense of justice."[22] Thus, the unity of the self represents both sides of the subjects as rational and reasonable. The priority of the right implies, as Rawls says, that "the Reasonable subordinates the Rational because its principles limit, and in a Kantian doctrine limit absolutely, the final ends that can be pursued."[23] This explains why the obligations that Sandel considers would not find a justified place under this perspective if they have not been critically scrutinized by principle of the Reasonable. The priority of the right over the good depends on a lexicographic criterion. According to the theory of Rawls the priority is justified because of the bases from where it is constructed. It is constructed from a particular standpoint: the standpoint of fairness. In this way the priority thesis becomes a practical response to the fact that in modern democratic societies there are strong disagreements about the good. Therefore, public deliberations and institutional decisions should be guided by a sense of justice and not by any conception of the good that can be seriously challenged by any other antagonistic conception of the good equally valid.

According to this perspective we should "bracket" the influence of our religious beliefs or philosophical views when we are deliberating political and legal issues. "If the citizens in a political community hold a multitude of incompatible moral, philosophical and religious views, we are led naturally to the demand that political justification proceed from a set of shared beliefs, ideals and values. To meet these demands citizens must *bracket* their differences and search for common ground."[24] "We should *bracket* our encumbrances in public and regard ourselves, *qua* public selves, as independent of any particular loyalties or conceptions of the good."[25]

This possibility is only open if we understand the term "moral persons" as an amalgam of two interconnected but different elements: the "legal" and the "ethical" sides of the self. The "legal" side is "an abstract conception that must not be understood ontologically (it is a normative conception); in legal relations it is fundamental rights and duties that form the basis of the legally regulated basic structure of society." The "ethical" side is composed by "a "comprehensive" [. . .] doctrine that determines the good life of individuals and the "strong evaluations" of their identity." Rainer Forst uses more explicit terms for this: "To recognize a person as an equal bearer of rights is one thing; it is quite another to recognize this person as the person who he or she is in all his or her attributes."[26]

One of the most important implications that the acceptance of this distinction implies is recognizing different "contexts of justification" as Rainer Forts has widely argued.

For Forst, as for many other modern deontological liberals, in the "context of ethical justification it is ultimately *you* (on whatever 'higher' ground) who decides about the direction of your life, in the context of moral justification it is *others* to whom you owe good reasons."[27] By taking this into consideration we can understand Forst's defense of

Rawls's liberalism as a theory that indeed recognizes the ethical side of the self. Nevertheless, it is important to notice that the emphasis is on how we can justify the existence of universal norms that can be accepted by anyone independent of their own conceptions of the good. In a strict sense, what this means is that liberalism is mainly a political (as different from an 'ethical,' 'metaphysical' or even, 'philosophical') theory. This is achieved by defending the difference that liberals sustain between "ethics" and "morality" and between the "ethical" and the "legal" person. To conclude, liberalism does not neglect the idea of an ethical side of the self; instead, it claims the protection of a free and autonomous development of any conception of the 'good' within a democratic society. For deontological liberalism moral norms do not operate as limitations or restrictions to ethical values but as the normative frame that protects them and makes them possible.

## THE LIBERAL DEFENSE FOR A NEUTRAL STATE

Until now we have seen that one important philosophical claim carried by the priority of the right over the good thesis is to consider individuals as autonomous beings who can choose rationally a conception of the good and lead their lives according to it; and that individuals can be reasonable enough to bracket their conception of the good when they get involved in public deliberations. This has lead liberal authors to distinguish between a private and a public side of the self. The former refers to our own personal way of understanding life and involves our ethical, philosophical and religious beliefs. From this "private side of the self" perspective individuals ask themselves: how should I live my life? Which is the best life to be lived? This, in turn, raises other kinds of questions. It submerges the self into the realm of morality which is concerned with the way individuals ought to treat others, with issues related to our obligations to our fellow man, and to our fellow citizens. Under this liberal perspective, talking about morality is to talk about justice and justice should prevail over any conception of the good.

With this in mind, now it is time to address the second question raised above: if liberals sustain, as they do, that principles of justice, upon which individual rights are based, are prior to any conception of the good life, then which scheme should the State adopt to act upon? The liberal response will be that the State has to remain neutral with regard to all conceptions of the good. The support for this answer is to be found in the priority of the self over its ends, desires and interests, which lead liberalism to advance a very specific claim about the role of public institutions.

Basing the principles of justice on the idea of individual autonomy provides liberalism with the necessary moral basis for claiming the existence of undefeatable individual rights, deontological liberals, such as

Kant, Rawls and Dworkin understand individual rights as normative shields that protect individuals against governmental decisions or against majority claims.[28] Modern deontological liberalism, as the kind defended by Rawls and Dworkin, by defining moral agents as free and autonomous persons who are *capable of rationally choosing* their own ends, is compelled to defend the idea that individuals, as such, are morally superior to any other kind of consideration which can affect in a direct or indirect way such freedom. Therefore, rational individual choices cannot be the subject of calculus of social interests or restricted by the majority rule.[29]

Various arguments in favor (and against) the neutrality of the State have been advanced, nevertheless, the reasons for this vary: While authors like Rawls or Dworkin defend the State neutrality in order to ensure that the State will not interfere in the development of personal autonomy, philosophers like Judith Shklar have done so to prevent oppression, instability or error on behalf of the State. Still others, like Bruce Ackerman and Charles Larmore have argued in favor of the neutrality of the State in order to ensure that political decisions are made in a rational way. These arguments can be called the *Moral Argument*, the *Argument of Fear*, and the *Dialogical Argument*.

### a. The Moral Argument

The moral argument in defense of State's neutrality has been defended by philosophers such as Rawls and Ronald Dworkin. Although both defend it in different ways, still the argument reduced to its essentials, states that a non-neutral government inverts the equation between agents and their ends. The non-neutral State, instead of leaving individuals to choose their own life plans, promotes or imposes one particular conception of good (or a group of a few conceptions) to choose from. Therefore, agents are not really 'choosing' but rather they are 'finding' or they are 'coerced' in choosing their conceptions of the good. In such a case, the State is not really placing individuals in a situation of a free choice. Let us remember that liberals conceive ends and interests as rational choices which are made by free individuals instead of conceiving them as something externally imposed or given, be it by the society, community, culture, family, God or nature. The core point of this argument is that the State, by not being neutral, "channels citizens in directions that they have not (yet) chosen"[30] and this situation directly damages personal autonomy.

Here the arguments are very loosely constructed. No doubt that much of the defense that this argument needs depends directly on the definition of *personal autonomy* adopted. Even though most of the various conceptualizations of this term reach the same conclusion regarding State's neutrality, there are paradigmatic examples that claim exactly the contrary. For example, for Joseph Raz 'personal autonomy' is a perfectionist concept that requires a non-neutral State.[31]

Gerald Dworkin has advanced a clarification of the various definitions of 'personal autonomy' that have been adopted by liberalism. He claims that:

> A person is morally autonomous if and only if he: 1. Is the author of his moral principles, their originator. 2. Chooses his moral principles. 3. The ultimate authority or source of his moral principles is his will. 4. Decides which moral principles to accept as binding upon him. 5. Bears the responsibility for the moral theory he accepts and the principles he applies. 6. Refuses to accept others as moral authorities, that is, he does not accept without independent consideration the judgment of others as to what is morally correct.[32]

If the value of autonomy relies on the capacity of being the author of my choices, autonomy also depends on the number of options from which I can choose. Following these formulations of the concept of autonomy, we can deduce that autonomy rejects any kind of external intromission that reduces the scope of options from which one can choose. In consequence, liberals have to affirm that any action of the State that is directed by a particular conception of the good goes against the others and as a consequence it tends to reduce the spectrum of choices, affecting thus in an irremediable way the autonomy of its citizens. Due to the intrinsic value attached to personal autonomy by deontological liberals, the State seems morally obliged to respect its development.

Is not surprising that Rawls sympathizes with the argument in favor of the neutrality principle. When Rawls argues about the truth of comprehensive doctrines and the acceptability of particular conceptions of the good he argues that these are so complex in a free society that even people who reason conscientiously and in a good faith will inevitably arrive at different answers: this is what Rawls calls the "Burdens of Judgment." Although the possibility that not all these doctrines can be true, the majority of them are reasonable in the sense that they do not reject the essentials of a democratic regime or of a sense of justice.

Still Rawls does not keep his argument at the level of skepticism to defend State's neutrality as authors such as Bruce Ackerman or Judith Shklar do. He pushes it a little bit further favoring the moral reasons we can have to defend the neutrality of the State. For Rawls it is not sufficient to say that the possibility of finding "true" or "false" doctrines requires from the State to remain neutral. It is at this point that we find one important characteristic of Rawls's defense.

Rawls understands the State's neutrality in the sense that the State should not act upon any conception of the good and not in the sense that the State should not promote or favor one conception of the good over another. For Rawls, this second kind of neutrality (neutrality of effect) is in fact impracticable.[33] He endorses what he calls "neutrality of procedure" and also some sort of "neutrality of aim."[34] In present days we can find, at least, three main versions of the neutrality thesis as defended by liberals. The first one, known as *neutrality of procedure* or *neutrality of justification*, refers to the claim that the procedure to identify and justify individual rights must not presuppose any conception of the good. The second version, known as *neutrality of aim*, sustains that the State should ensure to all citizens equal opportunity to advance any reasonable conception of the good. And the third kind, known as the *neutrality of effect*, claims that the State should not do anything that increases the likelihood of individuals to accept one particular conception of the good over another.

For the moment what is important is how Rawls seeks to defend such kinds of neutrality and for which reasons. His defense derives from three characteristics of his political liberalism: (1) the priority of the right, (2) the search for political legitimacy, and (3) the fact of reasonable pluralism.

Neutrality of procedure is a response to those objections that say that liberal neutrality fails to be neutral because at the end liberalism finished favoring *individual* plans of life over other more gregarian life plans. But as Rawls asserts, this problem only refers to neutrality of effect and not to neutrality of procedure which tends to offer moral reasons than all reasonable persons can accept independently of their own conceptions of the good. In this sense, the priority of the right thesis remains intact and the State succeeds in protecting personal autonomy.

This mechanism tries to achieve political legitimacy by constructing a fair system of cooperation among free and equal persons. No one is naturally superior or inferior to anyone else. Nevertheless, Rawls holds certain doses of skepticism regarding the validity of the conceptions of the good that constitute a plural society. Still, the existence of diverse and incompatible ways of life is another reason that contributes to the idea that the State should refrain from acting upon any specific conception of the good; this in order to prevent the State from justifying policies or institutions under an ethical criterion that can be reasonably rejected in a pluralistic society. Hence, for Rawls the reasons that justify policies and institutions in a liberal State are the product of an "overlapping consensus." Forst summarizes this conception of procedural State neutrality in the following way: "Liberal principles can be understood as norms that are justified by a general consensus among those who live according to these norms. They express the general interest."[35]

In this way Rawls applies the neutrality principle to the *reasons* that the State must provide in order to justify its policies and institutions and not to the *effects* that such dispositions may have. Rawls knows that it is impossible for the State to remain neutral in the face of promoting or favoring one conception over others. In fact, he knows that in a State that adopts the political liberalism perspective, many ways of life will cease to exist and others will gather adherents.[36] But for Rawls this does not mean that political liberalism is unjustly biased against certain conceptions of the good, say, individualistic conceptions against communitarians or associative ones. What is important is that all citizens know that they have the right to be as free and equal in choosing the ways of life that are closer to their values and interests. And this is what the State's neutrality must seek to ensure.

The argument of Rawls has as a starting point the defense of personal autonomy, and ensures it by procedural neutrality. Still, as I have said, there is another important defense of this argument that takes a different path. This is the "individualist approach" of Ronald Dworkin. Dworkin's liberalism differs from that of his peers in some substantial aspects. While liberals commonly base their theories on the value of individual liberty and freedom, Dworkin bases it on the value of "equal concern and respect"; this is, in the right that each individual has to non-discrimination and equal adjudication of social resources and guarantees.

Dworkin faces the problem by asking himself an archetypical political question: "What does it mean for the government to treat its citizens as equals?"[37] According to Dworkin there are at least two fundamental ways to answer this question: the liberal and the conservative. The liberal response, to which he indeed adheres, supposes that the "government must be neutral on what might be called the question of the good life [. . .] [it] supposes that political decisions must be, so far as possible, independent of any particular conception of the good life, or of what gives value to life. Since citizens of a society differ in their conceptions, the government does not treat them as equals if it prefers one conception to another, either because the officials believe that one is intrinsically superior, or because one is held by the more numerous or more powerful group."[38]

The way in which Dworkin has defined rights to be "Trumps" of the individuals that limit the power of a majority groups or the State is famous.[39] This characterization of rights is though more substantive than rhetorical. In *Taking Rights Seriously* Dworkin takes the right to equal respect to be a pre-political right. For him this right is not the product of the 'contract' but it precedes the contract.[40] Without the recognition of this right the contract will turn out to be an illegitimate contract. The right to equal treatment and respect then, becomes the "nerve of liberalism."[41] Under *equal treatment*, which is the formal side of this right, Dworkin understands the prescription directed to governments instructing them not to force citizens to pursue a particular plan of life since each individual has the right to pursue the life that better suits him or her without any repercussions. If the State promotes a particular conception of the good, explicitly or implicitly, it is implying that there are some conceptions of the good which are superior, better or more valuable. This violates the terms of treating individuals equally by recognizing some and degrading others. The substantial part of this right refers to the *equal respect* and *opportunity*. Thus Dworkin argues in favor of giving each citizen the same social resources and the same legal guarantees.

The difference that we find between the argument of Rawls and the one of Dworkin does not rely on their reasons to promote State's neutrality but in the ways they think about neutrality. For Rawls, neutrality means that the justification of policies and institutions has to be made without reference to any particular conception of the good, while, for Dworkin neutrality means that any public policy or institution should be directed to favor or to promote any particular conception of the good. The first one is a neutrality of justification (procedural), the second one, of adjudication. Calling into attention this distinction is not a paltry trick: here lies the most important difference between these two kinds of liberalism. While for Dworkin the principles of justice carry some ethical values, for Rawls this goes against a political conception of justice. This is why the liberalism of Rawls is understood as *political* while the one of Dworkin is understood as *ethical*.

Independent of these differences, which without a doubt are important, what must concern us for the moment is that both authors understand individual rights as the key elements to *implement* State's neutrality. For Rawls these rights offer a neutral justification for the State's actions and decisions. For Dworkin those rights bring the necessary way to treat each citizen with equal respect. Still, this has not been the only liberal perspective to defend the neutrality principle and the role of individual rights. Other views, such as the one described below, take rights as a sufficient element to *make* the State neutral. They work as a preventive mechanism to save us from oppression.

### b. The Argument of Fear

Under the perspective of the argument of fear the neutral State is not grounded on moral bases but rather on prudential considerations and the neutrality principle is taken as a protective mechanism rather than a morally grounded claim. It is thought to constrain the actions of the State so they would not become repressive, abusive or tyrannical. George Sher has distinguished three reasons that support the argument in favor of the State neutrality: oppression, instability and error. When he talks about "oppression," he refers specifically to the kind of pressure that the State's power can impose upon certain individuals or social groups and that eliminates any possibility of freedom. Sher describes this posture in the following way:

> To keep order, to protect citizens from external threats and from each other, and to provide essential services and public goods, a government must have both a (near-) monopoly on force and access to great wealth. But, quite obviously, these resources can also be used in less

salutary ways: to suppress dissidents, to consolidate and maintain personal power, and to create and sustain unjust patterns of advantage and privilege.[42]

This perspective towards the State and governmental authorities in general is not odd within the liberal lines. Certainly, it can be easily confused with the argument about the "defense of personal autonomy." Nevertheless, the viewpoint is quite different from it. Its origins can be traced to the work of Benjamin Constant[43] (among others, like Montesquieu), and in contemporary philosophy it has been defended through the "liberalism of fear" of Judith Shklar.[44] Both, Constant and Shklar, believe that the great powers conferred to the State, if not sufficiently controlled, can result in the most effective way to achieve oppression and tyranny. The liberalism of Shklar specifically, steps away from any "utopian" versions of it which, according to her, are mainly represented by the liberalism of natural rights and by the liberalism of personal development. "The liberalism of natural rights envisages a just society composed of politically sturdy citizens, each able and willing to stand up for himself and others."[45] For the liberalism of personal development "freedom, it argues, is necessary for personal as well as social progress [. . .] and morality is impossible unless we have an opportunity to choose our courses of action."[46] Under the liberalism of fear perspective, both ways of understanding the relationship between the State and individuals is erroneous in two ways: by thinking that individual rights, alone, will serve as an effective protective mechanism and by thinking that a "corrupted" government will stop itself in the name of progress and autonomy.

The difference between this perspective and the one defending the concept of "personal autonomy" is that this one defends the neutrality principle in a "negative" rather than in a "positive" way. The latter understands government and political power as a way to achieve freedom and personal autonomy. Hence, the State adopts neutrality not to affect personal autonomy and freedom. The State is taken to be an ally. Instead, the former claims neutrality because otherwise the State's power is a threat to freedom and tends to oppress different conceptions of the good that differ from its own. It takes government and political power as a constant threat to individuals. Here the State is taken as the enemy.

As mentioned above, the second reason in favor of State's neutrality according to Sher is instability. State power can be used by certain social groups to defend a particular conception of the good which leads to an unavoidable suppression and undermining of antagonistic conceptions. The only result of this mechanism would be a social panorama of imposing-resistance politics. "To avoid such conflict we are urged to place all efforts to promote the good strictly off limits."[47] The basic idea that this argument hands out is a way of conceiving neutrality as "modus vivendi." Neutrality is viewed as an instrumental agreement of 'live and let live,' as an accommodation among individuals that hold divergent conceptions of the good life.

The third and last reason discussed by Sher refers to the possibility of error: what if the government or its agents' idea of 'good' is not good at all? This perspective differs from the "epistemic argument" in a way. Those who defend the possibility of error are not skeptic towards moral knowledge. On the contrary, what this perspective argues "is not that the good cannot be known, but only that how well one knows it bears no relation to one's political power or influence."[48] Sher explains it in a deeper way: "Those with the deepest insights may be unable to affect public rhetorical skill to influence those who do have power, or because their potential audience is biased, preoccupied, or inattentive. And, conversely, those who do wield power and authority may hold views about the good that are shallow, incomplete, or simply wrong."[49]

At this point we can go back to Shklar's liberalism of fear. Shklar insists that the "instrumentalist" bases (we have called them 'prudential' before) that she defends are not at this moment any vice, but instead they are a virtue. The sense of instrumental reasoning that goes hand in hand with the liberalism of fear "amounts to a disdain for those who do not want to pay the price of utopian ventures, least of all those invented by other people. It refuses to take risks at the expense of others in pursuit of any ideal, however rational."[50] The defense for the neutral state principle according to this second argument is supported under the idea of fear, oppression, instability or error; for the supporters of this perspective individual rights are a good way to keep the "lion" tied to a leash instead of having it released.

## c. The Dialogical Argument

The last argument mentioned above is the one that I have called the "Dialogical Argument." There are many philosophers who have argued the idea that neutrality is a rational mechanism to settle disagreements. Bruce Ackerman in his *Social Justice in the Liberal State* has defended this argument and claims that the whole liberal project is based on the neutrality principle. For Ackerman, in the liberal State all discussions should be guided by the principle of neutrality in the sense that it constitutes the bases of "rationality." Neutrality is in this way understood as a dialogical exercise that discriminates "good reasons" from "bad reasons."[51] Ackerman defines "rationality" by saying that: "Whenever anybody questions the legitimacy of another's power, the power holder must respond not by suppressing the questioner but by giving a reason that explains why he is more entitled to the resource than the questioner is."[52] And he defines neutrality saying that: "No reason is a good reason if it requires the power holder to assert: (a) that his conception of the good is better than that asserted by any of his fellow citizens, or (b) that, regardless of his conception of the good, he is intrinsically superior to one or more of his fellow citizens." [53]

Consequently, someone engaged in a dialogical exercise has to explain why his or her position is better than that of the other. [54] But the only way to provide "good" reasons is by adopting a neutral perspective. In this way, according to Ackerman, neutrality is the dialogical mechanism that will lead us into the liberal principles of justice. Things do not finish here, neutrality is a mechanism to engage in rational dialogue and the only way for us to know which values should rule. Ackerman sustains that there is: "no moral meaning hidden in the bowels of the universe. All there is is you and I struggling in a world that neither we, nor any other thing, created." [55]

He appeals thus to the idea that there is "anything out there" to be found as realists tend to confirm. On the contrary, he sustains that the world has been already imprinted with our meanings. For him the principle of neutrality is not something that we can find in nature, because it is a creation of the human spirit for the construction of a public space. This perspective pushes him to defend a skepticism concerning the reality of transcendent meaning. Such a view of the world leads him to defend liberal neutrality from four main standpoints: (1) the "hard truth" that there is "no moral meaning hidden in the bowels of the universe," therefore (2) we all must "impress our own meanings on the world," (3) in turn no one may compel another person to live in a way that he/she, but not other, considers meaningful, and (4) therefore, the State's neutrality becomes a must under the liberal perspective which defends the protection of the free development of individuals. [56]

In this sense, Ackerman sustains a skepticism that doubts the possibility of knowing the correct ways of life and not the possibility of justifying general moral norms for ruling in public life. Accordingly, Ackerman sustains that we, as humans, tend to encipher meanings in the world, mainly because of the impossibility of finding knowledgeable values in nature. So we are the ones responsible for creating our own ethical views and justifying them as much as possible. But this might not be sufficient, and in fact is quite uncertain in the terrains of justice. Neutrality, understood in this dialogical way assures that the moral discourse will be backed up by good reasons preventing the State to rule by a possibly "wrong" (not neutrally constructed) conception of the good.

Not all philosophers who sustain the idea of a retreat to neutral bases for a rational dialogue sustain it under skeptical considerations like Ackerman. This is the case, for example, of Charles Larmore who also defends a justification of the neutrality principle based on a *rational dialogue* such as the one considered by Ackerman but without the skeptical mood. [57] According to Larmore, the principle of rational dialogue should be understood as: the capacity that individuals have to "respond to points of disagreements by retreating to neutral grounds, to the beliefs they still share, in order either to (a) resolve the disagreement and vindicate one of the disputed positions by means of arguments which proceed from this common ground or (b) bypass the disagreement and seek a solution of the problem on the basis simply of this common ground."[58]

Thus understood, the *rational dialogue* differs in one important aspect from Ackerman's proposal of a *neutral dialogue*: namely that for Larmore this principle of neutrality is not justified under the bases of an epistemological deficiency. On the contrary, for Larmore this norm has a moral justification that extends to the principle of neutrality. Under such conditions the neutrality principle is not to be defended for skeptical reasons but for moral reasons: so individuals can be able to achieve agreements on important substantive matters. In his characterization of the neutrality principle, Larmore does not exclude the idea of ethical conflicts that can arrive at agreements on their own soil. The principle of rational dialogue enters into question when these conflicts cannot find a mutual agreement. In this way, Larmore sees the neutrality principle as a conflict resolution mechanism. The conflicts that Larmore considers as the target of the neutrality principle are between two mutually consistent values that under given circumstances recommend two different courses of action which however cannot be performed simultaneously. The procedure in these cases is thus, according to Larmore, to seek, through the neutral dialogical process, some grounds for ranking the values, in order to settle the conflict. This procedure is not meant to disqualify as invalid one of the values; it just procures, under neutral standards, to identify which one of them is to be preferred under the given conditions. In this way, both dialogical models work towards the creation of an impartial mechanism for the justification of general norms. Both direct their schematization of the neutrality principle towards a procedural understanding.

The difference between these two formulations, the one of Ackerman and the one of Larmore, relies on the idea that for the former the ethical conflicts should be settled because individuals cannot be sure of the validity of their ethical beliefs, while for latter ethical beliefs and life plans, when reasonable, are valid in themselves this being the reason why there is a need for a procedure that can settle arising disagreements in a rational way.

As we can see, these three arguments in defense of a neutral State are strongly rooted in the deontological thesis about the priority of the right over the good. The first one considers that neutrality, either in justification or in adjudication, is the best way to protect personal autonomy. Individuals are considered holders of rights that should be protected by any kind of interference either from the State or from majority groups. The second one defends the idea that the only way to restrain the State is by taming it, reducing its power to a level of generality which keeps it farther away from the life plans of particular individuals. The suspicion is that State's power is so strong and wild that without any limits it can eliminate individual freedom. The third is based on the idea that principles of justice must be constructed in a neutral dialogical way either because it is extremely difficult (if not impossible) to *know* which ethical values are better or worse or because we need rational means to settle genuine conflicts between valid conceptions of the good.

Aside from the differences found in the arguments presented above, it is also important to notice that what liberals claim through the neutrality principle is a principle of restraint: either the State should restrain itself from acting against or in favor any reasonable conceptions of the good or, it has to restrain itself from acting according to one conception of the good or, it has to restrain itself from promoting, through policies and legal rules, the validity of some conceptions of the good over others.

As I have stated before, the three distinctions analyzed in this chapter will be addressed recurrently in this book. This is due mainly to the fact that they are some of the major characteristics of a deontological version of liberalism and have a direct impact in the way authors who attach themselves to this type of liberal thought understand tolerance.

Mainly, my arguments will surround the thesis of the priority of the right over the good. This distinction—that sustains a clear-cut difference between *ethical beliefs* and *moral norms*—is the one that helps Rawls to defend that "this priority means that admissible ideas of the good must respect the limits of, and serve a role within, the political conception of justice."[59] The priority thesis claims in this way that when any of these two kinds of values, ethical and moral, come into conflict, reasonable individuals should favor the moral over the ethical. This is indeed what the "autonomy of morality" means according to deontological liberals: "that there are no values or truths that can claim priority over it, in the sense either that morality rests upon them or that these values or truths can override morality. It is both normatively self-contained and has the final word within its own sphere of validity."[60]

If we take into account the autonomy of morality and relate it to the liberal conception of the self (which is the one that gives origin to it), it is possible to say, along with philosophers such as Bernard Williams, that under this conception of morality the construction of a self-identity is inevitably constrained by the boundaries imposed through the rules of morality.[61] Any conception of the good life must be guided by a moral sense in order to be reasonable, and in case of a conflict morality overrides any kind of ethical beliefs. Further, it will be argued that, although modern deontological liberals like Forst and Garzón (among others) believe that this distinction allows them to respond to all the normative conflicts that tolerance provokes,[62] these two theses—the "autonomy of morality" thesis and the "moral constrains in the construction of the self"—have negative impacts on the adequate understanding of the moral ideal of tolerance within modern deontological liberalism. I will explore all these problems in parts III and IV, but before that, it is important to deeply examine the arguments of this fundamental distinction.

## NOTES

1. John Rawls develops this distinction in several papers and also in his main books. The first introduction of this distinction was in his famous Chapter VII of *A Theory of Justice*, Oxford University Press, 1999, pp. 347–396. Still we can find some reference to it, sometimes not so explicit, in other papers written before to *A Theory of Justice*, like for example in "Justice as Fairness," *Philosophical Review*, 67, No. 1, (January 1955), "Constitutional Liberty and the Concept of Justice," *Nomos*, Vol. VI, *Justice*, 1963. After the publication of his *A Theory of Justice* we can find mainly four papers which he dedicated to this distinction: "Kantian Constructivism in Moral Theory," *Journal of Philosophy*, 77, (September 1980), pp. 515–572, "Justice as Fairness: Political not Metaphysical," *Philosophy and Public Affairs*, 14, (1985), pp. 223–252, "The Idea of an Overlapping Consensus," *Oxford Journal of Legal Studies*, 7, (1987), pp. 1–25, "The Priority of Right and Ideas of the Good," *Philosophy and Public Affairs*, 17, (1988), pp. 251–276. Years later, in his *Political Liberalism*, this difference became the spinal cord of his argument. Almost all these papers have been later published in a collection edited by Samuel Freeman published by Harvard University Press in 1999 and reprinted in 2001 from which I will be quoting them.
2. John Rawls, *Political Liberalism* (New York: Columbia University Press, 1996), 199–200.
3. Rawls, *A Theory*, 22 and ss; Ronald Dworkin, *Justice for Hedgehogs* (Cambridge, Massachusetts: The Belknap Press of Harvard University Press, 2011), 14–15, 255–270; Bernard Williams, *Ethics and the Limits of Philosophy* (Cambridge, Massachusetts, Harvard University Press, 1985), 6–7.
4. Michael J. Sandel, *Liberalism and the Limits of Justice* (Cambridge University Press, Second Edition, 1998), x. The same claim can be found in Michael J. Sandel, *Democracy's Discontent: America in Search of Public Philosophy* (Cambridge, Massachusetts, The Belknap Press of Harvard University Press, 1998), 10–11.
5. Rawls, *A Theory*, 119.
6. Rawls, *A Theory*, 11.
7. Rawls, *A Theory*, 491.
8. Rainer Forst, *Contexts of Justice: Political Philosophy beyond Liberalism and Communitarianism* (Los Angeles, University of California Press, 2002), 9.
9. Forst, *Contexts*, 21–22 (Emphasis added).
10. Rawls, "The Priority of Right," 451.
11. Sandel, *Liberalism*, 22.
12. Charles Taylor, *Sources of the Self: The Making of Modern Identity* (Cambridge University Press, 1992).
13. Rawls, *A Theory*, 97–101; Sandel, *Democracy's Discontent*, 14.
14. Sandel, *Democracy's*, 16.
15. Forst, *Contexts*, 16–29.
16. Forst, *Contexts*, 21.
17. Forst, *Contexts*, 22.
18. Rawls, *A Theory*, 491.
19. Rawls, "The Priority of Right," 454.
20. Sandel, *Liberalism*, 21.
21. Forst, *Contexts*, 17.
22. Forst, *Contexts*, p. 23; John Rawls, "Kantian Constructivism in Moral Theory," *Collected Papers*, 316.
23. Rawls, "Kantian Constructivism," 317.

24. For this argument consult, Steven Wall, *Liberalism, Perfectionism and Restraint* (Cambridge University Press, 1998), 44. (Emphasis added).

25. Sandel, *Democracy's Discontent*, 18. (Emphasis added).

26. Forst, *Contexts*, 27.

27. Rainer Forst, "Toleration, Justice and Reason," in *The Culture of Toleration in Diverse Societies: Reasonable Tolerance*, ed. Catriona McKinnon, Dario Castiglione (Manchester University Press, 2003), 77.

28. Rawls, "Kantian Constructivism," 319; Ronald Dworkin, *Taking Rights Seriously* (Cambridge, Massachusetts, Harvard University Press, 1978), 182.

29. Rawls, *A Theory*, 3–4.

30. George Sher, *Beyond Neutrality: Perfectionism and Politics* (Cambridge University Press, 1997), 15.

31. Joseph Raz, *The Morality of Freedom* (Oxford, Clarendon Press, 1985).

32. Gerald Dworkin, *The Theory and Practice of Autonomy* (Cambridge University Press, 1997), 35.

33. Rawls, "The Priority of Right," 460.

34. Rawls, "The Priority of Right," 458–459.

35. Forst, *Contexts*, 32.

36. Rawls, "The Priority of Right," 462–463.

37. Ronald Dworkin, *A Matter of Principle* (Cambridge, Massachusetts, Harvard University Press, 1985), 191.

38. Dworkin, *A Matter*, 191.

39. Dworkin, *Taking Rights*, 182.

40. Dworkin, *Taking Rights*, 181.

41. Dworkin, *A Matter*, 183.

42. Sher, *Beyond Neutrality*, 106.

43. Benjamin Constant, *Principles of Politics: Applicable to All Representative Governments* (Indianapolis, Liberty Fund, 2003).

44. Judith N. Shklar, "The Liberalism of Fear," in *Liberalism and the Moral Life*, ed. Nancy L. Rosenblum, (Cambridge, Massachusetts, Harvard University Press, 1989), 21–38.

45. Shklar, "The Liberalism," 26–27.

46. Shklar, "The Liberalism," 27.

47. Sher, *Beyond Neutrality*, 107.

48. Sher, *Beyond Neutrality*, 108.

49. Sher, *Beyond Neutrality*, 108.

50. Shklar, "The Liberalism," 33.

51. Luc J. Wintgens, "Les Possibilités et les Limits du Langage Libéral," *Archives de Philosophie du Droit*, Droit et Économie (1992): 211.

52. Bruce Ackerman, *Social Justice in the Liberal State* (Yale University Press, 1980), 4.

53. Ackerman, *Social Justice*, 11.

54. Wintgens, "Les Possibilités," 217.

55. Wintgens, "Les Possibilités," 141.

56. Ackerman, *Social Justice*, 368.

57. Charles Larmore, "Political Liberalism," *Political Theory* Vol. 18 No. 3, (Aug., 1990): 347. Larmore presents in this paper a stronger defense of the principle of neutrality than the one previously made in his Charles Larmore, *Patterns of Moral Complexity* (Cambridge University Press, 1987).

58. Larmore, "Political Liberalism," 347.

59. Rawls, "The Priority of Right," 451.

60. Rainer Forst, "Moral Autonomy and the Autonomy of Morality. Towards a Theory of Normativity after Kant," in *The Right to Justification. Elements of a Constructivist Theory of Justice*, Rainer Forst (New York, Columbia University Press, 2012), 46.

61. Williams, *Ethics*, 176–196.

62. Tim Heysse and Barbara Segaert, "Perplexities of Tolerance. Introduction," *Bijdragen. International Journal in Philosophy and Theology* Vol. 71 No. 4 (2010): 355.

# TWO

# The Rational and Reasonable

In *Justice as Fairness: Political not Metaphysical*, John Rawls defended the idea that a political conception of justice must be independent from any religious, philosophical or ideological doctrine. To put it otherwise, justice must be independent from those conceptions which are not necessarily shared or accepted by all the citizens of a democratic society. Later, in his *Political Liberalism*, Rawls tells us that such a conception of justice must be based on an "overlapping consensus" for reasonable comprehensive doctrines to be possible, or that justice must depart from a conception that all reasonable individuals can accept irrespectively of their own particular religious, philosophical and moral views.[1]

The theoretical framework of Rawls is undoubtedly anchored in the thesis of the priority of the 'right' over the 'good.' This, as we have seen, is the strongest tool that Rawls in particular and modern deontological liberals in general dispose of, for being able to address the main problems surrounding democratic societies (e.g., sustaining the existence of universal and categorical moral norms without affecting the idea of value pluralism and making irrelevant the political consensus) by detaching moral norms from any conception of the good and giving priority (normative and epistemological priority) to them over any other values so we can achieve just and general agreements among citizens that are divided in their ideas of a good life.

For Rawls, as for most deontological philosophers, this distinction works as a mechanism that enables us to answer the key question of democratic societies: "how is it possible for there to exist over time a just and stable society of free and equal citizens who still remain profoundly divided by reasonable religious, philosophical, and moral doctrines?"[2]

The idea of an overlapping consensus understood as the moral acceptance of the principles of justice by different reasonable comprehensive doctrines implies that all citizens, when involved in public deliberations, must argue from premises that most people could accept. Then, in such a case, citizens have to leave aside all their ethical, philosophical and religious views and compromise themselves with shared beliefs, ideals and values. As we have seen, to meet this demand, citizens must bracket their differences and search for common ground. In Rawls's perspective this process implies that the principle of tolerance is applied to philosophy itself. This process consists, precisely, in bracketing our conceptions of the good when we are involved in moral deliberations. Thus, for Rawls to talk about tolerance in a democratic society means that citizens have to keep their metaphysical convictions about the good and their religious beliefs in private; they must consider them as being exclusively personal.

The "bracketing strategy" (which is endorsed not only by Rawls but by several political philosophers such as Ackerman, Larmore, Nagel, Forst, Garzón, and others) requires that individuals exercise what Rawls calls the "sense of justice." This is defined as "the capacity to understand, to apply, and to act *from* the public conception of justice which characterized the fair terms of social cooperation."[3] According to Rawls, "given the nature of the political conception as specifying a public basis of justification, a sense of justice also expresses a willingness, if not the desire, to act in relation to others on terms that they also can publicly endorse."[4]

In the previous chapter I briefly discussed how the "bracketing strategy" and the "sense of justice" are related to the idea of being "reasonable." Now, in this chapter, my aim is to explain how these capacities are in the center of Rawls's conception of practical reason which is constructed mainly by the interaction of two principles of practical reason: the Reasonable and the Rational.

## JUSTICE AND PRACTICAL REASON

As we have already seen, the priority of the 'right' over the 'good' thesis constitutes one of the master keys to access the conception of justice of modern liberalism. The superiority that Rawls (as the biggest exponent of this type of liberalism) gives to this thesis is backed up by several reasons. One of them is that Rawls wanted to construct a conception of justice different from any teleological conceptions of justice. For example, away from an Aristotelian conception that understands justice as a particular virtue that only makes sense within a teleological frame that locates justice in relation to the 'good,' or away from a modern utilitarian conception that derives the 'right' from the 'good' and understands the former as the maximization of the latter.

Rawls, as Kant, inverts the relationship between these two realms by giving priority to justice over the good and by not understanding justice as the application of the good. This strategy was conceived by Rawls as the only way to protect, within a conception of public justice, the freedom and the individuality of persons in their choice of different life plans. For him, utilitarianism combines the desires of all persons into one coherent system of desires. Above this, utilitarianism seems to go against the idea that individual rights cannot be overridden by calculus or social interests. These considerations make out of the theory of Rawls a strict deontological theory (it is at this point where we find the stronger, though not the only, Kantian trait in the work of Rawls).

A second reason is that contrary to other liberal views, Rawls was interested in constructing a "freestanding" conception of justice. This means a conception of justice that is not dependent from any substantial conception of the good, but the product of a rational procedure developed in a reasonable context by free and equal citizens. Thus, justice is not only prior to the good in the sense of understanding individuals as prior to their ends and personal goals, but also in *constructing* the right *independently* from any idea of the good. "The gap between ethics and politics, in this sense of the discrepancy between personal and political values, is to be overcome by citizens themselves, not by submission to one single dominant conception of the good."[5]

A third reason might be that for Rawls justice cannot be defined by any kind of empirical factor or heteronomous ends such as happiness or by external independent 'authorities' such as God. Justice must be the product of a rational agreement between free and equal persons who wish to protect their main interests both as rational self-interested beings and as moral persons, moved to act through moral imperatives. Accordingly, Rawls's conception of justice is not theoretical but practical: justice as fairness is not the product of theoretical reason but the product of a *pure practical procedure*.[6] Justice so understood is obtained "when there is no independent criterion for the right result; instead there is a fair or correct procedure such that the outcome is likewise correct or fair, whatever it is, provided that the procedure has been properly followed."[7]

This procedure embodies all the relevant requirements of practical reason considered by Rawls and shows how the principles of justice follow from them. This procedure, that following Kant's moral philosophy Rawls calls "political constructivism," is built upon four basic features: (1) principles of justice are the result of a procedure (they are not out there to be found as realists tend to think), (2) we arrive at them through practical reason (and not through theoretical reason), (3) this procedure requires a rather complex conception of person and society to give form and structure to its construction, and (4) political constructivism as a procedure specifies an idea of the reasonable that applies to various subjects.[8]

In this way the political theory of Rawls is directed to justify the principles of justice that will govern the major social institutions, or what he calls the "basic structure of society."[9] One of his most important contributions to political and moral philosophy has been the idea according to which it is not necessary to engage in any metaphysical debate about moral truths to arrive at these principles of morality. Instead, according to Rawls, we need to consider which are the principles that all citizens could accept under idealized conditions of choice.

This idealized condition is called the "original position." In the original position, choosers are behind a "veil of ignorance" that does not allow them to know any relevant information about their identity or social position. This, according to Rawls, serves as a mechanism which prevents people from choosing in a partial way or based on their own interests. [10] By excluding all relevant information about the social position and personal interests of the participants in the original position, Rawls tries to protect the rational deliberation from bias and to achieve a common public perspective form. If citizens endorse the values of a democratic society the product of this procedure will be, according to Rawls, two principles of justices: "(1) each person is to have an equal right to most extensive scheme of equal basic liberties compatible with a similar scheme of liberties for others, and (2) social and economic inequalities are to be arranged so that they both (a) reasonably expected to be to everyone's advantage, and (b) attached to positions and offices open to all." [11]

According to what has been said, these principles are *constructed* according to a rational procedure and are taken to be objective insofar as they can be accepted by all citizens, independently of their particular social position and their specific personal interests. For Rawls all this is required to address the practical problem of disagreement and is sufficient to warrant a stable and fair system of social cooperation among citizens who are free and equal but hold different moral, philosophical, and religious views.

Now, following these fundamental characteristics of Rawls's conception of justice (as 'prior,' 'freestanding' and 'constructivist'), we can assert that his whole construction is based on a particular structure of practical reason composed by two main principles: the principle of the Reasonable and the principle of the Rational, which on their part have to work together with other two complementary conceptions: those of "person" and "society." [12]

The principles of practical reason are directed to sustain Rawls's whole normative project which starts from a fundamental idea about society. Justice as fairness takes society to be "a fair system of cooperation between reasonable and rational citizens regarded as free and equal." [13] In this broad and fundamental idea about society are presupposed several other ideas related to his conception of practical reason which, in a way, are the ones that help to conform and systematize it. We must notice that these other ideas that belong to the broadest one are there for us to see. In his conception about society Rawls takes 'people as citizens,' 'people as free,' 'people as equals,' and 'people as rational and reasonable,' also it understands society as a "fair system of cooperation."[14] All these elements compose the whole structure of practical reason that he proposes. Rawls takes such structure to be the best way to connect and relate systematically the ideas and principles that support his conception of justice for a democratic society.

In brief, the cornerstone idea of Rawls is developed together with two accompanying fundamental ideas: (1) the idea of citizens (those engaged in cooperation) as free and equal persons, and (2) the idea of a well-ordered society as a society effectively regulated by a political conception of justice.[15] To fully comprehend the second idea would require exploring Rawls theory of justice as a whole. As I have stated in the introduction of this book, my aim in the present chapter is to analyze the way in which Rawls sets the relationship between the "Reasonable" and the "Rational"; this relationship requires us to "bracket" our conceptions of the good and to have a sense of justice when we get involved in moral deliberations. Hence, this relationship relates the two principles of practical reason. No doubt this enterprise will require explaining some fundamental parts of his political conception of justice, but the stress will be placed on this fundamental relationship which, I believe, constitutes the core of the conception of practical reason from where Rawls derives his conception of justice as a whole.

## PERSONS AND THEIR MORAL POWERS

The moral status of free and equal citizens is underwritten into Rawls's conception of practical reason. Individuals are conceived as free and equal because they have the capacity to reason and they see each other as subjects of this same capacity. This conception of the person, then, is in virtue of the "two moral powers" and in the "power of reason" that individuals as human beings have. The last capacity, the power of reason, is broader in definition than the other two. Although Rawls defines it rather vaguely, it is possible to induce that the "power of reason" that he refers to is the capacity to judgment, thought, and inference connected with the moral powers.[16] Perhaps we can add to this idea all regular capacities of reasoning, weighing evidence, balancing values in case of conflict and the general intellectual skills in order to understand and interpret facts and experiences.

Instead, he explains in much more detail what he understands under the "two moral powers." According to Rawls, the two moral powers refer to the "capacity for a sense of justice and a capacity for a conception of the good. A sense of justice is the capacity to understand, to apply, and to act from the public conception of justice which characterizes the fair terms of social cooperation. Given the nature of the political conception as specifying a public basis of justification, a sense of justice also expresses a willingness, if not the desire, to act in relation to others on terms that they also can publicly endorse. The capacity for a conception of the good is the capacity to form, to revise, and rationally to pursue a conception of one's rational advantage or good." [17]

I have argued before that both, the capacity for a "sense of justice" and for a "conception of the good," are related to the two main principles of his conception of practical reason: the "reasonable" and the "rational." Hence, each moral power pertains to the two principles of practical reason: to be rational means to have the capacity for a conception of the good, being reasonable gives us the capacity for a sense of justice.

Against many philosophical views, such as the rational choice theory and the moral skepticism, [18] Rawls assures that although the Rational and the Reasonable are related in many ways there is no dependency relationship: the Reasonable does not derive from the Rational, nor does the Rational inform the Reasonable; they are two separate and independent concepts. While the Rational "applies to a single, unified agent [. . .] seeking ends and interests peculiarly its own" [19] the Reasonable seeks for "principles and standards as fair terms of cooperation." [20]

Under this perspective, rational agents are those capable of choosing ends and defining interests. Also, those that can adopt the most effective means to achieve its ends, are those that can balance the significance of their life plans and give a priority order to their ends and interests. In a word, rational agents are those capable of constructing, guiding and developing a conception of the good which is not only self-interested but which includes affections and attachments of many sorts (family, persons, country, community, etc.) as well. Nevertheless, according to Rawls it does not matter how complete or robust a life plan or a conception of the good of a rational agent might be; still by being the product of a purely rational agent it will lack moral sensibility. A proposal can be taken as perfectly rational given his or her strong bargaining position, but nevertheless being highly unreasonable. [21]

The principle of reasonableness is best characterized in Rawls's original position, as we already know. Such a situation imposes reasonable conditions for the choice of the principles of justices while the individuals are described as rational because following the principles of rational choice they pursue what they think it is best for them. So, the conditions of the original position are taken to be reasonable by Rawls because they consist in the exclusion of arbitrary information, biases and personal values. The original position, according to Rawls, works as a device for representation and modeling certain fundamental ideas implicit in the public political culture. Then, to be reasonable means to adopt a sense of justice that sets us in conditions in which we can accept the idea of reciprocity, which lies between the idea of impartiality and the idea of mutual advantage. Norms constructed through these conditions are viewed "as reasonable for everyone to accept and therefore as justifiable to them."[22]

Hence, there is a clear relation between the Reasonable and the Kantian categorical imperative, and the Rational and the hypothetical imperative, as I have argued in the previous chapter.[23] Rawls adopts the Kantian terms in a way that manages to configure the Rational as the representation of an empirical reasoning while the Reasonable as part of pure reason. In this way the Reasonable is the principle of morality and the Rational is the capacity to form and pursue a conception of the good. Regarding the priority of the right over the good, the Reasonable then has strict priority over the Rational.[24] Under this perspective, the sense of justice is the capacity that reasonable people acquire to form, limit and adjust their conceptions of the good to the principles of justice. The Reasonable limits the Rational, and in a Kantian doctrine limits it absolutely.[25] When in the original position the Reasonable frames the Rational and subordinates it absolutely, means that the principles of justice that are agreed on, are lexically prior in their application to the claims of the good.[26]

Despite the fact that Rawls considers both principles as separate and irreducible, the strict priority of the Reasonable over the Rational constitutes the grain that sustains his thesis about the unity of practical reason. This unity is represented by fully autonomous agents that "internalize" the requirements of both principles of practical reason. The idea of full autonomous agents becomes, in that sense, the cornerstone concept of Rawls's conception of justice. This is because, according to Rawls, a restricted sense of the Rational and the capacity of reasonableness are the key elements that guide citizens in the original position to choose as free and equals the principles of justice. And fully autonomous individuals are those that can rationally create and develop a conception of the good, constrain it through a sense of justice, and take responsibility for their ends.

Being aware of these arguments, now we need to ask ourselves: how does this work? How does Rawls understand the conceptions of the good? Which role do they play in the life of people? And, in which sense does the reasonable limit them? For answering this bulk of questions I will begin by explaining how Rawls sees and understands the construction and development of the conceptions of the good, understood as the result of our rational capacities. Later I will delve into the last question that relates the principle of reasonableness or what Rawls also calls the sense of justice.

## CONCEPTIONS OF THE GOOD AND RATIONAL PLANS OF LIFE

We have seen that the principle of the Rational informs us about the capacity of individuals to construct and advance their own conceptions of the good and plans of life. Now, how does Rawls conceive these conceptions and understand the construction of these life plans?

In *A Theory of Justice* Rawls relates the idea of the 'good' to the notion of a "rational plan of life": "The rational plan for a person determines his good."[27] A "rational plan of life" according to Rawls is defined as:

> first, a person's plan of life is rational if, and only if, (1) it is one of the plans that is consistent with the principles of rational choice when these are applied to all the relevant features of his situation, and (2) it is that plan among those meeting this condition which would be chosen by him with full deliberative rationality, that is, with full awareness of the relevant facts and after a careful consideration of the consequences. Secondly, a person's interests and aims are rational if, and only if, they are to be encouraged and provided for by the plan that is rational for him.[28]

For Rawls, the best plan of life is the one chosen with full information that can help us to assess its possibilities under a perspective of deliberative rationality. In *A Theory of Justice* Rawls insisted too much on the idea that rational agents were those who guide themselves by the principles of rational choice and that accordingly were committed to the primary goods that can make possible the achievement of their life plans. Later, in *Political Liberalism,* Rawls did not abandon the idea that the principle of the Rational serves as an effective means-ends principle, but he started understanding it also as a principle that serves to balance the ends and to give a structure of priority to the values that give significance to the life of individuals. Rawls, in this sense, does not understand rational agents in a purely egoistic, self-interested way, whose only worries are advancing and achieving their own particular ends and final goals, but as agents that have profound and sincere interests in certain values and take personal attachments as relevant for their lives, attachments to communities and places, including love of country and of nature.[29]

In this way, rational persons are not only those who know how to achieve effectively random ends and goals, but those who have the capacity to form, revise and rationally pursue a conception of the good. For Rawls a conception of the good "normally consists of more or less determinate scheme of final ends, that is, ends we want to realize for their own sake, as well as attachments to other persons and loyalties to various groups and associations."[30] Conceptions of the good, generally speaking, have different levels of sophistication: while "general" conceptions apply "to a wide range of subjects, and in the limit to all subjects universally," "comprehensive" conceptions are those that include "what is of value in human life, and ideals of personal character, as well as ideals of friend-ship and of familial and associational relationships, and much else that is to inform our conduct, and in the limit to our life as a whole."[31] "Fully comprehensive" conceptions are those that cover "all recognized values and virtues within one rather precisely articulated system, and the "par-tially comprehensive" conceptions of the good are those that comprise "a number of, but by no means all, nonpolitical values and virtues and is rather loosely articulated."[32]

According to Rawls the best candidates to be understood as "general" and "comprehensive" are the religious and the philosophical doctrines, such as Christianity or Marxism, that meet the demands of theoretical and practical reason. On the contrary, "full" or "partial" doctrines are less exigent conceptions. They are conceived as more modest, and probably not completely systematized, conceptions of a good life. They can be conceived as the ordinary common denominator between individuals who are not psychologically or morally compromised by any of the other type of conceptions. Still, this is not completely certain, as conceptions of the good under a deontological perspective such as the one of Rawls, are chosen in kind of an arbitrary way. Citizens are capable of revising and changing their conceptions on rational and reasonable grounds. Looking at things in this way it is obvious that for Rawls the conceptions of the good do not define the character or the personality of individuals: per-sons "are independent from and not identified with any particular con-ception"[33] of the good. This particular point of the formulation of Rawls has been recurrently criticized.

Michael Sandel, quoting several passages of *A Theory of Justice*, has described this situation of the arbitrariness in the choice of conceptions of the good in the following way:

> As Rawls describes it, once the principles of rational (i.e. instrumental) choice run out, 'We *must finally choose for ourselves* in the sense that the choice often rests on our direct self-knowledge not only of what thing we want but also of how much we want them.... *It is clearly left to the agent himself to decide what it is that he most wants.*' Since the princi-ples of rational choice do not specify a single best plan of life, 'a great deal remains to be *decided*...We eventually reach a point where *we just have to decide* which plan we most prefer without further guidance from principle.... [W]e may narrow the scope of *purely preferential choice,* but we cannot eliminate it altogether... *The person himself must make this decision,* taking into account the full range of inclinations and desires, present and future.[34]

Sandel's objections to the formulation of Rawls of the rationality princi-ple have been one of his main criticisms to Rawls's conception of justice in general.[35] The idea that conceptions of the good are chosen in a more or less arbitrary way by the individuals is translated, according to Sandel, by deontological doctrines in a way of understanding the 'good' as "nothing more than the indiscriminate satisfaction of arbitrary given preferences, regardless of worth."[36] By conceiving the 'good' in this way, says Sandel, it is not surprising that the 'right' has priority over it.[37] For Sandel, as other philosophers such as Taylor[38] and MacIntyre,[39] the problem here is related to the way in which Rawls conceives individuals as being prior to their ends and goals and that this choice is under the restrictions imposed by principles of justice. According to these authors insofar Rawls's formulation understands the self's integrity as granted "prior to the choice of its ends, it is incapable of developing attachments to those ends that are partly or wholly constitutive of its identity."[40] This objection belongs to the communitarian onslaught.

Although this debate is interesting, the purposes of this chapter are directed to pay attention to another implicit feature in Rawls's formulation. Perceiving the functions of the rational principle in this way, we can say that his formulation is very wide, leaving a lot of room for individual discretion and arbitrary choice. Each and every person would be completely and entirely free, without restrictions of any sort, to choose the conception of the good that better fits his or her ideals and final goals. But this does not make complete justice to Rawls's formulation. Definitely Rawls's formulation is wide, in the sense that it leaves enough room for individuals to choose the way they want to live their lives, but saying this is not the same as saying that his conception of justice does not put boundaries to people's choice. Referring to this particular point, Rawls says that in a constitutional democratic state, people are free to choose their plans of life, but this choice is constrained by the requirements of political justice.[41]

In this sense, the adoption of a conception of the good is restrained by the principles of justice which are considered as previously chosen in the original position. This kind of restrictions put to individual's choice is the one that makes possible the distinction between "reasonable" and "unreasonable" conceptions of the good. Let us remember that a purely rational conception of the good does not necessarily accord with the principles of justice. Rawls takes conceptions of the good to be limited by the principles of justice in two ways: a conception of the good is unreasonable firstly when what it affirms contradicts the public conception of justice, and secondly when what it affirms does not contradict the public conception of justice but neither accepts it (it does not form part of an overlapping consensus). Now I will turn to the limits imposed by the principles of justice to the conceptions of the good. These limits play a major role within Rawls's conception of practical reason, no doubt, but they also influence the construction of modern liberalism as a whole.

## THE REASONABLE

The idea of reasonableness plays a central role in Rawls's work. It is applied in several levels and in different stages of his theory. For instance, as far as we have seen, Rawls takes the Reasonable: (1) as a special place that models the ideal circumstances for the original position;[42] (2) as a characteristic of his ideal of the person. It is "part of a political ideal of democratic citizenship";[43] (3) as the criterion to assess his theory as a whole: Justice as Fairness must be understood, according to Rawls, as a 'reasonable' political conception;[44] (4) as an exclusionary mechanism because it marks the borderline between reasonable conceptions of the good life (legitimate) and unreasonable ones (illegitimate)[45] and, (5) as a conception that defines a "fully autonomous" person because she or he "freely accepts the constraints of the reasonable."[46]

Although in Rawls's conception of justice all these different senses of the term 'Reasonable' are interrelated with one another, here I am mainly interested in the second and in the fourth one: the idea of reasonableness understood as the individual moral disposition of citizens in a democratic society to act justly and as an exclusionary mechanism. In this way citizens are reasonable, according to Rawls, "when, viewing one another as free and equal in a system of social cooperation over generations, they are prepared to offer one another fair terms of social cooperation (defined by principles and ideals) and they agree to act on those terms, even at the cost of their own interests in particular situations, provided that others also accept those terms" and with the hope that their life plans will be taken as legitimate.[47]

The Reasonable understood in these two senses is closely related to what Rawls defines as the capacity of individuals to have a "sense of justice." The "sense of justice," as described and defined by Rawls, is composed by two central elements: (1) "the willingness to *propose* fair terms of cooperation and to *abide* by them, and (2) the willingness to *recognize* the burdens of judgment and to *accept* their consequences for the use of public reason in directing the legitimate exercise of political power in a constitutional regime."[48]

The first element that composes the "sense of justice" must be relatively clear by now. It refers to the idea that reasonable citizens are those capable of proposing fair terms of cooperation which are not derived from any particular conceptions of the good, e.g., they make proposals through reasons that can be shared by any other individual independently of their own religious, moral or philosophical doctrines. Reasonable individuals, in this sense, are those who guide their public deliberations through reasons shared by all. Then, the Reasonable viewed in this way is understood as a two-way street: "in offering fair terms we must reasonably think that citizens offered them might also reasonable accept them. And they must be able to do this as free and equal, and not as dominated or manipulated, or under the pressure of an inferior political or social position."[49] Accordingly, the first element of the sense of justice refers to other central criterion of Rawls's theory of justice: the idea of "reciprocity."[50]

This other criterion, as we have said before, "lies between the idea of impartiality" which is altruistic and moved by the general good, and the idea of mutual advantage "understood as everyone's being advantaged with respect to one's present or expected situation as things are."[51]

Brian Barry in his *Theories of Justice* claims an incompatibility in Rawls's perspective between the impartiality idea (understood as altruistic) and the mutual advantaged (understood as seeking a profitable outcome).[52] According to Barry, Rawls's contradiction is found in two conceptions of justice: one based in the prudential aspect of justice which is covered by the idea of self-interests and mutual advantage, and another based on the idea of justice as impartiality which is covered by the idea of reasonable citizens who seek agreement.

Catherine Audard has argued that the mistake in Barry's argument is that he foresees that Rawls's moral understanding of justice is distinctive because it does not simply equate justice to impartiality: "Rawls rejects the thick altruistic assumptions of such a concept. Instead, Rawls's concept of justice includes both aspects but in an innovative way, in what he calls "justice as *reciprocity*"."[53] Audard's idea is backed up by something that was discussed earlier: Rawls's conception of justice departs from a conception of practical reason that takes two aspects of it: the prudential aspect (the Rational) and the moral aspect (the Reasonable). Henceforth, the idea of reciprocity is a mechanism that combines both: the prudential aspect of cooperation and mutual advantage and the moral aspect of impartiality. We already know that Rawls's understanding of the impartiality criterion is to take into consideration the value and the interests of others following the idea that all are free and equal. According to Rawls the idea of reciprocity that is underwritten to the Reasonable does not only cover the altruistic idea of impartiality but also the concern of the self as moved by its own interests. Rawls in this sense will answer Barry's objection saying that "the reasonable society is neither a society of saints nor a society of the self-centered."[54] Reasonable persons seek to advance their own particular interest in an environment of social cooperation. Although what would happen when the self-interests are not achievable in an environment of fair cooperation? What would happen if the interests of a person do not correspond to the idea of impartiality? The answer of Rawls would be guided by the priority of the 'right' over the 'good': "Citizens are reasonable when, viewing one another as free and equal in a system of social cooperation over generations, they are prepared to offer one another fair terms of cooperation of political justice; and when they agree to act on those terms, *even at the cost of their own interests in particular situations*."[55]

Does this mean that, in fact, Barry was right in pointing at this tension? If there is a need to call for the priority thesis perhaps it is because there can be a contradiction or a tension within the idea of reciprocity so understood that has to be solved. And if the reasonable has priority under the idea that the principles of justice allow us to pursue our rational interests, then it appears that the principles of justice are not any more accepted under moral terms than under prudential ones. If this is so, the answer to Barry's claim is still standing and the tension continues to exist. Solving the tension through a priority principle means exactly that — *solving a tension* — and not dismissing it existence. Without the priority principle, no doubt, this could become a serious problem for Rawls's conception of justice.

But aside from this problem, however interesting, there is still another important point which must be addressed now. Does the idea of reciprocity imply that all reasonable people can always reach an agreement on what constitutes fair terms of social cooperation?

This question begs the second element that constitutes the sense of justice: the recognition of the "burdens of judgment." The "burdens of judgment" is a technical term that Rawls uses to refer to the sources and the causes of reasonable disagreement between persons. The burdens of judgment explain how is it possible that two reasonable agents, given their moral powers (share in common human reason, similar powers of thought and judgment — both can draw inferences, weight evidence, and balance competing considerations), can disagree in fundamental aspects of social cooperation and justice without compromising their reasonableness.

As reasonable and rational agents we make different kinds of judgments: "As rational we have to balance our various end and estimate their appropriate place in our way of life [...] as reasonable we must assess the strength of people's claims, not only against our claims, but against one another, or on our common practices and institutions, all this giving rise to difficulties in our making sound reasonable judgments."[56] Due to several sources the conclusions drawn by two reasonable and rational agents might fall into disagreement.

Rawls mentions six sources that can cause disagreements: (1) evidence that is hard to assess and evaluate, (2) giving different weight to considerations that we agree on, (3) having differences in the interpretation of concepts and ideas which are vague and indeterminate, (4) our experiences regarding the way we assess evidence and give weight to moral and political values, (5) giving different force to normative considerations, and (6) facing the diversity of values, problems in selecting them, and in setting priorities and adjustments.[57]

This characteristic of being reasonable or of having a sense of justice makes, in Rawls's perspective, practical reason public. The principles of practical reason (both, Rationality and Reasonableness) create publicly engaged citizens who reason in public terms. For this reason, recognizing the existence of these sources and the fact that they generate burdens on our judgments is a requirement for being reasonable, thereby, practical reason compromises us with the idea of tolerance and to the "fact of reasonable pluralism."

Pluralism is the social context from which Rawls departs his whole political conception of justice. For him: "[A] democratic society is always marked by a diversity of opposing and irreconcilable religious, philosophical, and moral doctrines."[58] Rawls knows that diversity is caused by the development of free institutions but he does not understand it as a "mere historical condition that may pass away." On the contrary, for Rawls pluralism "is a permanent feature of the public culture of democracy."[59] Under this perspective, political power has only two venues: oppression through the mere use of power or through the definition of legitimate restrictions. Political liberalism opts for the second one and it is where the principle of toleration, understood as the practical representation of the sense of justice, plays a major role.

Before entering in the relation between 'tolerance' and the 'sense of justice,' which is left for part III, where I will discuss three different justificatory mechanisms of tolerance, we should ask ourselves what exactly Rawls understands to be "legitimate restrictions" and in which cases can these be displayed? These are important questions for a conception of justice such as the one of Rawls. Fundamentally, because what these kinds of conceptions of justice are seeking is legitimacy and not only stability which could be found with the use of mere political power. Rawls understands that the idea of legitimacy is an integral part of the idea of rational and reasonable agreement. Justifiable political power can only be displayed according to constitutional standards agreed by rational and reasonable agreements. Now, the second part of our question, namely: "In which occasions or against whom the political power can be displayed?" is still pending.

Clearly, as it was recently argued, the principle of reasonableness makes a sharp distinction between 'reasonable' and 'unreasonable' individuals. Therefore, we must ask ourselves if those unreasonable individuals are the ones Rawls is envisioning as subjects of political coercion. If, as we have seen, the Reasonable is what guides individuals in the original position, then, the principles of justices are the product of practical reason. Any person who does not accept such principles of justice is, therefore, unreasonable in the sense of not correctly developing a sense of justice. Citizens who do not have a sense of justice in the sense described are to be taken as unreasonable, and if their unreasonableness jeopardizes the stability of a democratic society, political power can be used to control it.

Political power in this sense is understood as the limitation that public institutions can develop against unreasonable conceptions of the good.

Nevertheless, we must still ask ourselves about the public relation between reasonable and unreasonable individuals or groups of individuals. Are unreasonable ones always the subject of intolerance or not?

## NOTES

1. Rawls, *Political* , 134.
2. Rawls, *Political* , 47.
3. Rawls, *Political* , 19. (Emphasis added).
4. Rawls, *Political*, 19.
5. Catherine Audard, *John Rawls* (England, Acumen, 2007), 8.
6. Sandel, *Liberalism*, 176
7. Rawls, *A Theory*, 75.
8. Rawls, *Political*, 93–94.
9. Rawls, *A Theory*, 10.
10. Rawls, *A Theory*, 118–123.
11. Rawls, *A Theory*, 53.
12. Rawls, *Political*, 107.
13. Rawls, *Political*, 103.
14. Rawls, *Political*, 14–15.
15. Rawls, *Political*, 14.
16. Rawls, *Political*, 19.
17. Rawls, *Political*, 19.
18. For Rawls the paradigmatic example of this kind of perspective is the one introduced by David Gauthier, *Morals by Agreement* (Oxford, University Press, 1986).
19. Rawls, *Political*, 50.
20. Rawls, *Political*, 49.
21. Rawls, *Political*, 53.
22. Rawls, *Political*, 49.
23. Rawls, *Political*, 48 note 1.
24. Rawls, "Justice as Fairness", 401 note 20.
25. Rawls, "Kantian Constructivism", 317.
26. Rawls, "Kantian Constructivism", 319.
27. Rawls, *A Theory*, 358.
28. Rawls, *A Theory*, 358–359.
29. Rawls, *Political*, 51.
30. Rawls, *Political*, 19.
31. Rawls, *Political*, 13.
32. Rawls, *Political*, 13.
33. Rawls, *Political*, 30.
34. Sandel, *Liberalism*, 161–162.
35. This criticism can be found from his *Liberalism and the Limits of Justice*, to his more recent collection of papers Michael J. Sandel, *Public Philosophy: Essays on Morality in Politics* (Cambridge, Massachusetts, Harvard University Press, 2005).
36. Sandel, *Liberalism*, 167.
37. Sandel, *Liberalism*, 167.
38. Taylor, *Sources*, 34–37.
39. Alasdair MacIntyre, *After Virtue* (University of Notre Dame Press, 2007), 246–247; Alasdair MacIntyre, *Whose Justice? Which Rationality?* (London, Duckworth, 1988), 336.
40. Stephen Mulhall and Adam Swift, *Liberals & Communitarians* (Massachusetts, Blackwell Publishing, 1996), 160.
41. Rawls, "Justice as Fairness", 408–409.
42. Rawls, "Justice as Fairness", 401 note 20.

43. Rawls, *Political*, 62.

44. Rawls, "Kantian Constructivism", 340; *Political*, 58; John Rawls, "The Idea of an Overlapping Consensus", in *Collected Papers*, 430.

45. Rawls, *Political*, 58.

46. Rawls, *Political*, xlviii–306.

47. Rawls, *Political*, xliv.

48. Rawls, *Political*, 54. (Emphasis added).

49. Rawls, *Political*, xliv.

50. Rawls, *Political*, 50.

51. Rawls, *Political*, 50.

52. Brian Barry, *Theories of Justice* (Los Angeles, University of California Press, 1989), Chapter 6.

53. Audard, *John Rawls*, 37.

54. Rawls, *Political*, 54.

55. Rawls, "The Idea of Public Reason Revisited", in *Collected Papers*, 578.

56. Rawls, *Political*, 56.

57. Rawls, *Political*, 57.

58. Rawls, *Political*, 4.

59. Rawls, *Political*, 36.

# THREE

## The Moral System

In the first two chapters, modern deontological liberalism has been characterized as a theory of justice based on three main features:

(1) It defines the 'right' independently from the 'good.'
(2) The 'right' is not directed to maximize the 'good.'
(3) The 'right' has priority over the 'good.'

In this sense deontological liberalism seeks to defend:

(4) A theory of justice that provides moral reasons that can be shared by all individuals independent of their own conceptions of the good life, and
(5) A political perspective that assumes the idea that rational individuals can chose and cherish valuable life plans and that they are reasonable enough to give priority to the principles of justice over their own conceptions of the good; that is, reasonable individuals are guided by a sense of justice within their own practical deliberations.

Accordingly, modern deontological liberalism assumes that moral norms (or the principles of justice) are *autonomously* justified, *universally* binding and *prior* to any other kind of normative claims. To support this claim about moral norms, deontological liberalism relies on certain sources of normativity and on a particular structure of practical reason that had given support to them. Liberals of this sort, such as John Rawls, Ernesto Garzón, Rainer Forst, Charles Larmore, and Bruce Ackerman, among others, embrace a Kantian deontological moral theory as the normative structure of their theories.

It is important to notice that not all deontological accounts of liberalism necessarily represent 'political liberalism' as the one defended by John Rawls, but all kinds of 'political liberalism' are related in one way or another to moral deontologism. This is mainly because political liberalism is constructed under the base of certain presumptions that only a Kantian structure of practical reason can give normative support to. For example, the priority of 'morality' over any other normative claim; a conception of the self which is prior to its ends and rationally capable of choosing them, and the existence of individual rights inherent to all human beings which are considered to be universally valid.

According to deontological liberals, these normative claims are assumed to be the ones that provide liberalism with a structure of practical reason that can solve, on the one hand, the problem of the limits of tolerance, and the so called "moral paradox" of tolerance, on the other. Before we enter into the discussion of these problems that derive from the idea of tolerance it is important to analyze the conceptual and justificatory structures that modern liberal authors have in mind.

Hence, my concern in this chapter is to analyze the moral premises of the deontological account of liberalism. To achieve this, I will briefly refer to the main characteristics of a deontological normative system; the rules and principles that guide a deontological understanding of practical reason.

## THE DEONTOLOGICAL MORAL SYSTEM (DMS)

Liberal deontological moral theories have an undeniable Kantian trait. No doubt there have been great modifications around Kant's moral philosophy in the works of contemporary moral and political philosophers—take for instance the great modifications that were argued before John Rawls has made to it—still and despite this, it is rather difficult to say that some contemporary deontological moral theories do not respond to a Kantian tradition of practical reason.

In *A Theory of Justice,* John Rawls defines deontological theories as those that: (1) define the 'right' independently of the 'good' and/or, (2) do not interpret the right as maximizing the good.[1] In broad terms, this frame of practical reason is interested in emphasizing the fact that the *right* moral action implies acting according to our moral duties, which are imposed by rules agreed upon in advance, and without regarding the consequences (beneficial or prejudicial) of such acts.

In *Right and Wrong,* Charles Fried states that the deontological theories defend posture (1) because "The goodness of the ultimate consequences does not imply the rightness of the actions which produced them."[2] And in *Privacidad, autonomía y tolerancia,* Martín Diego Farrell says that deontologism defends posture (2) because right action entails respecting certain previously accepted norms that agree upon what is right or what is wrong, then "the process through which we arrive at a result has priority over the result itself."[3]

Generally speaking, deontological perspectives sustain that correct moral actions entail a conscious acceptance of and compliance with moral obligatory norms, which are the ones that determine what is *right* and what is *wrong*. For the deontologists, these norms end up creating a border of limits that make morally incorrect, on the one hand, the pursuit of self-interested desires such as subjective values that cannot be required from anyone else except from us and, on the other hand, the possibility of qualifying as correct actions those that focus only on the outcomes. In moral philosophical terms, this entails that deontological moral theories reject both utilitarianism and any kind of moral egoism. Thus, deontological theory considers the possibility of qualifying certain acts as inherently wrong prior to any conflicting circumstances and independent of the consequences that acting according to them can generate.

It is important to take note of this last characteristic because it is precisely one of the characteristics that distinguish it from its archenemy: consequentialism. Contrary to the deontologists, consequentialists reject the idea that right actions are those that comply with determined general norms for action. From this perspective, moral or immoral acts are determined by the value of the ultimate consequences brought out by our actions and not by the compliance with moral duties. Then, a right action entails doing things in such a way that the act itself maximizes the individual or the general 'good' or some other value previously agreed upon.

The rationale behind the deontological perspective is still found in the three pillars of the Kantian moral philosophy: (1) the autonomy of persons, (2) human dignity, and (3) moral universality.

For Kant, these three concepts are interdependent. The autonomy of the people is based on the possibility of orienting our actions in accordance with those moral principles that we have accepted internally and with those we direct our plans of life.[4] Human dignity is a quality ascribed to all autonomous individuals. For Kant, in a way, human dignity consists in the capacity that every rational being has not to obey any other law than that which is self-imposed. And according to Forst's interpretation of Kant "moral persons are members of a 'kingdom of ends' who mutually recognized one another as free and responsible beings. As members of this kingdom, they are subject only to the laws that are strictly universal on the one hand, and can be regarded by each person as his or her own, self-given laws on the other hand."[5]

In the *Groundwork of the Metaphysics of Morals,* Kant says that: "Although in thinking the concept of duty we think of subjection to the law, yet at the same time we thereby represent a certain sublimity and dignity in the person who fulfills all his duties."[6]

Still, the formulation of moral autonomy as the capacity of a rational agent to self-legislate creates an apparent tension with the claim that moral laws are universal laws. For philosophers like Javier Murguerza this situation "settles him in perplexity."[7] According to him, how are we to sustain the idea that laws and moral judgments are capable of being universal while, at the same time, we sustain the idea of being autonomously legislated? The difference is to be found in the next words of Kant:

> *only to laws given by himself but still universal* and that he is bound to act in conformity with his own will, which, however, in accordance with nature's end is a will giving universal law. (…) one never arrived at a duty but instead at the necessity of an action from a certain interest. This might be one's or another's interest. But then the imperative had to turn out always conditional and could not be fit for a moral command. I will therefore call this basic principle the principle of the autonomy in contrast with every other, which I will accordingly count as heteronomy.[8]

Then, under this Kantian perspective deontological philosophers get rid of the conflict. In this respect, Garzón states that the Kantian self-legislation already contains a note of universality, which radically distinguishes it from the one that could be the result of an act of freedom which only responds to the individual interests of each person.[9] Sharing the same perspective, Forst says that "with this argument Kant seeks to explain the normativity of moral norms such that they are represented at once as 'laws' and nevertheless as 'products' of autonomy. "The moral law holds absolutely, but at the same time it is the law of freedom that summons its addressees to autonomy and responsibility."[10]

Considering that deontological philosophers see the tension between autonomy and universal laws solved in that way, we can infer that the three pillars of a DMS are no more different than the three basic formulations of the Kantian categorical imperative: (1) "Act only according to that maxim whereby you can at the same time will that it should become a universal law without contradiction" (*Universality principle*). (2) "Act in such a way that you treat humanity, whether in your own person or in the person of any other, never merely as a means to an end, but always at the same time as an end" (*Human dignity principle*). (3) "Therefore, every rational being must so act as if he were through his maxim always a legislating member in the universal kingdom of ends" (*Autonomy principle*).[11]

However, saying that the three basic notions correspond to the formulations of the Kantian imperative still does not tell us much about the premises of liberal deontological moral theories. In order to get there, we must take into consideration the principles that have been mentioned before. Indeed, those principles are the ones that make up the entire deontological framework. In other words, according to the DMS, anyone who accepts the validity of these principles is, likewise, committed to the value of the autonomy of the people. This is because for the moral conception held by deontological liberals, acting in a right way is acting in accordance with what has been autonomously accepted. Under this perspective, all genuine moral judgments ultimately rest upon a deep level of the agent's will. This implies that, at the very least, we should not act under social pressure or out of fear of legal sanctions, nor out of psychological compulsion. Up to what point is it compatible to sustain this moral perspective while at the same time, arguing in favor of the authority of the Law, is something that I will have to leave as an open question due to the limits I have imposed on myself. However, it seems to me that the subject deserves a lot of attention. From here it may be concluded that under a moral deontological philosophy the individuals have a leading role in the construction of moral norms. This perspective leads deontological authors to establish a first principle that gives shape to their structure, namely: *t he principle of moral autonomy.*

This principle excludes, first and foremost, every possibility to develop moral norms under a communitarian ethics or from a particularistic conception of morality. As it has been explained before, deontological liberals such as Rawls or Dworkin, for example, reject the possibility of imposing ethical communitarian values or values of majoritarian social groups upon individuals, they also reject the idea of making judgments and decisions taking only into consideration the particular and contingent circumstances at hand and without the guidance of general moral principles.[12]

If we take a closer look to the principle of moral autonomy we will notice that it entails two fundamental ideas that merge up at the end: the universal character of moral norms, and that all human beings are equal. Under these two conditions, from a moral point of view, no one is more valuable than anyone else. This means that all people are equally *responsible* for the rightness of their actions and equally bound to *respond* with reasons for all their actions.[13] In this context, the phrase *"right action"* means responding with an autonomous will and respecting the dignity of all humanity. "To be autonomous means to be situated in a space of norms and to be capable of acting in accord with reasons."[14] With a certain degree of confidence, we could say that this is the moral obligation par excellence in the *Deontological Moral System.*

Nonetheless, it is valid to question whether this obligation has exceptions; that is to say, are there any extreme situations in which non-compliance with our moral obligations can be justified? Are there any practical life situations that exempt us from our moral obligations, such as, for example, decisions or acts within the political realm? If the deontological system is to be coherent with its own bases, then the answer must be 'No': it is not possible to justify our non-compliance. In the first place, the answer is 'No' because the DMS shields itself behind the principle of *the inviolability of morals.*

We have seen that moral autonomy pinpoints the source of moral obligations. In this sense, the principle of inviolability becomes relevant because it tells us where some of the limits to the enforceability of these obligations reside. What this principle dictates is that *no one who is morally autonomous is exempt from fulfilling his or her moral obligations*. In other words, anyone who claims to encounter a concrete situation that makes it prima facie impossible to fulfill a moral obligation bears the burden of proof. He or she has to provide good reasons to justify his or her non-compliance with morality.

In second place, the negative answer comes from another principle of the DMS: *the inderogability of morals*. According to this principle, no one can derogate the principles that have been autonomously chosen. What this principle states is a prescription according to which all ethical and moral evaluations are applied to persons qua persons: "the institutional actions are likewise subjects of moral evaluation in that they are also voluntary actions of autonomous individuals."[15] An individual as a reasonable human being finds it impossible to act in a morally right way and to escape moral prescriptions at the same time. Henceforth, no one can establish a system of applicable norms to a determined field of the practical sphere (ethical, political or legal) without simultaneously derogating some moral principles.

We must observe the characteristically Kantian trait that lies beneath these last considerations. We must also not lose sight of another trait of the same nature that underlies the same principle of inderogability. This other trait states that morality is autonomous, in the sense that it does not leave room for any other kind of justifying reasons which are different from the moral ones, "the autonomy of morality means that there are no values or truths that can claim priority over it, in the sense either that morality rests upon them or that these values or truths can override morality. It is both normatively self-contained and has the final word within its own sphere of validity."[16]

This helps mould the Kantian identity of DMS vis-à-vis the boundaries and the enforceability of morals. In order to do so the DMS claiming the autonomy of morality stipulates its *supreme character*. According to the autonomy of morality, there are no reasons that can impose themselves upon moral ones. Denying this principle, while at the same time thinking that we are acting morally, is tantamount to allowing ourselves to be cornered by irrationality, because to commit ourselves to certain moral principles, accepting them as universally valid, and in the face of morally relevant situations neglecting to act in accordance to them, is to act in a irrational way. Thus, following Rainer Forst, the normative conception of a deontological perspective presupposes:

(1) a normative concept of the *person* in his or her dignity as a rational, autonomous being;
(2) an "absolutely" valid *moral law (Sittengesetz)*;

(3) *moral laws* (or norms) that derive their validity from the operation of the justification procedure of the categorical imperative.[17]

In this sense, and to conclude with Forst's claim, "the *autonomy of morality* is based on the *moral autonomy* of reasonable persons who bring forth a realm of normativity."[18]

This structure of practical reason is the one that allows deontological liberalism to sustain four of its basic philosophical claims: (1) The priority of the *right* over the *good*; which, as we have seen, gives a special priority in the legal, political and ethical spheres to individual basic rights. (2) The independence of the sources of moral normativity from any metaphysical or natural presumptions and their belonging exclusively to the autonomous will of each and every rational being. (3) To sustain a distinction between the *rational* and the *reasonable,* which leads liberalism to accept the 'fact' of plurality of rational, still incompatible and incommensurable, ways of life which are limited by general moral norms (they are reasonable). (4) To defend the idea that morality is a complete and self-sufficient system of practical norms.

With this bulk of considerations regarding the theoretical structure and the practical consequences of liberal deontological moral theories, now it is time to analyze the ways in which tolerance has been conceptually understood and normatively justified by them. Later, in part IV, I will address some critiques to this scheme of practical reason and I will denounce the tensions that exist between tolerance, understood as a moral ideal, and this structure of practical reason.

## NOTES

1. Rawls, *A Theory,* 26 and ss.
2. Charles Fried, *Right and Wrong* (Cambridge, Massachusetts, Harvard University Press, 1978), 9.
3. Martín Diego Farrell, *Privacidad, autonomía y tolerancia: Ruidos disonantes en ética* (Buenos Aires, Argentina, Hammurabi, 2000), 27.
4. Immanuel Kant, *Groundwork of the Metaphysics of Morals* (Cambridge University Press, 1997), 2.
5. Rainer Forst, "Moral Autonomy and the Autonomy of Morality. Toward a Theory of Normativity after Kant", in *The Right to Justification,* 47.
6. Kant, *Groundwork,* 46.
7. Javier Muguerza, *Desde la perplejidad* (México, Fondo de Cultura Económica, 1990), 688.
8. Kant, *Groundwork,* 40–41.
9. Ernesto Garzón Valdés, "La Alternativa del Disenso. La Propuesta de Javier Muguerza", in *Derecho, Ética y Política,* Ernesto Garzón Valdés (Madrid, Centro de Estudios Constitucionales, 1993) 473–489.
10. Forst, "Moral Autonomy", 47.
11. Kant, *Groundwork,* Section II.
12. Jonathan Dancy, "Ethical Particularism and Morally Relevant Properties", *Mind,* New Series Vol. 92, No. 368 (1983): 530.
13. Forst, *Contexts,* 256.

14. Forst, "Moral Autonomy", 45.
15. Garzón, "Moral y política", 555.
16. Forst, "Moral Autonomy", 46.
17. Forst, *Contexts*, 47.
18. Forst, *Contexts*, 47.

*II*

# The Liberal Idea of Tolerance

# FOUR

# Regarding the Concept

Today's debate about tolerance is divided by a series of irreconcilable postures regarding its concept and foundations. In contemporary philosophical literature, it is possible to find examples of widely dissimilar stances, such as the following:

> (1) On a conceptual level, (a) those who claim that tolerance is a "value-neutral"[1] concept, and therefore applicable to every case involving opposition or divergence, as against (b) those who claim that tolerance is a normative concept that only applies to the cases involving moral divergence or opposition.[2]
>
> (2) On a justificatory level, (c) those who argue that tolerance is a "calculation" rather than a "value"[3] ; a "monster motivated by fear," "intimidated [...] by distrust in its own power or by fear of the others power,"[4] as against (d) those who argue that, since tolerance is a moral value, it can only be justified by reasons of the same nature.
>
> (3) On an instrumental level, (e) those who contend that tolerance holds no intrinsic value but rather serves as a medium for the realization of other values, and (f) those who consider that tolerance is a value in itself.[5]
>
> (4) On a theoretical level, (g) those who claim that tolerance arises out of a commitment with ethical skepticism,[6] as against (h) those who maintain that tolerance may only be invoked by those who defend a moral objectivism.[7]

In addition to this, and in order to get a better idea of the vastness of the scenario of tendencies, we could also add to the list a complete framework of the ramifications derived from each and every one of these positions.

My purposes in this chapter are to present a brief and schematic map of the conceptual divergences that stem from the way this concept has been constructed by modern liberal authors. Later, in the next two chapters, I will dwell into more specific problems related to the relationship between tolerance understood as a moral ideal or as a virtue of justice and the philosophical structure of deontological liberalism. But in order to accomplish that, first we need to analyze some main conceptual characteristics about 'tolerance.'

## DISAGREEMENTS REGARDING THE CONCEPT OF TOLERANCE

In 1983, Manuel Vicent published a short story entitled *Keep your dirty hands off Mozart,* where he describes:

> A father willing to endure the aversion his children's habits provoked on his moderate leftist sensibility, residual of a bourgeois heritage. For years he tolerated the atrocious group of friends that gathered in his daughter's bedroom, all for the sake of keeping an open dialogue and to protect their individual freedom to develop. The worst thing was not that they would breeze past him without deigning to greet him but rather the goat stench that lingered behind. That they would wipe their muddy boots on the carpet, descend upon the bookshelves and pawing his books with dirty fingernails, that they would drink the whisky and urinate without flushing the chain. All this he was willing to tolerate. Until on day, on May 14, 1980, his daughter stepped out of the den, with greasy hair and yellow stained nicotine fingers; crossed the room and headed towards the library with the intent of showering her cronies Mozart's 40th symphony. Tolerance had reached its limit: the father [...] bolted out of the couch propelled by a spring and let out a deafening scream: not Mozart!!! Do not put your filthy hands on Mozart!!![8]

The attitude of Vicent's character is quite similar to that of Mary Warnock when she states:

> I am tolerant if one of my daughters' boy-friends wears sandals with his suit or a stick with his tweed coat, and I not only make no mention of this outrage, but actually express myself pleased when they announce their intention of getting married. I am exercising the virtue of toleration if I am still on good terms with my son, though when he stays in the house I can never clear the breakfast before lunchtime, nor be certain that there is any whisky left in the bottle for when the Chancellor calls.[9]

The attitudes described by both Vicent and Baroness Warnock coincide in several points: they are both in a 'hierarchically' superior position (mother or father) which enables them to be subjects of tolerance in relation to their children. They both feel that certain conditions have been violated (rules of etiquette in Warnock's case and minimum rules of decency in Vicent's case). And they both exercise a tolerant attitude for the sake of what they consider to be a more important value: which in this case may be their children's freedom to develop.

If we accept these conditions as the conceptual core of tolerance, then we will agree with Annette Schmitt when she says, embracing Peter Nicholson's proposal, that an act of tolerance is possible *"if and only if a person A omits, for determined reasons, to intervene (non-rejection) against Y action of person B, in spite that Y(B) injures (deviance) X relevant conviction of A (disapproval) and A has and can (power) act against Y(B)."* [10]

Even though this conceptual frame is widely accepted by moral and political philosophers, the interpretations that they attach to it are, for the most part, decidedly different. This, in great part, can be explained trough the *dependence* that the concept of tolerance has with distinct normative theories in the sense that philosophers like Rainer Forst or Glen Newey have understood such dependency. [11] In sections IV and V, I will argue that the concept of tolerance is not only *normative dependent* but it is also *contextually dependent*. But for the moment I will put this issue aside and I will return to the conceptual differences. As it was previously acknowledged, it is possible to find within the literature of liberalism at least two theses that defend irreconcilable postures about the concept of 'tolerance.' These stances are: 1) The wide scope thesis (or the wide thesis), and 2) The narrow scope thesis (or the narrow thesis). [12]

Authors who advocate the *wide scope thesis* call for a 'value-neutral' concept, detached or independent from the reasons that justify an act of tolerance. Ontologically speaking, for the authors who defend the wide scope thesis, tolerance is an attitude that does not require either positive or negative value in order to be accounted for, nor is it a subject to a concrete normative framework. With this they seek to expand the limits of application of the concept of tolerance.

In contrast with the previous view, philosophers who advocate the *narrow scope thesis* claim that tolerance is a 'moral ideal' and accordingly that it is a normative concept. This characteristic reduces the scope of its application to those cases where moral and ethical convictions are in play. Therefore, for them tolerance is considered as a 'virtue' or a 'principle' subject to a moral justificatory framework.

Delving into the subject of disagreements, the wide scope thesis claims that in order to recognize an act of tolerance it is only necessary to consider two 'conditions' or 'circumstances' of toleration: [13] (1) the existence of an action that 'injures a relevant conviction,' and 2) to have the 'power' or the 'competence' to act against such action.

This simple idea has generated heated debates amongst the supporters of both stances. For the authors of the narrow thesis, to speak of 'tolerance' without contemplating as part of that concept a third circumstance which considers *the pondering or balancing that exists between the value of an injured conviction and the reasons that justify the non-intervention*, is not to properly speak of tolerance.

The recognition, or lack thereof, of toleration's third circumstance is the source of the first confrontation between these two stances. Perhaps, taking into consideration the postulates of both theses, we could then argue that this conflict is only apparent, i.e. that the inclusion or exclusion of the third circumstance of tolerance brings with it different consequences, depending on the standpoint from which the concept is formulated. If, on the one hand, what we are attempting to build is a purely descriptive concept of tolerance, then it could be presumed that the exclusion of the third circumstance would not entail the same consequences that it would have if, on the other hand, the problem that we were attempting to resolve concerns normative matters.

Some authors of the wide thesis, such as A. Schmitt, claim that phrases such as "'X' is tolerant" or "action 'Z' is the expression of tolerance" have no reason to raise a positive or negative evaluation—that "an evaluation of 'X' and 'Z' is only possible if the reasons why this tolerance is practiced are expressed. When a government tolerates certain minorities for the sake of a security policy, tolerance becomes a political instrument. But if the government's goal is to protect the freedom and equality of all members of society, then it is practicing tolerance as a democratic virtue."[14] Henceforth, according to these comments, the risk that is taken is that of compromising the neutrality of the concept.

On the contrary, supporters of the narrow thesis consider it impossible to speak of tolerance without taking into account the balancing of reasons that lead us to non-intervention. Those who adhere to such a thesis argue that if this facet of tolerance (and other variants that we will touch upon later) is not taken into consideration, then we will run the risk of confusing it with other attitudes such as, for example, *compromising* (that is to say, consenting to something that is not believed to be fair, reasonable or true) purely for the sake of resolving a difference; the same goes for *patience* understood as the capacity to endure pain or tribulations calmly or without complaint, and also for *acceptance* meaning agreeing either expressly or by conduct with the acts of another person.

Following this outline, it seems that the difference between someone who compromises and someone who tolerates is that the former has no intention whatsoever of intervening: on the contrary, his or her desire is to put the dispute to an end as soon as possible, without thereby entailing any sort of utilitarian end or value judgment. In that situation, the person who compromises will display features of indifference. "The patient person who rejects an action is not linked with a tendency for intervention, but rather acts upon the hope or certainty that his object has a transitory existence."[15] The one who accepts on the other hand does not maintain his opposition to that which is being rejected; on the contrary, he eliminates it from his value or normative system the norm that previously prohibited the act.

This is an important point, since it distances tolerance from mere acceptance or rejection in conceptual terms, placing it somewhere in between.[16] It also clarifies the notion that one who is (in)tolerant is not by definition (un)compromising. We must not lose sight of the fact that the differences between tolerance and these other attitudes emerge from the conceptual requirement of including the idea of weighing of values within the tolerant subject's system, e.g., between the value of a relevant conviction and the reasons for not intervening against the damaging action.

Before we start discussing in detail the variants of the "circumstances of tolerance," it is important to stress another significant difference between these two theses: for the authors of the wide scope thesis, 'tolerance' means: knowing that something *differs* from our convictions and having the adequate *power* either to stop it or to let it pass. While for the authors of the narrow scope thesis, which is the scope adopted by most modern liberals as we have seen, 'tolerance' means: knowing that something *bad* is opposing one of our *relevant* convictions and, in spite of having the (physical) *power* or the (moral) *competence* to stop it, *for whatever ultimate reasons*, we let it pass.

It would then, in this sense, seem that there are two types of disagreements: one of a formal nature, which consists in the fact that for the wide scope thesis the *first* and the *second* 'circumstances' are *necessary* and *sufficient* for the concept of tolerance, while for the narrow scope thesis, while they are also necessary, they are however not sufficient. This is because the third circumstance of tolerance is also necessary so as not to confuse it with any other kind of attitudes. The other disagreement is of a substantive nature and is related to the idea that for the wide scope thesis, the concept of tolerance can be applied to any sort of rejection, while for the narrow scope thesis the concept only applies to rational disagreements.

We shall now return to our point of departure. As noted above, it can be argued that the problem of inclusion/exclusion represented by the third element of tolerance is a pseudo-problem. This can be argued by taking the perspective that both conceptual stances are not necessarily antagonistic and that, in fact, they have different methodological routes or that they seek different conceptual aims. In such a vein it could be stated that one seeks to answer the question: when did an act of tolerance take place? Whereas the other is looking for an answer to the question: when must an action be tolerated? Or, which actions are candidates for tolerance?

When looking at the problem from this perspective, apparently the situation could be summarized into two possibilities: (1) that there is no such debate precisely due to the fact that, since each stance takes a different methodological route, their arguments will never meet, and this will render them both intact after the "debate," and (2) that alternatively, and independently, from the methodological differences, one can consider that one of them is correct.

But there might be a third possibility in-between: the recognition that both have different methodological aims, but even in that case, arguing that one of them is correct. This is due to two considerations: (1) mentioning the reasons for conflict is not the same as evaluating the justificatory quality of those reasons; mentioning the reasons that lead us to choose a particular course of action does not compromise the descriptive neutrality (as the wide thesis claims), and (2) if they are used as reference for considering the reasoning that leads an agent to take a particular course of action, those reasons may also serve us to explain (descriptively) certain conduct. This third possibility is accepted by philosophers such as Joseph Raz and Juan Carlos Bayón,[17] who argue that "the concept of an explanatory reason presupposes or may be analyzed from a justificatory reason standpoint: an explanatory reason is a *belief in a justificatory reason*, so that this last concept becomes primary in terms of giving an account of the former one."[18]

The same perspective could be explained with the distinctions drawn by H. L. A. Hart in *The Concept of Law*. Hart distinguishes between two possible points of view that may be adopted in relation to rules: the *internal point of view*, and the *external point of view*. For Hart, the first one is the one adopted by a member of the society who accepts and recognizes the rules as guidelines for action. The second, the external point of view, is the one adopted by an impartial observer: "An observer is content merely to record the regularities of observable behavior in which conformity with the rules partly consists."[19]

For Hart, "statements made from an external point of view may themselves be of different kinds. For the observer may, without accepting the rules himself, assert that the group accepts the rules, and thus may from outside refer to the way in which *they* are concerned with them from the internal point of view."[20]

If this proves to be correct, then it is possible to argue the correctness of this third possibility in the sense that, indeed, both stances seek different methodological aims, but the exclusion of the *third* "circumstance of tolerance" is a must for both. In the case of the wide thesis, excluding it runs the risk of providing an incomplete and therefore defective description of the acts of tolerance. In the case of the narrow thesis, it would run the risk of not knowing the justificatory quality of the tolerated act.

Let us say that the authors of the wide thesis accept this and consider the matter settled. Nonetheless, other disagreements regarding what is meant by the *relevance* of an injured conviction and the *power* and *competence* to intervene against the object that is being tolerated exist.

## NOTES

1. Annette Schmitt, "Las circunstancias de la tolerancia", *Doxa. Cuadernos de filosofía del derecho*, 11 (1992): 71–85. Andrew Jason Cohen, "What Toleration Is", *Ethics*, 115 (2004): 68–95.

2. Peter Nicholson, "Toleration as a Moral Ideal", in *Aspects of Toleration: Philosophical Studies*, ed. John Horton, Susan Mendus, (London/New York, Methuen, 1985); Rodolfo Vázquez, *Liberalismo, Estado de Derecho y minorías* (México, Paidos-UNAM, 2001); Ernesto Garzón Valdés, "No pongas tus sucias manos sobre Mozart: Algunas consideraciones sobre el concepto de tolerancia", in *Instituciones Suicidas: Estudios de ética y política*, Ernesto Garzón Valdés (México, Paidós-UNAM, 2000), 181–198; D. D. Raphael, "The Intolerable", in *Justifying Toleration: Conceptual and Historical Perspectives*, ed. Susan Mendus (Cambridge University Press, 1988), 137–153.

3. Jesús Silva-Herzog, "Razones para la Tolerancia", in *Tolerancia y Pluralismo*, ed. Rodolfo Vázquez (México, Ediciones Coyoacán, 2005), 85.

4. Aurelio Arteta, "La tolerancia como barbarie", in *Tolerancia o barbarie*, ed. Manuel Cruz (Barcelona, Gedisa, 1998), 53; Richard Vernon and Samuel V. LaSelva, "Justifying Tolerance", *Canadian Journal of Political Science*, 17, 1 (1984): 3–23.

5. T. M. Scanlon, "The Difficulty of Tolerance", in *Toleration: An elusive virtue*, ed. David Heyd (Princeton University Press, 1996), 226–239; John Horton, "Toleration as a Virtue", in *Toleration: An elusive virtue*, ed. David Heyd (Princeton University Press, 1996), 28–43.

6. Geoffrey Harrison, "Relativism and Tolerance", *Ethics*, 86, 2 (January, 1976): 122–135; Gordon Graham, "Tolerance, Pluralism, and Relativism", in David Heyd, *Toleration*, 44–59.

7. Rodolfo Vázquez, *Entre la Libertad y la Igualdad: Introducción a la Filosofía del Derecho* (Madrid, Trotta, 2006), 127–61.

8. Manuel Vicent, *No pongas tus sucias manos sobre Mozart* (Madrid, Debate, 1983).

9. Mary Warnock, "The Limits of Toleration", in *On Toleration*, ed. Susan Mendus and David Edwards (Oxford, Clarendon Press, 1987), 125.

10. Schmitt, "Las circunstancias", 72 and *ss.*

11. Forst, "Toleration, Justice", 75; Glen Newey, *Virtue, Reason and Toleration: The Place of Toleration in Ethical and Political Philosophy* (Edinburgh University Press, 1999), 19, 35–39.

12. Susan Mendus, *Toleration and the Limits of Liberalism* (London, MacMillan, 1989), 15; Catriona McKinnon, *Toleration: A Critical Introduction* (London, Routledge Press, 2006), 19.

13. Glen Newey distinguishes between *conditions* and *circumstances* of toleration. The first ones he defines as "the terms which a given act has to meet if it is to qualify as an act of toleration" while, the second, as "the *opportunities* for acting tolerantly". Then according to Newey "the conditions of toleration are the standard by which we are to decide whether or not a given agent has in fact acted tolerantly in response to those circumstances", Newey, *Virtue*, 21. In fact I agree with Newey's distinction, still, I will use the term 'circumstances' to refer to what Newey calls "conditions" because this is the way most of the authors here quoted does. However, I still consider that Newey's distinction is more accurate.

14. Schmitt, "Las circunstancias", 84.

15. Vázquez, *Liberalismo*, 77.

16. McKinnon, *Toleration*, 35.

17. Joseph Raz, *Practical Reason and Norms* (Princeton University Press, 1990); Juan Carlos Bayón Mohino, *La normatividad del Derecho: deber jurídico y razones para la acción* (Madrid, Centro de Estudios Constitucionales, 1991).

18. Raz, *Practical Reason* , 18–19.

19. H. L. A. Hart, *The Concept of Law* (Oxford, Clarendon Law Series, 1997), 87.

20. Hart, *The Concept*, 87.

# FIVE

## On Relevant Convictions

There are different types of injuries and all of them vary in their levels of intensity. For example, many legal systems in the world recognize at least four different degrees of injuries: very mild, mild, severe and very severe; and two types of injuries: physical and mental. There are other legal norms that speak of moral injuries, such as those contemplated by almost every civil code and constitution in the occidental world (for example, injuries to the right of honor).

In sum, there are many types of injuries, and all vary in degree. But regarding the problems I will address in this part of the chapter, there is no need to delve deeply into the discussion of the concept of 'injury' or 'harm.' Although these terms are certainly subject to several interpretations and of great importance for the subject at hand, for the moment I will consider them as uncontroversial concepts. This is because the actual importance is premised on the type of injured 'conviction' rather than on the type of 'injury' or 'harm' suffered by it.

However, it is important not to oversee the fact that, in order to speak of tolerance, the existence of an 'injury' is a necessary condition, and that this injury must be inflicted by someone else. In other words, one of the conditions that allow us to speak of tolerance is the existence of an action[1] Y that injures the conviction X, and that Y was inflicted by an agent different from that holding X. And it must also not be forgotten that X must be *relevant*. Now, the problem that I will address is, the way the expression *relevant conviction* has been understood.

Luis Villoro has said that a "conviction corresponds with the beliefs we deem to be vitally important, those that satisfy our ends and give meaning to our existence, those that orient our life's necessary actions, although not necessarily the most probable or proved."[2]

In other words, a conviction plays a very *important* role within our set of values or in the normative system that harbors it. But, can any conviction be a candidate for tolerance? How do liberal authors define which convictions are *relevant* for tolerance?

According to Schmitt, "the importance of a conviction may be measured by observing, for example, whether the disgust (or irritation), namely, the rejection provoked by the injury is so big that it manifests the existence of a *tendency to respond with an intervention*."[3] Hence, according to her assessment, if we observe that the reaction is of such a magnitude that the injured person is forced to act against the action, whether to slow it, stop it or forbid it, we probably have a *relevant* conviction.

But this, in fact, does not really answer the question. The intensity of the reaction displayed by an individual does not define what should be understood by *relevance* of a conviction. The intensity of the reaction, as described by Schmitt, is precisely produced because the conviction injured was relevant and not the other way around. In other words, what makes the conviction a *relevant* conviction is the reaction produced by the injury. If the conviction had not been *relevant* prior to the injury then, according with Schmitt's definition, we would not be speaking properly of tolerance.

The point here is not the *intensity* of the reaction caused by the injury of a relevant conviction but rather who or how are we to define the *relevance* of a conviction? Joshua Halberstam has asserted that not every conviction is a candidate for tolerance.[4] Because this is precisely so, who is to decide or how is to be decided the *relevance* of a conviction? Should we accept that all the convictions considered by an agent as "relevant" can be candidates for tolerance? It seems to me that this is the crux of the matter within the deontological liberal thought.

Using Annette Schmitt and Mary Warnock's works as a starting point, we can say that those who adhere to the wide thesis would answer the second question affirmatively. Those who defend this thesis believe that the relevance of the conviction is not to be determined by any external objective criteria but by a mere subjective whim of the agent. Accounting for such understanding of 'relevance' by way of the *intensity* of the reaction caused by the injury or by way of the subjective or passionate decision of the agent without considering any other justificatory criteria, is a way not to compromise their conceptual posture. However, if this posture is brought to a justificatory level it would corner them into sustaining that the idea of tolerance is an exclusive concept of subjectivism or relativism. This is because there is no other criterion of 'relevance' beyond the wishes, passions, whims or personal preferences and desires of each individual (no matter how illegitimate they might be). The narrow thesis authors, on the contrary, would answer the same question negatively. The guiding idea behind this answer is that tolerance is a moral value, a virtue of justice or a principle, that must take as *relevant convictions* only those that are considered rational.

Both stances differ radically at this point, the latter takes a meaning of 'relevance' in a very narrow way limiting it only to those convictions that depart from a rationally chosen conception of the good, while the former understands it in a very wide sense (without limits), considering that any conviction that an agent regards to be relevant can be a legitimate candidate for tolerance including prejudice or false beliefs. Following both ways of understanding the relevancy of a conviction for tolerance, we can make an inquiry into the reasons that some philosophers have in mind to defend these perspectives. This can be done by analyzing the different types of normative systems from which convictions are derived.

According to Schmitt we can find at least six different normative systems from which some convictions derive, these are: *1. Aesthetic mandates, 2. Social conventions, 3. Prejudices, 4. Principles of means-end rationality, 5. Religious conventions,* and *6. Moral conventions (ethical beliefs).*

This list can be considered a good starting point since the wide scope thesis considers all convictions derived from these systems as relevant and the narrow thesis does not consider that all the convictions derived from these systems enjoy the *relevance* envisaged. Henceforth, the list provided by Schmitt gives us the opportunity to analyze the reasons that each stance provides to support their perspectives.

It is pertinent to begin with the analysis of the *religious conventions* because, historically speaking, they have paved the way for a debate on tolerance and also because they relate to one of the most intriguing and thorniest types of tolerance nowadays. Additionally, they represent some of the most difficult cases theoretically and practically speaking.

It is commonly thought that those individuals who hold religious beliefs have very strong feelings about our place in life and about the way we should behave with others. Regularly, they guide themselves by ideas about the eternal life and about supra-empirical entities which tell them how to guide their conducts and behaviors towards others. They tend to believe that whoever does not adopt or follow the 'words' of God is doomed to eternal perdition. Heretics and atheists will lose all possibility to access paradise or similar promised land in their afterlife, and their lives will be marked by sin.

Benjamin Constant, for example, was aware of the problems that we can face when trying to define and to describe the power that religious convictions infuse in the believer's consciousness:

> This feeling relates closely to all noble, delicate, and profound passions. Like all of them it has something mysterious about it. For common reasoning cannot explain any of these passions in a satisfactory manner. Love, that exclusive preference for an object we been able to manage without for a long time and which so many others resemble, the need for glory, that thirst for a fame which must outlast us, the enjoy-

ment we find in devotion, and enjoyment contrary to the habitual in-
stinct of our egoism, melancholy, that sadness without cause, in the
depths of which there is a pleasure we could not begin to analyze, a
thousand other sensations we cannot describe, which fill us with vague
impressions and confused emotions: affinity with religious feeling. All
these things aid the development of morality. They make man break
out of the narrow circle of his interests, they give the soul that flexibility, that delicacy, that exaltation smothered by habituation to life in the
community and the calculations it necessitates. [5]

Following Constant's appreciation, religious convictions are one of the
most rooted beliefs that human beings can cherish (when they cherish
them). They are a mixture between practical, theoretical and metaphysical claims that tend to reconstruct in a systematic way an explanation for
every event, for every cause and effect, and for every belief humans can
hold. In this way, and using Rawls terminology, religion qualifies as a
*fully comprehensive conception of the good*. [6]

Though, it has been argued before that, precisely, one of the main
problems of liberalism when it faces the problems of religion is to consider them as any other conception of the good. When discussing religious
beliefs Michael J. Sandel asserts that it is a liberal mistake to ground
religious liberty not on respect for the ethical value of religion but on
persons' free choice to lead a religious life. This perspective is rooted in
the priority of the right over the good and in the priority of the self over
its ends as we have seen. Liberalism, in this way, understands religious
beliefs as something that has been deliberately chosen by individuals.
Sandel claims that liberals protect religious beliefs as they protect freedom of choice or freedom of expression and not as something inscribed
in their personality. [7] For Sandel, then, religion has strong practical implications in the deliberations of any religious person. Religious convictions,
understood in this way, constitute part (or all) of the self. This brings a
problem for deontological liberalism according to Sandel, because it
creates a very serious tension between the priority of the right over the
good when it is applied to the religious convictions of individuals. [8]

But if, for philosophers like Sandel, religious convictions create certain
kinds of tensions between religious beliefs and the principles of justice,
for liberal philosophers the distinction between the right and the good
works precisely in the other direction: the sphere of the rights works to
confront and to dissolve religious disagreements in the sense that it
should always prevail over the good. When liberals deal with these types
of convictions they vindicate their position by taking into account a very
important matter that arises as a limit of tolerance: the fact that we cannot
tolerate something that we are not able to prevent, deter or forbid (we
will have a closer look at this in the following chapter). Deontological
liberals, in this sense, consider that these limits became much stronger
because of the role they give to "individual rights." The recognition of

these rights, as seen thus far, according to this kind of liberalism, creates a restriction for toleration in such a way that when a conduct, act or belief is explicitly allowed by these basic individual rights, any religious, ideological, aesthetical, or philosophical belief of a reasonable conception of the good has reached a limit.

This is, in fact, a core idea of deontological liberalism. Take, for instance, John Rawls's perspective on the matter. In his *The Idea of an Overlapping Consensus*, Rawls raises the question: "How can a political conception of justice express values that, under the reasonably favorable conditions that make democracy possible, normally outweigh whatever other values conflict with them?" to which he answers: "The most reasonable political conception of justice for a democratic regime will be, broadly speaking, liberal. But this means, [. . .] that it protects the familiar basic rights and assigns them a special priority; it also includes measures to ensure that all persons in society have sufficient material means to make effective use of those basic rights. Faced with the fact of pluralism, a liberal view removes from the political agenda the most divisive issues, pervasive uncertainty and serious contention about which must undermine the bases of social cooperation."[9] Here the Reasonable works as an exclusionary mechanism in the way it was defined in chapter 2.

For Rawls, the way to construct a cooperative democratic society is by assuring that all individuals "within the scope allowed by the basic liberties and the provisions of a just constitution, [. . .] can pursue their way of life on fair terms and properly respect its (non-public) values."[10]

Closely related to Rawls's line of thought is the one of Rainer Forst. For Forst, "tolerant citizens are 'reasonable' in accepting that the 'context of justification' for ethical beliefs and general norms are different: they see that an *ethical objection* does not amount to a legitimate *moral rejection*; and they also see that they have a moral duty to tolerate all those ethical beliefs and practices that they disagree with."[11] The idea behind Forst's claim is that if ethical beliefs cannot be thought as legitimate enough as to defeat moral reasons, a fortiori, any other kind of beliefs different than the ethical ones cannot defeat this type of reasons either. Forst's idea is that moral principles, as those conceived as individual rights, are justified by the criteria of *reciprocity* and *generality*. As we will discuss in one of the next chapters (chapter 8), these two criteria are the normative bases that Forst uses to argue the justifiability of mutually binding norms and the limits of toleration.[12]

If adherents of deontological liberalism, such as Rawls and Forst are, sustain the difference between *ethics* and *morality*, and the priority of the later over the former, it would be difficult for them to accept (or, at least, it would sound odd for them) that in cases of religious convictions, nowadays, someone attempts to argue, as John Locke did in his time,[13] reasons why a society or a State should *tolerate* people who adopt a different religious creed from the one of a majority group or from the official one, and it would sound especially strange if this argument lacked any mention to universal moral rights. Due to this distinction, from a liberal perspective it is quite hard to speak of tolerance towards heretics, atheists, Muslims, Jews, Catholics, etc. According to its own bases, we must have legal and political guarantees that protect our universal *right* to adopt, profess or choose any religious creed that we desire and to profess it publicly.

This could certainly be counter-argued with the events occurred since 9–11 or with what some newspapers have called "the modern Holy War": with the religious conflicts between Middle East and big parts of the Western world, as well as with the conflicts that arise amongst ethnic and religious communities within European countries such as is the case with Belgium, Holland, Northern Ireland and France, among others in Europe; or Bolivia, Ecuador, Guatemala, Mexico and Peru, in Latin America, or Israel, Palestine, Egypt and Syria in the Middle East.

However, and in spite of these examples, many deontological liberals such as Rawls, Nino, Forst or Dworkin may state, that it is because they do recognize these types of rights that these events are subject to the most profound moral criticism. Of course, this argument is based exclusively on the liberal idea that all human beings have universally recognized their right to exercise, hold and profess any kind of religious, ideological or philosophical belief.

The liberal argument to limit tolerance within the frame of basic rights can be clarified with the case of the Danish newspaper *Jyllands-Posten* that in November 2005 published cartoons depicting the Islamic prophet Muhammad. This event led to a series of violent protests by the Muslim community, whose members accused the cartoons of being culturally insulting, islamophobic and blasphemous, stating that their intent was to humiliate the Muslim minority residing in Europe. On the other hand, the supporters of the Danish newspaper argued the right to freedom of expression. This case shares the same general characteristics as the recent terrorist attacks in France against the satirical newspaper *Charlie Hebdo*, where al-Qaeda terrorists brutally killed 12 people to "avenge" the prophet.

We should keep in mind that during these events the convictions at play were considered as *ethically relevant*, and that public opinion referred continuously to the word 'tolerance' and its role within a plural society. However, it is hard to consider that when the State has already taken matters into its own hands, that this problem is within the realm of *tolerance*; on the contrary, we are dealing with a problem of conflict of rights (between freedom of expression and the right that protects honor) and their effective application. No doubt that the weight attributed to each one of these rights is a subject of discussion. It greatly depends on the standpoint we are using to interpret the rights in question, in other words, which one is more important or bears more weight. Several legal philosophers, for example Robert Alexy, have defended different kinds of interpretations and arguments about how we should attribute specific weight to certain rights. Aside from these discussions, the point I am trying to make here is that, specifically, this problem is not a problem of tolerance as it was argued by some public intellectuals, but it was a problem related to the techniques of legal adjudication.

Going back to the argument above, if the liberal premises impede us to talk about forbearance when we talk about rights, then, when we talk about rights we are also impeded from talking about tolerance.

For instance, Richard Vernon and Samuel LaSelva, defend this same argument in the following way: "the recognition of rights of any kind makes tolerance unnecessary. If to have a right is to have a *protected* choice, then rights and tolerance arguments differ in at least one fundamental respect: the justification of forbearance in the face of disapproval is central in the case of tolerance; but in the case of rights no question of forbearance or of its justification can arise." [14]

Assuming the idea that our convictions hold normative boundaries which are based on a moral normative system would help us to define which convictions deontological liberalism takes to be *relevant* in the context of tolerance. A stance, as the liberal one, that takes seriously the existence of individual rights will somehow limit the possibilities of (in)tolerance in the public sphere towards certain actions, conducts and beliefs, even though that some individuals might consider them as bad or false. [15] In this sense, liberal moral principles outline the boundaries between what is tolerable and what is intolerable or what should not be tolerated within the public sphere.

Albeit that most liberals accept that moral norms put boundaries over different conceptions of the good, there are situations in which the convictions at play fall beyond the reach of the normative force of moral norms. These kinds of situations belong to what has been called the "private sphere." In this realm we can find all kinds of beliefs and conflicts that are not necessarily constrained by moral principles. We have to ask ourselves if these moral boundaries also apply in the "private domain." When dealing with religious matters it is difficult to make a clear-cut distinction between the 'private' and the 'public' spheres. Of course, in part this is due to the fact that she or he who holds a religious belief has the certainty of knowing our divine destiny, and that for these individuals those beliefs have, without a doubt, a type of normative-ethical force. Nonetheless, it can be argued that through the prism of liberalism, in the private sphere, these boundaries should also be assumed by any reasonable person independent of any particular religious doctrine.

Let us remember that for John Rawls a "reasonable" person is "ready to propose principles and standards as fair terms of cooperation and to abide by them willingly, given the assurance that others will likewise do so." [16] A reasonable person has the capacity to argue with reasons that can be generally shared. Ernesto Garzón Valdés has argued that the reasonableness of persons depends on their capacity to give and accept what he calls "bridge reasons." Reasons that can be shared and understood by any individual that wishes to take part in the public deliberation;[17] this excludes, by definition, reasons that belong to personal religious, metaphysical or ideological beliefs that lack the characteristic of being "shareable." These are the same kind of reasons that other authors have called "moral reasons"[18] or "public political reasons."[19] Most deontological liberal authors define them as reasons that can be accepted by any person, independent of his or her own particular conception of the good, and to fundamental general norms of conduct. So, a reasonable person is the one who accepts these kinds of reasons and guides his or her conducts towards others according to them, while an unreasonable one rejects them.

This is why Rainer Forst says that "persons are tolerant to the extent that, even though they disagree with others about the nature of the good and true life, they tolerate all other views within the bounds of reciprocity and generality. This is why toleration is a *virtue of justice* and a *demand of reason.*"[20]

We have seen until now that for deontological liberal philosophers, tolerance is a personal attitude adopted only by reasonable persons.[21] In this sense, tolerance turns out to be a demand of justice, a moral ideal. Taking into account this perspective that understands a tolerant person as a reasonable one, in the case of religious toleration we can distinguish between the *reasonable believer* (i.e. the one who adopts a more modest position facing his or her religious doctrine or set of beliefs and is willing to respect other people's ways of life by bracketing his or her believes when judging others' lives), and the *fanatic believer* (who holds an unwavering religious stance and truly believes that anyone who thinks differently is doomed to perdition and, therefore, he/she seeks to use any kind of social repression to ensure the dominance of his or her own conception of the good in the name of salvation). Religious toleration, then, is only possible for the reasonable believer, for the one who accepts the demands of justice; the one, that has a "sense of justice."

Still, as already mentioned, the moral boundaries of tolerance may become blurred within the 'private domain' and, no doubt, may even change. Accordingly, the example provided by Mary Warnock will serve as a starting point which will help us become better acquainted with the arguments that each thesis offers in order to determine the 'relevance' of the convictions that are candidates for tolerance within this 'private sphere.'

What Warnock is briefly telling us is that if she were to learn that one of her daughter's 'boyfriends' wears sandals with his suit or carries a walking stick while wearing a tweed jacket, in different circumstances (in the case that they were not engaged) she would consider it an intolerable 'outrage.'

One interpretation of this example provides us with a good guideline from which we can analyze the *aesthetic mandates*. The reason Warnock tolerates this 'outrage' is because she considers her daughter's happiness to be more important than her boyfriend's limited sense of aesthetics. On the other hand, another interpretation states that it is rather likely that Warnock is engrossed in a *prejudice* which implies that men who dress in a certain way are neither 'good' nor 'successful,' which will lead her to consider whether she should or should not tolerate this situation, given that the 'poorly dressed' man is planning to marry her daughter.

Warnock intentionally formulates this clearly trivial example to show us the ineffectiveness of the narrow scope thesis. According to her, the adoption of the narrow thesis is an unnecessary way of reducing the scope of the concept of tolerance, since this thesis only allows us to speak of the cases where matters of *moral* or *ethical relevance* (rational or reasonable) are in play. For Warnock, the reality of this concept is quite different. According to her, in everyday life, this term is generally used in many situations where we cannot draw a clear distinction between preferences and tastes and what is considered to be morally or ethically relevant. She simply does not "believe that a distinction can be drawn, [. . .] between the moral and the non-moral, resting on the presumption that the moral is rational or subject to argument, the non-moral a matter of feeling or sentiment."[22]

It is for this reason that Warnock prefers to distinguish between two types of concepts of tolerance: a weak concept, which enables us to speak of tolerance in the context of our tastes and preferences (non-moral) being affected and a strong concept, or tolerance with regard to what we morally disapprove. The proposal of a double concept, or better of a double function of the concept proposed by Warnock is inadequate for two reasons: first, because if what Warnock desired was to avoid the ambiguity of the term she instead, with this double function that she is attributing to it, renders it even more confusing and difficult to manage. Consider many other distinctions that surround the concept of tolerance, such as: "private and public tolerance,"[23] "negative and positive tolerance,"[24] "horizontal and vertical tolerance,"[25] etc. In this sense, Warnock's distinction would only serve to amplify the situation: "weak public tolerance," "strong public tolerance," "weak vertical tolerance," "strong vertical tolerance," and so on. This situation will only make it more difficult to define and respectively recognize acts of tolerance.

The second and the more important reason is that Warnock's proposal regrettably leads us back to square one. What differences can we find between Warnock's weak sense and the wide thesis, or between her strong sense and the narrow thesis? On the contrary, her proposal places us at the same crossroads: either we accept that tolerance may be used for any kind of rejection that goes without any intervention and thus renders it a morally trivial concept, or we accept that tolerance is a moral value which only comes into play, at the expense of reducing its scope, in those cases involving situations of which we morally or ethically disapprove. In other words, the distinction proposed by Warnock does not differ from the one that we have called the narrow/wide theses discussion—which is the one that she was trying to resolve in the first place.

Going back to the two interpretations offered before the example of Warnock, the defenders of the narrow thesis in the first case would infer that the relevancy of the conviction is at risk because it is based upon fashionable reasons, which are irrelevant from a moral or from an ethical standpoint. Taking into consideration the premises upon which the narrow thesis is constructed, it is possible to infer that it is not only irrelevant from these points of view, but is also irrelevant from the perspective of tolerance. According to this thesis, the reasons that justify the suppression of the intervention against the tolerated subject should be of a moral nature. In this case we are unable to understand how we could explain a genuine pondering of values that allows to talk about an act of tolerance; in any case we could better speak of a sentiment of disgust or resignation instead of an act of tolerance.

It is important to note this matter because, if we understand tolerance as a moral ideal when the injured conviction is an ethical or moral conviction, then the reasons for refraining from acting against the tolerated agent, according to a moral deontological stance, should necessarily be moral reasons. This issue will be addressed in greater detail below and in further chapters. However, it may be noted now that the reason for this is that moral reasons are taken, by modern deontological liberalism, to be ultimate reasons for action.[26] This is important because herein lies a second disagreement: the types of reasons that both theses have in mind in order to justify an act of tolerance.

For those who adhere to the narrow thesis, the reasons given for non-intervention following violation of a relevant conviction must, due to the type of relevance they have in mind, be exclusively moral reasons. Otherwise we could not properly speak of tolerance as a 'moral ideal' or as an 'ideal of justice.' On the other hand, those who adhere to the wide thesis consider that the reasons for non-intervention—or the reasons that justify an act of tolerance—may be of different kinds: moral, prudential, faith based and even prejudice based or pragmatic.

If we consider the wide thesis, the second interpretation of Warnock's example could lead us to think that even if her conviction were based on a prejudice—that is, an unjustified belief—it would still create a conflict of values within its normative system. For example: her daughter's immediate happiness at the expense of a lifetime of hardships and limitations (which is where the prejudice is hinged) versus her daughter's future happiness with the inevitability of the immediate pain produced by the disappointment she will experience by not marrying that man.

However, when it comes to preferences and prejudices, the relevance of the conviction, according to the narrow thesis, is always at risk. Peter Nicholson, a champion of the narrow concept, has said that if "[t]oleration is a matter of moral choice, our tastes or inclinations are irrelevant."[27] The problem, in this case, is centered on the fact that Warnock's conviction is a *weak conviction*, in the sense that it lacks any rational base. Under a deontological perspective it is difficult to sustain that something believed as non-tasteful for one individual would allow the moral possibility of either rejecting it or imposing it on another.[28]

The crux of the matter is that while the wide thesis does not consider the existence of a *balancing* (the third circumstance of tolerance) between different values, the narrow thesis considers it as a necessary condition. Recall that on this point the narrow thesis is clear: it claims the existence of a third circumstance of tolerance which talks about the balancing of reasons for and against toleration. For those who defend this thesis, the existence of a balancing of values is a sine qua non requirement in order to invoke the idea of tolerance as a moral ideal.

It is worth noting that this balancing of values is not as peaceful as it may sound. In most cases the balancing exercise incarnates a genuine conflict of values which, as I will argue, under the premises defended by the narrow thesis (adopted by deontological liberals), can take the form of 'tragic' cases or genuine moral dilemmas. This is because for the authors who adopt this conception of tolerance the convictions that raised problems of tolerance should be *relevant* and the reasons justifying the act of tolerance should be *moral*. Under this scenario there is a high risk that the decision over whether or not to tolerate certain actions can leave behind some moral residue (as a sense of regret) for the agent of tolerance (I will address this problem in chapters 16 and 17).

It has been stated that the *intensity* of the rejection is, for the defenders of the wide thesis, one way of defining the *relevance* of a conviction, while for the supporters of the narrow thesis that the *intensity* cannot define what *relevance* should be. In that case, following the line of reasoning presented by the narrow thesis, we should now inquire about what could the *types* of rejections (and not the *intensity*) can tell us about the *relevance* of a conviction.

One of Peter Nicholson's more interesting points is his distinction between two types of rejection: *dislike* and *disapproval*.[29] This distinction will, undoubtedly, help us to pinpoint which types of convictions are considered *relevant* for the narrow thesis. The distinction between 'dislike' and 'disapproval,' as formulated by Nicholson, is based on the difference between *moral* and *non-moral convictions*. Nicholson says that by "disapproval" we generally understand a rejection based on moral reasons, while by "dislike" we understand an irrational feeling or non-moral rejection.[30] The narrow thesis, which Nicholson advocates, states that if we understand tolerance as a moral value then, in order to apply the concept, we must exclude rejection based on *dislikes* and only accept rejection based on *disapproval*. It is important to notice that Nicholson does not make an implicit distinction between *ethical beliefs* and *moral reasons*. But following his reasoning is possible to see that he will not have a problem accepting that acts of tolerance begin with something that we ethically disagree. In this sense, 'disapproval' can also be considered as an *ethical objection* and not only as a morally based one.

Therefore, if we take into account the fact that for one of the theses, the existence of genuine tragic conflict between values or principles is a consequence of tolerance and that for the other one it is not, then it all takes a new meaning. The wide thesis does not rule out rejection by *disapproval* because as we have seen under it, tolerance ranges from cases of moral and ethical disapproval to cases of aesthetic and fashion dislikes and the reasons that may justify non-intervention do not necessarily have to be moral reasons. On the contrary, the authors of the wide thesis believe that this would limit the scope of application and reduce tolerance's explanatory power.

According to the narrow thesis's authors, this posture trivializes the idea behind the concept. They state that, the idea of tolerance is based (1) on a conflict of values (between the objected conduct and the reasons that justifies the non-intervention), and (2) on the tolerator's reasonableness or sense of justice to justify the choice made between them.

A frequent argument used by the wide thesis authors to include dislikes as part of the concept of tolerance, is that otherwise, matters such as racial prejudice would be excluded from the vocabulary of tolerance. Peter Nicholson argues against this saying that: "The addition of 'dislike' may well be important for the historical or sociological study of toleration, where 'toleration' is a descriptive term. A definition of the moral ideal, however, must exclude 'dislike.' [. . .] we must see the moral ideal of toleration solely in terms of disapproval, i.e. of the making of judgments and the holding of reasons over which moral argument is possible."[31]

Until which point are liberals allowed, theoretically speaking, to include dislikes such as racial prejudice within the concept of tolerance? Is it possible to think, under the liberal perspective, of tolerance towards Blacks, Jews or Latinos based on race? We should not forget that in order to speak of tolerance we not only need to have a rejection of *Y*, but also need the power or competence to prevent, detain or prohibit *Y*. It seems that as far as problems of racial prejudice are concerned, it is not possible to find such a condition.

What is important of Nicholson's distinction is not the difference between moral and non-moral convictions but the one between convictions that can be subject of an argument and convictions that cannot. This difference is not a trivial one, because the emphasis now is put on convictions that are based on reasons that can be rationally defended and convictions that are based on prejudice or false beliefs or on pure emotions. In such a case, rational convictions, or convictions that can be subject of an argument, are not necessarily only those of a moral or ethical nature but also of another kind, such as for example, certain aesthetic convictions (as we will see, this coincides with Garzón's and Forst's acceptance of including these kind of objections within the realm of tolerance). As Rawls puts it, a belief is justified when, and because, it would survive if the subject were to bring all of his or her beliefs into "reflective equilibrium."[32] "A reasonable man—continuing with Rawls—knows, or tries to know, his own emotional, intellectual, and moral predilections and makes a conscientious effort to take them into account in weighing the merits of any question. He is not unaware of the influences of prejudice and bias even in his most sincere efforts to annul them."[33] It is indispensable to remember at this point that when Rawls defines what he understands by 'conceptions of the good,' he not only includes rational criteria such as 'means-ends' principles or self-interests desires but also affection and attachments of many sorts, such as, family, persons, country, community.

In that sense, then it is clear that a pure *rational* criterion is not sufficient for deontological authors. There is another ingredient that we should take into consideration when we talk about convictions that can be candidates for tolerance: namely the *relevancy* for the life of the tolerator. Convictions for tolerance not only have to be *rational* in the sense above described but they also have to play an important part in what authors, such as Bernard Williams, like to call our *ground projects*.[34] Convictions must be central to a person's self, the loss of all or most of these would remove meaning from his or her life, and, therefore, leave him or her unclear why they should go on at all.[35] In Williams's words: "A man may have, for a lot of his life or even just for some part of if, a *ground* project or set of projects which are closely related to his existence and which to a significant degree give meaning to his life."[36]

In this sense, it will be argued that those convictions that meet the requirements of *rationality* and of *relevancy* are the ones that can be candidates for tolerance. This means that tolerance not necessarily has to be reduced to moral convictions or to mere dislikes in Nicholson's simplistic terms.

If Warnock could rationally defend her suspicion about her daughter's boyfriend of being a man of no success, and this being a conviction that has ruled her life in a profound way—as Williams describes it—then it is possible that her case could qualify as a case for tolerance.

Now, if we pay attention, the second circumstance of tolerance is one of the main tenets of a liberal account of tolerance. Hence it is probably best to move on with this discussion and address the conditions that have to be present in order to be able to speak of the 'competency' and 'power' required for tolerance, before we enter in more specific discussion about these kind of conflicts that surround the mere idea of tolerance.

NOTES

1. I will understand the term 'action' as both positive interventions or *doing*, as well as, omissions or *not doing*.

2. Luis Villoro, *Creer, saber, conocer* (México, Siglo Veintiuno, 1982), 119.

3. Schmitt, "Las circunstancias," 73.

4. Joshua Halberstam, "The Paradox of Tolerance," *The Philosophical Forum*, 190, (1982–83): 191.

5. Constant, *Principles*, 132.

6. Rawls, *Political*, 13.

7. Sandel, *Democracy's*, 62–64.

8. Sandel, *Liberalism*, 133–134.

9. Rawls, "Overlapping Consensus," 439.

10. Rawls, "Overlapping Consensus," 438.

11. Forst, "Toleration, Justice," 78.

12. Forst, *Contexts*, 36 and ss.

13. John Locke, "A Letter Concerning Toleration, being a Translation of the Epistola de Tolerantia," in *On line Library of Liberty, The Works of John Locke*, 5 (2010): 1–36. I do not think that the thesis I am defending here enters into a disagreement with the one of Locke. In that sense, I am not trying to develop a critique of Locke, but am simply reviewing the evolution that liberal thinking has had since his time.

14. Vernon, LaSelva, "Justifying," 12–13.

15. Forst, *Context*, 41–45.

16. Rawls, *Political*, 49.

17. Ernesto Garzón Valdés, "¿Puede la razonabilidad ser un criterio de corrección moral?," in *Instituciones Suicidas*, 245–246.

18. Forst, *Contexts*, 43.

19. Rawls, *Political*, xix.

20. Forst, "Toleration, Justice," 78–79.

21. Forst, "Toleration, Justice," 78–79.

22. Warnock, "The Limits," 126.

23. The difference between private and public tolerance comes from the distinction made in chapter 1, between the "public" and the "private" spheres. Specifically, this distinction refers to the different kinds of spheres where acts of tolerance can take place. Normally, private tolerance is understood as the one exercised between individuals within their private sphere, while public tolerance is exercised by the authority or a majority group. The former is not intended to have an impact on social-political discourse, while the latter is considered as an exercise that is aimed at having an impact by changing public institutions and policies.

24. Negative and positive tolerance, are conceived as two different conceptions of toleration. "Negative tolerance" consists in tolerating an action because the consequences of not doing it are far more serious. In other words, there are those who justify tolerance because they believe that to do otherwise would represent a higher moral cost than the one incurred by the suppression of a conviction. Clearly, this conception does not attribute tolerance an intrinsic value; on the contrary, it leaves a distinct instrumentalist taste compared to its counterpart, "positive tolerance," which does consider that tolerance holds value in itself and that from there we derive a *duty* to tolerate. This conception takes the justification or tolerance as a moral duty which is independent of the consequences (favorable or unfavorable) that they may generate.

25. Garzón Valdés distinguishes between two types of tolerance: one that makes reference to a situation of tolerance where there is a relationship of supra-subordina-

tion between the subject and the object of toleration, this is what he calls "vertical tolerance," and the other, called "horizontal tolerance" where an act of tolerance takes place among equals or between individuals in the same hierarchical position. Garzón, "No pongas tus sucias manos . . ." *op. cit.*, p. 183. I will discuss this point in the next chapter.

26. Carlos S. Nino, *Ética y Derechos Humanos: Un Ensayo de Fundamentación* (Argentina, Astrea, 2005), 111.

27. Nicholson, "Toleration," 160.

28. This impediment, I believe, will apply for the majority of the moral standpoints, whether objectivist or relativist. The objectivists know that it is morally irrational to try to impose a subjective belief, while the relativist knows that one cannot impose a belief on another because, from their doctrinal standpoint, it would be morally incorrect; in other words, they believe that two people may emit different moral judgments over one same act and both judgments could be considered valid.

29. Nicholson, "Toleration," 160.

30. Nicholson, "Toleration," 160.

31. Nicholson, "Toleration," 160.

32. John Rawls, "Outline of a Decision Procedure of Ethics," in *Collected Papers*, 5.

33. Rawls, "Outline of a Decision," 12.

34. Bernard Williams, "Persons, character and morality," in *Moral Luck,* Bernard Williams (Cambridge University Press, 1999), 12–13.

35. Williams, "Persons, character," 13–14.

36. B. Williams, "Persons, character," 12.

# SIX

## About the Power and Competence to Tolerate

The previous chapter gave us the opportunity to appreciate the fact that most of the authors who speak about the concept of tolerance refer to the necessary power or competency to detain, stop or prohibit the object of tolerance. Such is the case of Annette Schmitt, for example, who considers that without this 'circumstance' we could not properly speak of tolerance, or Peter Nicholson who affirms that "[t]he tolerator has the power to try to suppress or prevent (or at least to oppose or hinder) what is tolerated."[1] It is also the case for Rodolfo Vázquez who says that, "the tolerator must possess, [...] the competency or faculty that will allow him to factually intervene against an action that injures his convictions"[2] or Mary Warnock, who believes in tolerating her daughter's boyfriend because she has certain influence over her daughter.

The idea behind this circumstance of tolerance is to denounce the limitations that we have to tolerate conducts we disapprove of. These boundaries that shorten our possibilities to talk about tolerance may be extended or reduced depending on the type of limits we accept: either they can be exclusively referred to a physical or social power, to certain normative criteria that concede authority or competence or to both. The natural limits that cut our possibilities to tolerate refer to the impossibility to tolerate a storm or a heat wave, as to the impossibility to tolerate an earthquake. We regularly say that we endure or suffer this kind of natural event but not that we tolerate them. This is, mainly, because we cannot do anything to change them or to stop them.

Many authors, such as Bernard Williams, have rightly criticized the full acceptance of this kind of limitations. This is because, as Williams puts it, if the only accepted limitations to be tolerant are related to *power*—this is, superior in strength or majority in numbers—then the weak (physically or socially speaking) would have no possibility of tolerating. This is the case that Bernard Williams refers to when arguing that the majority groups are not the only ones in power to tolerate. This because what Williams understands as 'toleration' "is a matter of the attitudes of any group to another and does not concern only the relations of the more powerful to the less powerful."[3] For him, tolerance is not a luxury that only the most physically powerful can afford. Thinking otherwise would undoubtedly reduce the scope of tolerance to a very limited number of people. That notwithstanding, a mild version of the natural limitations component is regularly accepted. At least, the one that accepts the impossibility to speak about tolerance towards certain natural disasters or events that fall outside of our human possibilities to prevent them or stop them.

Now, turning to the second kind of limitations, what should we understand by 'competence'? There is no doubt that the term 'competence' entails the idea of regulative norms and rights. Following Robert Alexy, the idea of "adequate competency" is a situation in which "the deontic status is opposite to one of subjection."[4] That is, the tolerating subject holds a position of superiority vis-à-vis the agent's act that is tolerated. According to Alexy's definition, in every situation in which someone has the competency to do something, there is a person who is in a state of subjection.

With this in mind, it is easier to understand where these 'situations' of superiority come from. For the supporters of both theses, the typical cases that serve to ground the tolerant subjects' competencies are found within normative systems: *legal, moral* and *social.*[5]

The case of superiority, or competence based on social norms, may be exemplified by a situation where the head of a company bans smoking on the premises of his enterprise. According to this perspective, the employee who smokes does not have the necessary competence whether or not to tolerate the rules set by his boss, and if he challenges them, it might cost him/her the job. If we then imagine the opposite scenario, where the boss, despite his declared aberration to smoking, stills permits it on the premises of his company, we could say that he or she is a tolerant person.

Let us now assume that the company I am referring to is a company that processes crude oil, stores dynamite or engages in mining. In those cases, the smoking ban could not be judged as an act of the boss's intolerance toward the smoking employees. In fact, allowing smoking would constitute an act of moral or legal irresponsibility. In this case, we can say that the boss is acting coherently with the norms of a legal system that prohibits the consumption of cigarettes in high risk places such as mines, gas stations or factories that manufacture flammable products.

As noted above, Vicent's character presents himself as a person who is very tolerant with his daughter, as is the case with Warnock. They are both aware that they hold a certain moral superiority (that of a father or a mother), because they both presume they can somehow influence the (moral or social) rectitude of their children's acts. This is why we can say that Vicent's character allows them to paw his books and drink his whisky. It is clear that without this competence he would not be in a position to tolerate his daughter's intent to show her cronies Mozart's 40th symphony, and that Mary Warnock can tolerate the fact that her daughter's boyfriend wears sandals with his suit or carries a walking stick while wearing his tweed coat.

It seems that it is very complicated to think of a situation of tolerance that does not entail a hierarchical supra-subordination relationship. As we have seen, the tolerator always finds himself/herself in a position of superiority compared to the one being tolerated; hence, tolerance is not found amongst equals, as argued by Ernesto Garzón Valdés.[6] In other words, tolerance implies being in a position from where one can deliberately allow something of which one disapproves. Therefore an act of tolerance may only be predicated when the tolerator has the power to prohibit or detain the object that is being tolerated. I believe that these requirements have, so far, been made clear.

However, it is still hard to believe that all situations of competence are as clearly regulated as those we have so far analyzed. It is possible to think of several situations where the relationship of supra-subordination is only temporary or transitory. This would be a type of superiority based on moral or social 'roles.'[7] These sorts of situations, grounded on a kind of 'social convention,' blur the alleged cases of tolerance between peers that some authors consider to be possible.

In order to affirm this possibility, one must consider the differences that could be generated among peers who find themselves in situations of inequality. In other words, I may have the same legal, moral or social status that a friend of mine has — in fact, let us suppose that I have exactly the same status in all aspects as he or she does — still it is not the same if we meet at his or her house or at mine. It is not the same if we meet at his or her office or at mine, or if we meet in a public park or in the university hall. We do not treat each other in the same way when we meet at a friend's party as when he or she is chairing a faculty committee. These types of circumstances change our perception of superior/inferior status and thus alter the role as the subject/object of tolerance.

The notion underlying this idea is the psychological *make-up* worn by all of us in different situations, as we play our roles of parents, friends, colleagues, mates, etc. These types of situations manage to change our perception, and with it alter our impression of ranks of supra-subordination. But they also manage to diminish our capacity to appreciate what is an act of tolerance and what is not. And this vulnerability that I am referring to is increased if we combine the idea of *the role based superiority* with the stance adopted by authors such as Nicholson concerning the competence derived from the moral relevance of our convictions.

Nicholson says that: "the tolerator is claiming that his disapproval is morally justified and that he has a right to act on it if he wishes: he does not merely possess *power* but also the *authority* to exercise it."[8]

Let us suppose that someone is in a socially accepted position of superiority (as the owner of a house), and that someone else (a dinner guest) infringes one of his/her convictions (arriving empty handed when having promised to bring dessert). Which would be the quality that grants him or her the competence not to tolerate such conduct: being the owner of the house or sustaining a moral norm that prohibits the breach of a promise?

Now let us imagine another situation, in which the owner of the house is a compulsive smoker and the dinner guest arrives at his house with his newborn baby; does the father of the baby have, in this situation, competence (derived from a morally relevant conviction: the health of his child) not to tolerate his friend's smoking in the presence of his child, even though he is a guest at his friend's house? Or is his only way out to leave with his child or not take him in the first place?

The 'role' based competence serves as a clue that informs us if we actually have the competence to tolerate. However, it certainly does not lack importance, and may even gain strength when complemented by the morally relevant based competency of an injured conviction.

However, it is still unclear whether the acceptance of this proposal belongs to the supporters of the narrow thesis or to those of the wide thesis. This is because both the narrow and the wide theses are, in accordance with their theoretical presuppositions, willing to accept all the possibilities of 'competence' that I have hereby explained. For example, contrary to what one might first think, the supporters of the wide theory are open to embrace a competence based on the moral relevance of the convictions as the one expressed by Nicholson. The 'role' based competence will serve as a tool for me to argue that tolerance is not only a "normative dependent concept" but also a "contextually dependent" one.

## TOLERANCE AMONG EQUALS

Until now it has been argued that one of the conceptual requisites for tolerance is the existence of a supra-subordination hierarchical relation between the object and the subject of tolerance. Although this has been widely accepted among specialists, there is another perspective that claims that tolerance can be displayed among equals. This perspective claims the existence of acts of tolerance between people who are not in different moral or physical hierarchical situations. Moreover, this same perspective claims that those kinds of acts of tolerance are symmetrical or reciprocal; both individuals tolerate each other for the same reasons and the same conducts.

One of the most serious attempts to argue in favor of this possibility (of talking about tolerance among equals) is that of Ernesto Garzón Valdés. According to him, the second circumstance of tolerance does not necessarily refer to a supra-subordination relationship, independent of which context we are referring to, either a public or a private one. The public normally understood, as stated before, as that in which the parts represent a political and/or social groups that make up a community, while the private as the one displayed by participants as private individuals. In other words, the former takes place on a political or social level and the latter on an interpersonal level.[9]

For example, M. A.'s tolerant attitude towards the cigarette smoke expelled by Garzón is for Garzón himself a typical case of private tolerance. John Locke's *Letters Concerning Toleration,*[10] addresses typical cases of public tolerance.[11]

In what follows, I will analyze Ernesto Garzón's arguments to defend such a possibility and I will defend the necessity of this supra-subordinations relation between the subject and the object of tolerance in both, the private and the public realm. Another claim that will derive from this analysis is the *conceptual irrelevance* of the distinction between 'public' and 'private' tolerance, or the claim that the concept of tolerance does not entail any differences whether it is applied in a public or in a private context. In this sense, if the only difference depends on the context or on the number, or on the political quality of the actors that certain act of tolerance involve then this distinction is completely contingent on conceptual grounds.

This claim becomes relevant at this moment because Ernesto Garzón tries to avoid it by introducing in his conceptual analysis another difference: the one between *vertical tolerance* and *horizontal tolerance*. And it is here where his claims about the 'second circumstance of tolerance' come into play.

Garzón, as other philosophers such as Comanducci, Schmitt, Nicholson and Mendus, accepts as a condition for tolerance the *competence* and *power* to stop, detain or impede the tolerated act.[12] However, he also assures that this type of competence cannot be equated to a relationship of authority between the one who tolerates and the one who is being tolerated.

The examples of tolerance that imply supra-subordinated relationships of authority, according to Garzón, are as frequent as those in which such a relationship does not exist.[13] Following this, Garzón traces a line that divides the cases of tolerance where the relationship of authority exists (vertical relationship) and the cases where it does not exist (horizontal relationship).[14]

Garzón defends the existence of a horizontal tolerance in the private sphere, using as an example M. A.'s aberration of cigarettes referred to previously. This relationship, where tolerance comes into play, is mainly based upon, "M. A.'s belief that tobacco harms his health"[15] and on Garzón's need to be engulfed in a cloud of smoke.

But, according to Garzón, M. A's tolerant attitude is not completely based on the power that M. A. could wield in order to stop or restrain Garzón's habits. In other words, Garzón thinks that M. A. is not in a hierarchically superior position in comparison to him.

Because of this, Garzón argues that:

> When M. A. (...) tolerates me smoking in his presence, he does not do so by virtue of some position of authority, rather perhaps, because he thinks it is not convenient to reduce his circle of interlocutors over an alleged salvation of his physical health, or because he considers that the saying *mens sana...*, is not always true, or because he considers that those who seem to suffer a "terminal weakness of will" (...), may also, between one cigarette and another express some interesting judgments.[16]

M. A. puts precisely all these reasons into play because he believes that he has in his hands the *power* or the *competence* to prohibit Garzón from smoking in his presence. But what Garzón is trying to make us realize is that both he and M. A. have an equal hierarchical position. And that no matter what their hierarchical horizontality is, M. A. has the ability to "tolerate" the cigarette smoke he expels. So after all, that he does have a sort of "competence" to do so; a competence that, according to Garzón himself, "derives from the capacity that each individual has to defend himself against harm or offense."[17] In this case, what could be the basis for this type of competence? Could we not rather say that the type of claim (or conviction) which M. A. sustains is derived from a sort of competence that grants him the moral authority to prohibit, detain or stop Garzón's bad habits that affect him? Otherwise, we are unable to understand from where the 'competence' that Garzón refers to, derives. It seems that Garzón is cornered into choosing between one of two possibilities: a) either denying the conceptual necessity that states that tolerance must always imply a supra-subordinate relationship (of competency and subjection or power and powerless) and therefore deny the second circumstance of tolerance, or b) accept the conceptual necessity of the second circumstance and then maintain two completely different concepts of 'competence': one where *competence* means being free from subjection (vertical tolerance)[18] and the other, where *competence* means something entirely different in which there is a no defined deontic quality (horizontal tolerance).

The truth is that this second way of understanding the term 'competence' is difficult to comprehend. Especially if we accept that 'competence' is a term from which the term *authority* is derived. For example, when we say that someone has the authority to do this or that, it is because we are likewise saying that they have the adequate competence to do it. Thus, the concept of authority denotes a hierarchically defined quality granted by the same idea upon which the term 'competence' rests on.

It is also difficult to understand that, if we accept the existence of different forms of substantiating 'competence,' it is precisely from there that the different types of authority derive. For example, depending on the type of competence we are referring to, be it based upon a certain moral, legal or social quality, we could speak of different types of authority: ecclesiastical, jurisdictional, academic or family. This is because all of them denote a determined deontic quality, independent of the normative system from which they are derived.

If we accept this, it seems that the meaning of 'competence' under the second perspective loses a great deal its force and basically any reference to tolerance between equals ceases to make sense; at least from the point of view of private tolerance.

Following the same line of reasoning it is possible to say that the case between Garzón and M. A. is resolved precisely because of the "competence" that M. A. grants to the justification of his judgment that tobacco seriously damages the health of the smoker and of those who are near the smoker. If we agree on the fact that from this claim derives a sort of (moral) authority, then we would be able to argue that Garzón is in a state of subordination.

In spite of this, under his theoretical framework it does not sound plausible to support the idea that a rational agent may legitimately uphold the existence of a moral (or any other kind of) reason that can justify damaging the health of a third party. Of course, in this moment I am referring to the cases where the circumstances do not admit causes of justification, such as self-defense or the so-called state of necessity. Besides, thanks to the Kantian moral deontologism that Ernesto Garzón sustains an imperative such as the one presented by these cases becomes inviolable. Unlike other types of moral theories, such as for example, consequentialism, in which under some circumstances it could be acceptable to harm the health of another, if the consequences of doing so could maximize some other value held by a greater number of people.

It is possible to sustain the possibility that M. A. tolerates the cigarette smoke expelled by Garzón for other reasons which he considers to be even more commendable than the health of his lungs; it could be the case, for example, that M. A. thinks that the friendship they share is more worthy than a few hours of fresh air. Or perhaps M. A. actually does not tolerate Garzón's smoke but rather he endures it or suffers it, in which case, Garzón would be in a position of superiority with respect to M. A., a position that could be based upon different types of social or psychological conventions, such as: age, Garzón's academic standing, the respect he inspires in him, etc.

Whichever way it is done, this perspective looks more related to the idea of tolerance than to say that M. A. and Garzón are in a situation of equality, since M. A., in this case, would have the moral authority to impede Garzón from physically harming him. Alternatively, it could be said, that he actually does not tolerate Garzón's smoke, but rather suffers it. In both cases, none of them are in an equal hierarchical position.

We saw a case of "private horizontal tolerance," but there are also, according to Garzón, cases of "public horizontal tolerance." The relationship between these variables allows him to introduce another classification: a *symmetrical* or *asymmetrical* relationship between the tolerator and the subject of tolerance.

Garzón argues that "in the case of vertical tolerance, the triadic relationship is always asymmetrical; in the case of horizontal tolerance it could be present in a symmetrical and an asymmetrical relationship."[19]

It could be said that denying the possibility of horizontal tolerance, likewise entails denying a symmetrical triadic relationship. This is so because the symmetrical relationship that Garzón speaks of is peculiar to what he calls *horizontal tolerance*. Vertical tolerance, by definition, cannot be symmetrical. Therefore, if we deny the existence of public horizontal tolerance, we are denying the symmetry within the triadic relationship.

It could be argued, as Garzón does, that in cases of private horizontal tolerance symmetry is possible but not necessary. In other words, a conjunction of triadic relationships is not always present. For Garzón, the case of M. A. could play both a symmetrical and an asymmetrical role; M. A. can tolerate and not expect to be tolerated by Garzón (asymmetry), or tolerate and expect to be tolerated (symmetry). However, it was argued above that this case is not of *horizontal* tolerance. Therefore, the argument here presented denies the symmetry of the triadic relationship.

Let us suppose for a moment that there is a possibility that M. A. does tolerate Garzón's smoke and that Garzón, likewise, tolerates one of M. A.'s acts. This supposed *symmetry*, which might come into effect, does not necessarily imply that they are in a situation of equality. It has been argued before that in some cases the situation of supra-subordination varies depending on the justification of our moral judgments when confronting certain acts and on the 'role' we are currently playing.

For now, let us call this matter settled and turn our attention to the cases of *public* horizontal tolerance which, according to Garzón, are always symmetrical.[20] This is so because according to him the *reciprocity* of tolerance in these cases is indispensable. For Garzón, a case that exemplifies this type of tolerance is the theory of a hypothetical social contract.[21]

It has been said before that under Garzón's conceptual framework, denying the horizontal quality of tolerance entails likewise denying the possibility to speak of symmetry in the triadic relationship. We have just done that with the private horizontal tolerance represented by the M. A.'s case. If in what follows, the argument that interprets the social contract as something different from an act of tolerance (neither reciprocal amongst equals—which would be horizontal symmetry—nor a *simpliciter* tolerance—that is to say, vertical asymmetry), taking it as rather an agreement of wills between individuals who find themselves in the same circumstances, then we will be in a position to deny the symmetry of the triadic relationship, and therefore its horizontality. If the argument that will be presented is able to achieve this, then it seems that we will be in a position to disregard as well the *conceptual* relevance of the public/private dichotomy, which among other things, Garzón speaks about.

For the case at hand, it does not matter much under which version of the social contract we consider our situation, whether Hobbesian, Lockeian or Rousseaunian. I am aware of the marked differences between the various theories—Hobbesian, Lockeian or Rousseaunian—of the social contract. Nonetheless, I consider that the argument presented below can be applied indifferently to all three of them. It this sense, it seems to me that none of them can afford to speak of a reciprocal tolerance between individuals who subscribe to it. Nonetheless, the argument I will present focuses on the Hobbesian theory of the social contract because it is the one that Garzón refers to.

In each of these three classical versions the "state of nature" is defined as a state of utmost equality. However, it must be remembered that for an author such as Hobbes, this situation of equality, equality de facto, is one of the main conditions that generate diffidence among individuals. This is the context in the work of Hobbes, along with shortage of goods, which creates the supposed "war of everyone against everyone."[22] Hobbes would say that three main causes of the dissension of men—competition, diffidence and glory—derive from the sum of these elements.[23]

The state of nature is an imaginary situation in which men cannot act in accordance with the dictates of right reason, due to the absence of a power so overwhelmingly strong that could guarantee that all individuals will act in such a way.

The dictates of reason that I am referring to, captured by Hobbes within the scope of natural laws in the *Leviathan*, only bind individuals *in foro interno*. Hobbes says that in a way individuals are convinced that if all of them obey these mandates they will achieve common peace; they are convinced that if they obey these laws they would finally guarantee their *primum bonum*: life.[24]

However, the internal acceptance of said laws is not enough. Those who are in this horrifying state of nature have to take one step further. They have to take this presumption to another level which will help them abandon the state of nature and arrive at the desired state of peace. This step to another level, according to Hobbes, can only be taken through consensus: the supreme principle that legitimizes his political society.

In this vein, we can argue that the social contract as construed by Hobbes does not entail acts of tolerance. On the contrary, we are dealing with an agreement of wills, a contract, or a voluntary acceptance of the parts involved which think that this contract is the only effective remedy to get rid of an unbearable situation. But the contract itself, or the agreement of wills itself, is not an act of reciprocal tolerance. It is an "agreement" between individuals in order to overcome a state of anarchy, which is considered by them to be an evil in itself.

For the case in point, let us recall an argument made at the beginning of this chapter: *tolerance* does not mean *acceptance*. Tolerance means restraining, for a given period of time and for specific reasons, an objection which is based on a rational and relevant conviction that has been injured or hurt.

This is not the same as accepting, which implies abandoning our conviction. Acceptance in other words would be tantamount of recognizing that such and such a prohibition or permission, which we had contemplated for specific circumstances, was wrong: that it was wrong from a moral standpoint or that it was wrong from a coherent intra-systemic point of view, and which, irrespective of our perspective, we must get rid of.

To say that the social contract is an act of tolerance is to say that at the end, after its hypothetical acceptance, whenever we desire, we can reactivate the prohibition or permission that we had temporarily "restrained." This leaves us with only two exit routes in order to stop tolerating: detaining or stopping the particular act that we disapprove of or ridding ourselves of the prohibition: in other words acting or accepting. As it has been argued by the social contract philosophers, the transit from a state of nature to an organized society is based on the idea of accepting the rules (and the punishments that follow) and the rights of the social game with a hint of irrevocability.[25]

Javier de Lucas, for example, in his work, *To stop talking about tolerance* says that: "the situations of "horizontal tolerance" [argued by Garzón], in the public sphere are either irrelevant or inexistent [. . .] what Garzón describes as such ("the social contract hypothetically supposed to be the remedy for the costs of anarchy") [. . .] are not examples of horizontal tolerance, but rather expressions of the terms within which he frames the foundational political consensus, i.e. of rights: one who settles in terms of equality does not intend to be tolerant, but recognition [of his] rights."[26] We can find the same thought in Rawls when he says that "those who engage in social co-operation choose together, in one joint act, the principles which are to assign basic rights and duties and to determine the division of social benefits."[27]

In this way we can argue that neither the symmetry of the triadic relationship nor the horizontality of tolerance seems to be plausible distinctions. Along the same line of reasoning it can also be stated that the dichotomy between "private-public" does not hold any conceptual relevance as Garzón presumes. It does not imply a different conceptual structure. It refers to different contexts of justification of tolerance and it refers to the different boundaries to which tolerance is submitted in the public or in the private sphere.

## NOTES

1. Nicholson, "Toleration," 160.
2. Vázquez, *Liberalismo*, 76.
3. Bernard Williams, "Toleration, a Political or Moral Question?," in *In the Beginning was the Deed: Realism and Moralism in Political Argument*, ed. Geoffrey Hawthorn (Princeton University Press, 2005), 129.
4. Robert Alexy, *Teoría de la Argumentación Jurídica* (Madrid, Centro de Estudios Constitucionales, 1993), 234. (Here I will be quoting the Spanish translation of Robert Alexy, *Theorie der Juristischen Argumentation: Die Theorie des rationale Diskurses als Theorie der juristischen Begründung* (Frankfurt am Main, Suhrkamp Verlag, 1983).
5. Schmitt, "Las circunstancias," 78–81.
6. Garzón, "No pongas," 184. This point will be discussed in the next section of this chapter.
7. W. D. Ross, *The Right and the Good* (Oxford University Press, 2003), 19.
8. Nicholson, "Toleration," 161. (Emphasis added)
9. Garzón, "No pongas," 186 and ss.
10. Locke, "Four Letters".
11. Warnock, "The Limits," 125.
12. Paolo Comanducci, "Sobre el problema de la tolerancia," in *Tolerancia y pluralismo*, 67–79; Schmitt, "Las circunstancias," 71–85; Nicholson, "Toleration," 161; Mendus, *Toleration*, 9.
13. Garzón, "No pongas," 184.
14. Garzón, "No pongas," 185.
15. Garzón, "No pongas," 184.
16. Ernesto Garzón uses this example in the text that I have been quoting. The initials correspond to the name of one of Ernesto Garzón's colleagues and friends. Out of respect of this person wishes, I have omitted his name, even though Garzón does use it in the text that I am quoting. Garzón, "No pongas," 184.
17. Garzón, "No pongas," 187.
18. It is Robert Alexy who defines "competence" in this way: Robert Alexy, *Teoría de los Derechos Fundamentales* (Madrid, Centro de Estudios Constitucionales, 2002), 234 (Here I will be quoing the Spanish translation of Robert Alexy, *Theorie der Grundrechte*, Suhrkamp-Verlag, 1986). Meanwhile, Ernesto Garzón accepts this same definition: "In effect, the demand of competence so as to determine the deontic quality of the act allows us to distinguish between tolerating and enduring or suffering.," Garzón, "No pongas," 183. As pointed out by Robert Alexy, the opposite of competence is subjection. "The slave does not tolerate the punishments of the master: he endures or suffers them." Alexy, *Teoría de los derechos*," 234.
19. Garzón, "No pongas," 186.
20. Garzón, "No pongas," 187.
21. Garzón, "No pongas," 187.
22. Thomas Hobbes, *Leviathan* (London, Penguin Classics, 1985), 185.
23. Hobbes, *Leviathan*, 185
24. Norberto Bobbio, *Thomas Hobbes* (México, Fondo de Cultura Económica, 1995), 48–49.

25. Bobbio, *Hobbes*, 52. According to Bobbio, irrevocability is one of the three fundamental attributes of the Hobbesian doctrine of the State. The other two are absolute character and indivisibility.

26. Javier de Lucas, "¿Para dejar de hablar de la tolerancia?," *Doxa. Cuadernos de filosofía del derecho*, 11 (1992): 121. (The parentheses and the translation of the title are mine.)

27. Rawls, *A Theory*, 10.

*III*

# Tolerance in Modern Liberalism

# SEVEN

## Tolerance as Reasonableness: John Rawls's Conception

Taking into consideration the description in section I of the *Deontological Moral System* and the conceptual aspects considered by modern deontological liberals discussed in section II, we can assume, first, that modern deontological liberalism defends a moral conception of tolerance. Or, that deontological liberalism understands tolerance as a virtue of justice that can only be justified and limited with and by moral reasons. Ernesto Garzón Valdés and Rainer Forst have developed a detailed and profound study about this particular conception of tolerance. Certainly, related to the conceptual structures and the means of justifying tolerance both of them share many things in common, still the best way to present them is separately. In this way we will be able to penetrate in the particularities of each proposal. Nevertheless, the criticisms that will be raised against the deontological conception of tolerance in the next chapters tend to be general in two ways: first, they will be directed to the proposals that will be analyzed along this third part (Rawls, Garzón and Forst), but also they attempt to cover all deontological moral theories. Considering this, then, the deontological theories of Garzón and Forst, next to the one of Rawls, are to be understood as a representative for modern deontological liberal perspectives in general.

### TOLERANCE AND REASONABLENESS

From the explanations given in chapters 2 and 3 we can deduce that in Rawls's political philosophy tolerance is composed by three main characteristics: (1) tolerance is an ideal of justice, (2) tolerance must be sup-

91

ported by moral reasons, and (3) tolerance is a dispositional property of reasonable individuals.

These three characteristics of Rawls's conception of tolerance are important to have in mind since they represent a *continuum* of ideas within the rest of deontological liberal perspectives such as the ones hold by Ernesto Garzón Valdés and Rainer Forst that will be analyzed in chapters 8 and 9.

In the case of tolerance as an ideal of justice we must remember that for Rawls the principles of justice are created over the base of reasonableness in an original position. The principle of the Reasonable in the way understood by Rawls is laid out "by looking to the public culture itself as the shared fund of implicitly recognized basic ideas and principles."[1] In this sense, the original position simply "models what we regard—here and now—as fair conditions."[2] In that sense, tolerance for Rawls becomes the practical tool of the reasonable that helps us, within the original position, to construct the principles of justice. A tolerant agent is the one who adopts and cherishes the principles of justice created in a context of reasonableness.

This conception of tolerance links it with the idea that tolerance must be supported by moral reasons. Tolerance as reasonableness is justified if it is backed up by reasons guided by the principle of reciprocity. The only values that can be considered justified in a democratic society are those which respect and advance a fair system of cooperation. These values are only those which can be considered as moral-political values, excluding from this picture ethical values. Tolerance guided in this way by the principle of reciprocity can only be reasonable if the reasons proposed for its justification are moral-political values. In Rawls's political conception the sole standard for correctness is reasonableness.[3] Of course, the ideal form of reasonableness is translated in the adoption of a sense of reciprocity and the acceptance of the burdens of judgment.

Individuals in a democratic society conceive themselves as free and equal and they also regard "themselves as self-originating sources of valid claims."[4] But these must be compatible with the principles of justice.[5] If an individual suspends his/her sense of justice he/she will be left largely with the rationale which, as argued before, is insufficient to produce justified claims in a democratic society. This is why Rawls says that "the reasonable always binds *in foro interno*,"[6] so there are no contradictions between a rational conception of the good and reasonable moral norms. In this sense, the reasonableness is a dispositional property of individuals that consider themselves (*internally*) as free and equal and as sources of valid claims. So tolerance, accordingly, is a tool that must be applied to philosophy in itself. This perspective does not represents a *continuum* in Rawls's work, but it is the last understanding of tolerance that he gave.

From *A Theory of Justice* to the publication of *Political Liberalism* there is a considerable change in Rawls's understanding of tolerance. In *A Theory* Rawls justifies tolerance by alluding to the principles of justice; particularly, by making a reference to his first principle.[7] His argument for toleration does not run in the light of our knowledge about any religious, philosophical or moral doctrines but in the bases of the original position where we do not have any knowledge about these doctrines and practices. Then, for Rawls the question is whether we must tolerate a religious sect that does not accept the principles of justice derived from the original position? If such a sect does not put freedom in danger it must be tolerated by everyone.[8] The oddity in this formulation is that Rawls does not explain what can constitute a "danger for freedom" and, therefore, every single conception of the good, as intolerant it can be and without accepting the principles of justice, must be tolerated under these grounds if, and only if, it does not put freedom in danger.

The twist he makes to the principle of toleration in *Political Liberalism* is that tolerance is no longer justified by the principles of justice but by the principle of reasonableness. With this new formulation Rawls extends the application of toleration to other areas of life, including philosophy in itself.[9] The idea of applying toleration to philosophy in itself takes tolerance as a guide for formulating the principles of political-morality. As it has been said, principles of political-morality are constructed in such a way that they must include any philosophical perspective. By 'philosophy' Rawls clearly includes all different kinds of religious, moral or ideological doctrines that exist in a democratic society. Thus, we cannot formulate 'freestanding' principles of justice without a concern for the principle of toleration.[10] Toleration so conceived works as a mechanism of the Reasonable in the construction of the principles of justice. One problem arises from this formulation and it is that the principles of justice will not work anymore as the limits for tolerance being understood in this way as Rawls proposed in his *A Theory of Justice*. The new perspective of tolerance would have to settle new limits as well. Where does Rawls find the limits for tolerance?

In chapter 2, it was explained that the principle of the Reasonable has two constituting elements. The first one, denominated the "reciprocity" element, consists in the idea that reasonable persons are those who have the desire to propose principles that others could reasonably accept and act according to them. The second one was called the "burdens of judgment" and consists in the idea that reasonable people will accept the possibility that their conceptions of the good might not be correct or true, and therefore, should not be imposed on others.

These two elements can be considered as the *moral* and the *epistemological* ideas of the principle of Reasonableness. Steven Wall has referred to the first idea as the "agreement disposition" and to the second idea as the "epistemic charity."[11] Accordingly, a reasonable person in Rawls's terms is one who has an "agreement disposition" to find principles of justice that all can accept and is "epistemically charitable" if he/she accepts that others can reasonably disagree with him/her, even when he/she thinks they are correct. As Wall correctly affirms, these two ideas complement each other: "If one is not epistemically charitable one will likely reject the agreement disposition; and if one accepts the agreement disposition, one will likely be epistemically charitable." [12]

But if we take into consideration Rawls's recognition of unreasonable persons, then it is possible to say that both ideas are compatible but there is no necessary connection: one person can be epistemically charitable, this is, can recognize the burdens of judgment, and still reject the principles of justice. Or, someone can agree with the principles of justice and not be epistemically charitable. At this point the principle of tolerance should be able to provide an answer.

Clearly the question of tolerance does not arise when we are dealing with someone's act that fully cherishes the sense of justice (that is reciprocal and accepts the burdens of judgment). Then the limit between justified and unjustified tolerance lies between the reasonable and unreasonable acts or practices developed by people who: (1) reject both the principles of justice and the burden of judgment, (2) only reject the principles of justice, or (3) only do not accept the burdens of judgment.

From these three possibilities, under Rawls's conception of justice only the first two cannot be tolerated. Those that are not epistemologically charitable but accept the principles of justice enter into the realm of the tolerable. The problem for Rawls is found in those who reject the principles of justice. This is due to the fact that those are the ones who jeopardize the existence of an overlapping consensus and put at odds the stability of a democratic society.

In this way, according to the formulation of Rawls, tolerance is the practical representation of a sense of justice. It is born from the development of our practical capacities of being rational and reasonable: first, by accepting that there are moral reasons for us to not promote controversial conceptions of the good and to agree on fair terms of cooperation, and second by accepting the possibility that our own conceptions of the good are subject of burdens of judgment.

Rawls is not as explicit as other philosophers are about the mechanism that justifies an act of tolerance. In that sense, philosophers such as Forst and Garzón, will be of great help to clarify all the ambiguities that Rawls's proposal suffer. The next two chapters are fully dedicated to this explanation.

## NOTES

1. Rawls, *Political*, 8.

2. Rawls, *Political*, 26.

3. Rawls, *Political*, 127.

4. Rawls, "Justice as Fairness", 406.

5. Rawls, "Justice as Fairness", 406.

6. Rawls, *Political*, 54.

7. Rawls, *A Theory*, 191.

8. Rawls, *A Theory*, 192.

9. Rawls, *Political*, 10

10. Steven Wall, *Liberalism, Perfectionism and Restraint* (Cambridge University Press, 1998), 72.

11. Wall, *Liberalism, Perfectionism*, 73.

12. Wall, *Liberalism, Perfectionism*, 74.

# EIGHT

## Tolerance and the Two Normative Systems: Ernesto Garzón Valdés's Conception

In *Keep your dirty hands off Mozart*,[1] Ernesto Garzón defines tolerance as a dispositional property that is "tested in diverse and reiterated circumstances" which he calls, like other philosophers, *circumstances of tolerance*. Before I explain the justifying mechanism that Garzón proposes, I would like to delve into some important aspects of his concept of tolerance.

We must pay attention that Garzón uses the expressions: "tested" and in "reiterated circumstances." These expressions entail a semantic distinction prior to his concept of tolerance. They refer specifically to the difference that other philosophers such as Annette Schmitt, Paolo Comanducci and Andrew Jason Cohen, make between "tolerating" and "being tolerant."[2] Schmitt claims that "while (. . .) the act of tolerance constitutes in the omission of an intervention, the property of "being tolerant" requires a tendency to practice tolerance every time determined circumstances are present."[3] Comanducci, in accordance with Schmitt, asserts that: "the notion that it is a disposition that lasts over time is not included in the concept of tolerance (and of tolerating)."[4] According to him, propositions such as: "In that circumstance, and only in that, John Doe has tolerated action X" or "In that circumstance, and only in that, John Doe has shown evidence of tolerance," do not strike him as a *stretched* use of this term."[5]

In other words, for Schmitt as well as for Comanducci, *tolerating something* may only be a one-time matter and does not require a per se disposition to "be tolerant." The first is understood as an adjective, the second as a verb.[6] Garzón in this same sense affirms that "we do not say that someone is tolerant if he/she only once tolerates an act he/she is inclined to prohibit, and then prohibits it when the same circumstances occur."[7]

Glen Newey, from the perspective of virtue ethics, has claimed something very similar. He calls it the *dual-predictability* phenomenon of virtues. This dual-predictability, he explains, "has somehow to account for the fact that agents who are $\phi$ often fail on relevant occasions to perform $\phi$ acts, and that an act may be $\phi$ even though the agent performing it is not."[8] Following the dual-predictability of Newey it is possible to say that someone has acted tolerantly without having the disposition to be a tolerant person.

When Garzón speaks of tolerance as a dispositional property he is referring, then, to the activity of "being tolerant" or to the dispositional property, and not to the "act of tolerating." It is important to bear this distinction in mind, because with it we can present a fact that will subsequently be useful in order to approach other aspects of his proposal that are relevant, such as, for example: (1) the fact of whether Garzón understands tolerance as a moral disposition or as a passing attitude, and (2) the way in which he relates the mentioned conception of tolerance with its mechanism of justification. A second point that I would like to address regarding his conceptual frame is closely related to the way he understands the formal structure of tolerance. Garzón affirms that tolerance is composed of a triadic relationship represented by a person '$a$' that tolerates ('$T$') an act '$X$' of another person '$b$' who is the recipient of '$T$' in a specific circumstance '$c$.'

This relationship can be simplified with the formula he uses: $aTbXc\ t$ $1 ..... t\ n$.

First of all, it seems to me that this formula not only shows the relationship between the three elements he has in mind when defining tolerance, but also reinforces the previous point. If tolerance is a dispositional property it would necessarily have—that is, by definition—to manifest itself reiteratively; that in this formula is represented by the times '$t\ 1 ... t$ $n$.'

Therefore (and repeating something I have already stated, but that I consider necessary to stress) the interest of Ernesto Garzón lies in the cases that pertain to *being tolerant* and not in isolated acts of tolerance. This is important, because it is from here that a much more comprehensive claim than that of knowing what constitutes an act of tolerance is derived. If this is so, we can initially assume that what he is interested in is in analyzing tolerance as a virtue: as a moral ideal.

By addressing the concept of tolerance as a dispositional property Garzón is actually alluding to the virtue of being tolerant. It is also important to note the fact that virtues in general share this same trait. We do not say that someone is brave or has courage if one only displays their bravery or courage in one single occasion. For something to be considered a virtue it has to be displayed and present consistently. This point will be discussed in further detail in chapter 16.

Now, for the purposes of this chapter it is important to notice that Ernesto Garzón considers that there are three necessary and sufficient *circumstances of tolerance*: (1) the injury of a relevant conviction, (2) the adequate competence to intervene against a tolerated act, and (3) the balancing of the arguments in favor of or against the prohibition or permission of the act in question. Since in chapter 6 I have already analyzed and discussed several parts of Ernesto Garzón's conceptual framework, throughout this chapter, the central point of my analysis will revolve around the way in which Garzón interprets, articulates and schematizes the interaction between circumstances (1) and (3).

## BASIC NORMATIVE SYSTEMS AND JUSTIFICATORY NORMATIVE SYSTEMS

Ernesto Garzón argues that when we talk about tolerance we are referring to two normative systems. On the one hand, the tendency to forbid the act in question which can be finally tolerated comes from a system to which it is normatively bound. He calls this system: the *basic normative system*. Garzón says that this *basic normative system* is what defines the kind of tolerance we are dealing with, which can vary from case to case. In this sense, Garzón argues in favor of the possibility of speaking of different types of tolerance: moral, religious, scientific, aesthetic, political and even a tolerance that refers to conventions of fashion. Overcoming the tendency to prohibit an act is the result of considering the principles and rules that belong to a superior normative system. He baptizes this other system with the name of *justificatory normative system*.[9] Ultimate justificatory reasons belong to it.

Hence, the different types of convictions that an individual may hold derive from the different "basic normative systems" (BNS), which in turn are the ones that define the type of tolerance we are dealing with. The ultimate reasons, the ones that invite us to refrain from intervening when an act injures one of our relevant convictions (which come from one of our basics normative systems), are inferred from the "justificatory normative system" (JNS). It is from this JNS from where the "reasons of tolerance" are inferred, which, under the deontological perspective held by Garzón, are only moral reasons. The difference made by Garzón between the BNS and the JNS is not different from the one between 'morality' and 'ethics,' and the whole justificatory frame that Garzón refers to is the one considered by the priority thesis.

Certainly, this structure can make us think that under Garzón's perspective tolerance only involves moral choices, and that 'our likes or inclinations are irrelevant.' But this is not so. For him saying that tolerance only involves moral or ethical choices is to assure something that is overly radical. At this point, as it is obvious, he disagrees with Peter Nicholson who says that "toleration is a matter of moral choice, and our tastes or inclinations are irrelevant."[10] For Garzón this stance takes things to the extreme, narrowing the scope of tolerance and dissipating the importance that the different basic normative systems hold in the life of particular individuals.

In fact, Garzón argues that since these types of systems also have boundaries, their "violation means their destruction."[11] "He who tolerates *refrains from prohibiting* or *derogating a prohibition*, and this last notion could, as shown by Alchourrón and Bulygin, have grave systematic consequences. Like every normative system it accomplishes the function of guiding human behavior and so its injury or elimination is not something trivial."[12]

In other words, what Garzón has come to say is that practices such as wearing sandals with suit or actions such as pawing someone else's Mozart records should not be regarded as irrelevant or banal prohibitions from the perspective of tolerance. This is so because the systems from which these convictions are derived accomplish a function in the everyday life of each and every individual, e.g., guiding their conduct.

The problem of tolerating something, according to Garzón, is resolved thanks to the interaction between both normative systems. This means that if an act 'X' is prohibited within a basic normative system, what tolerance requires is to put this prohibition under the critical evaluation of the justificatory normative system.

It is important to note the fact that it is not necessary that an act of tolerance of 'X' should emerge from this evaluation, although it may be the case that JNS does reaffirm the prohibition contained in the BNS, and consequently, that it would not be *derogated* from the BNS. Clearly, the reaffirmation of the JNS of a conviction held in a BNS would close the doors to tolerance, widening, so to speak, the circle of the non-tolerable.[13]

It is true that the relationship between the basic normative system, the justificatory normative system and the person that sustains it is not an easy one. Garzón combats this complexity with a set of logical and conceptual rules which explain the inter-systemic relationship between both normative systems:

> I) The act object of tolerance, by definition, must be prohibited in a BNS.
> II) The prohibition can only be raised through reasons that stem from a JNS.
> III) It is resolved to tolerate an act X after a careful balancing between the BNS and the JNS.
> IV) If the conflict that causes X for the BNS and the JNS is overcome, we can no longer speak of tolerance.

V) The tolerance based on a moral JNS entails a moralization of the BNS.[14]

It is easy to understand the need to have a basic normative system in order to speak of tolerance. Strictly speaking, how are we to speak of an act that injures the content of a prohibition, without a normative system which contemplates such a prohibition? In other words, how can we properly speak of 'disapproving something' when we do not hold a normative prohibition of such act? This is clear: in order for a prohibition to exist it is necessary for it to be contemplated in a system of values or rules.

What is not so obvious any longer is why, when Garzón refers to the content of the basic normative systems, he only alludes to prohibitions. This may be due to the fact that the normative systems, according to Garzón, are formulated in a negative way, i.e. in the typical deontological form: as "demands" of the sort "you will not." Does this then mean that, according to him, the mechanism of tolerance is only set in motion when someone violates one of these prohibitions or deontological demands?

Under his perspective, the basic normative systems are articulated as follows. Within them: "[. . .] the acts or activities that we dislike or disapprove of are prohibited; to prohibit what we like or approve of is a clear symptom of masochism or dementia, because *if tolerance means suspending a prohibition*, it does not make any sense to say that we tolerate that which is allowed or considered worthy of praise by our basic normative system."[15]

However, I am not convinced that tolerance only involves acts that attack certain prohibitions. There may be cases in which someone holds a "strong permission" in his/her basic system and another person prohibits him/her from doing something that is permitted by him/her. In a case like this, it is possible to consider that there could be a violation of a conviction; thus, in principle, it could trigger the mechanism of tolerance. I am adopting the distinction between "strong permissions" and "weak permissions" that was made by Alchourron and Bulygin.[16] These two philosophers sustain that 'strong permissions' are those that are explicitly shown in the rule of a system $\alpha$, while the 'weak permissions' are the result of the absence of a prohibition expressed in the system $\alpha$.

In a case like this, where 'strong permissions' are involved there are no reasons to think that an agent intends to tolerate something that was already permitted in his/her value system. This would effectively make it a case of "deontic redundancy" or allowing what is allowed, and accepting what is accepted. This is what Garzón has in mind when he claims that "it does not make sense to say that we tolerate that which is permitted in our system."[17]

However, in the case that we are supposing, what can or cannot be tolerated is for someone to prohibit something that is considered to be deontologically permitted under our value system. This would be the case, for example, for someone who in his or her value system would allow everyone to speak their mind, as against someone who prohibits this type of freedom. In that case, this person would be injuring a value that the tolerating subject considers significant, e.g. that all people have the opportunity to speak their minds.

Let us imagine the case of an academic seminar in which one of the main rules is the discursive participation of all the participants, that is to say, everyone has the permission to speak and give their opinion regarding the topic that is being discussed at their table. However, the moderator does not share the same ideas as one of the participants, and thus simply does not allow his/her to speak. In this case, it seems to me that any participant that internally adopts this permission cannot tolerate the attitude of the moderator, denouncing his/her totalitarian and inacceptable attitude in this respect.

For the time being, this idea seems plausible. However, I will leave it where it is, in order to delve into other important matters.

If we pay attention to the second of Garzon's rules, which states that *derogating* or *suspending* a prohibition can only be achieved through reasons that stem from a JNS, we will be able to see an important fact within the basic normative systems when dealing with an instance of tolerance: *their self-insufficiency*. In Garzón's perspective, this self-insufficiency is provoked by the same logical rules that govern the construction of the normative systems.

In a case of tolerance, the assurance of the self-sufficiency of the basic normative system is, according to Garzón, a sign of a logical contradiction within the system itself. A basic system that likewise prohibits and permits an act 'X' must be considered a pathological system. The syndrome is the lack of logic within the system, and the sickness is the contradiction between two norms. Therefore, if a normative system is in a situation that simultaneously allows and prohibits 'X,' the only option left is to take out the *broom of logic* and set aside the norm with lower status. But what happens with equally ranking contradictory norms? This is something that will be discussed later. For the moment, we should only consider that according to the systemic rules that Garzón states, these kinds of conflicts are logically impossible.

Still, in the case we were dealing with, it must be considered that derogating the norm with lower status has nothing to do with tolerance. As Garzón argues, "the prohibition (or permission) that we eliminated because of logical coherence was the result of a defective intra-systemic legislation; in truth, we were wrong with respect to the deontic qualification of the act that it pretended to regulate."[18]

If this is so, then the elimination of a prohibition in a BNS is not an act of tolerance, but rather the medicine that heals the pathology of an incoherent system.

It is for this reason that in the case of tolerance the self-insufficiency of the basic system plays a very important role in Garzón's scheme. Coupled with the fact that if it were self-sufficient, there would be no need to sustain a justificatory system, and, according to this stance, without the existence of a justificatory system to evaluate the norms contained within the basic system, there would be no tolerance at all.

We have seen that for deontological liberal systems this distinction is fundamental: the one between 'morality' and 'ethics,' which as I said before corresponds to the one made by Garzón between the JNS and the BNS.

In this sense we must agree that under this deontological framework, tolerance is understood as the *discrepancy* that arises between a relevant conviction that belongs to a BNS and a moral norm of the JNS, and when the two systems coincide we can no longer speak of tolerance. Furthermore, Garzón argues that the prohibition expressed in the BNS, after its critical or justificatory revision, not only maintains the same deontic quality, but is rather reinforced, it is *moralized* (remember Garzón's structural rule of his justificatory proposal that states that *the tolerance based on a moral JNS entails a moralization of the BNS*).

This *moralizing* process is also present in cases of discrepancy; that is to say, it is not exclusive to the instance of coincidence between both systems. The extent to which the *moralizing justificatory revision* that Garzón speaks about allows us to understand tolerance as a dispositional property is something I will discuss in future chapters.

Before moving on to the next justificatory proposal, we must consider one final matter. When Garzón distinguishes between *reasonable* and *unreasonable* tolerance,[19] the difference lies in the fact that reasonable tolerance is based upon *good reasons* and unreasonable tolerance upon *bad reasons*. But, in any case, what does he mean by 'good' and 'bad' reasons? What parameter does he uses to measure the 'goodness' or 'badness' of the reasons of tolerance?

The first clue we can find is that Garzón compares what he calls *unreasonable tolerance* with what Marcuse once called *repressive tolerance*.[20] It may be recalled that Marcuse insisted on the notion that "pure" tolerance or a tolerance that without limits or unrestricted, would invariably tend to oppression. Marcuse asserts that the reasons offered by capitalist societies are bad reasons for tolerance because tolerance is extended to policies, conditions and modes of behavior which should not be tolerated because they are hindering, if not destroying, the chances of creating an existence without fear and misery.[21] Thus, from Marcuse's perspective indiscriminate tolerance, i.e. the tolerance that allows everything, tends to eliminate itself or to self-destruct. The absence of limits to tolerance makes out tolerance a vacuous concept that allows everything.

Based on this, Garzón defends the idea that in order for tolerance not to deny itself, or to become unreasonable, it must be surrounded by a fence of insurmountable reasons: by a fence of "intolerances." These reasons also allow us to define the scope of what is tolerable with greater certainty. Specifically, Garzón points out that "intolerance would not only be inner denial of tolerance, but a *sine qua non* condition of it."[22]

Regardless of however paradoxical this may sound, the truth is that without a fence to limit its scope of action, whatever we call it, tolerance tends to disappear. For Garzón *reasonable tolerance* not only has to be confined within a border of *intolerances* but it needs to contemplate another criterion. The other criterion that Garzón has in mind is one that has been widely defended by many liberal philosophers who have tried to answer this very same question, including J. S. Mill, D. D. Raphael, John Rawls, and as we will see now, Rainer Forst. All these authors agree on the idea that 'good reasons,' understood as good for tolerance, are those that are based on a stance of *impartiality*, namely a stance that takes into account the interests of others as autonomous beings capable of directing their own lives without causing harm.[23]

In chapter 5 I have already discussed the idea of *impartiality* that Garzón, among other liberals, holds. For not repeating the same ideas here, it is worth just to keep in mind that Garzón believes that all moral judgments need to be supported by reasons that can be accessible and acceptable by anyone. This, in the political liberalist fashion, excludes any metaphysical, religious or ideological claim form the rational deliberation. Garzón backs up this idea on Gerald Gaus's *conditions for accessibility*.[24] These conditions are the ones that Garzón uses in order to explain the idea of rational reasons as those which can be shared by any reasonable human being.

## NOTES

1. Garzón, "No pongas, " 181–198.
2. Schmitt, "Las circunstancias, " 71; Comanducci, "Sobre el problema, " 71; Cohen, "What Toleration Is, " 76–78.
3. Schmitt, "Las circunstancias, " 72.
4. Comanducci, "Sobre el problema, " 71–72.
5. Comanducci, "Sobre el problema, " 72.
6. Cohen, "What Toleration Is, " 76.
7. Garzón, "No pongas, " 185.
8. Newey, *Virtue*, 87.
9. Garzón, "No pongas, " 187.
10. Nicholson, "Toleration, " 158–173.
11. Garzón, "No pongas, " 188.
12. Garzón, "No pongas, " 188.
13. This consideration appears in Ernesto Garzón Valdés 's text "El sentido actual de la tolerancia, " in *Teoría del discurso y derechos constitucionales*, Robert Alexy (México, Cátedra Ernesto Garzón Valdés, ITAM/UAM/ ELD/ INACIPE, Fontamara, 2004), 14.
14. Pablo Navarro, "Reflexiones acerca del concepto de tolerancia, " *Doxa. Cuadernos de Filosofía del Derecho*, 13 (1993): 279.
15. Garzón, "El sentido actual, " 16. (The italics are mine.)

16. Carlos Alchourrón and Eugenio Bulygin, *Análisis Lógico y Derecho* (Madrid, Centro de Estudios Constitucionales, 1991), 218.

17. Ernesto Garzón Valdés, "Algunas reflexiones más acerca del concepto de tolerancia. Comentarios a los comentarios de Pablo Navarro, " *Doxa. Cuadernos de filosofía del derecho*, 14 (1993): 424.

18. Garzón, "Algunas relfexiones, " 14–15 (Parentheses added).

19. Garzón, "No pongas, " 195.

20. Herbert Marcuse, "Repressive Tolerance, " in *A Critique of Pure Tolerance*, ed. Robert Paul Wolff, Barrington Moore Jr., Herbert Marcuse (Boston, Beacon Press, 1969), 105–107.

21. Marcuse, "Repressive Tolerance, " 105.

22. Garzón, "No pongas, " 195.

23. Garzón, "No pongas, " 198.

24. Ernesto Garzón Valdés, "¿Puede la Razonabilidad ser un Criterio de Corrección Moral?, " in *Instituciones Suicidas*, 246.

# NINE

## Tolerance as a Virtue of Justice: Rainer Forst's Conception

Rainer Frost's analysis of toleration covers three different stages: the *conceptual* analysis, the study of different *conceptions* of toleration, and the *justificatory* analysis of tolerance.

Forst distinguishes between the *concept* and the *conceptions* of toleration, understanding the former as the analysis of the necessary components that enable us to speak about tolerance while the later as the study of different ways in which those components have been understood in different times and places. In what follows I will explain how Forst conceptualizes tolerance and which of the different conceptions of tolerance he favors. This exercise will give us a better understanding of Forst's justificatory mechanism of tolerance.

According to Forst, the conceptual components upon which tolerance is built are: *objection, acceptance* and *rejection.* Forst says that the *objection* component refers to the tolerator's belief that certain practices are judged as wrong or bad. He is fully aware that this component is the cornerstone of the concept of tolerance: "if this component is absent, there is either indifference or affirmation—two attitudes that are incompatible with toleration."[1] Any of these two attitudes finds itself within the idea of conflict. Objection and conflict are the heart of the concept of tolerance, if there is no objection there is nothing to be tolerant about. As Tim Heysse points in his analysis of Forst "social conflict defines the requirements of the notion of toleration."[2]

Regarding this component of the concept, it is important to notice that for Forst the substantive nature of the objection does not have to be necessarily moral. As for Garzón, Forst thinks that "it would be inappropriate to exclude other forms of normative critique, such as, for instance, aesthetic critique."[3] At this point the similitude of Forst's formulations with those of Garzón is obvious. Both claim that the objection must be normatively substantive, but that it is not necessarily restricted to moral reasons. Thus, for both philosophers the convictions that might be considered as candidates for tolerance can belong to different normative systems: aesthetic, ethical, fashionable, religious and so on. This is a very important feature that we must keep in mind together with the acceptance component. Later I will argue that under a deontological perspective of practical reason the way in which Forst reconstructs these components might make out of tolerance a suicidal (self-destructive) concept.

The second component of tolerance is the *acceptance* component. Forst understands it as the one that counteracts the *objection* component. Still, we must acknowledge that for him *acceptance* does not mean to cancel the negative judgment, but to give positive reasons *"which trump the negative ones in the relevant context."*[4] In the case where the objection and the acceptance component are considered *moral* it leads to the 'moral paradox' or the 'dilemma of tolerance.' That is, the normative conflict between two equally valid moral requirements. Nevertheless, as we will see later, Forst thinks that this type of conflict can be solved.

The third component that Forst considers as necessary is the *rejection* component. The reasons to *reject* are the ones that create the "fence of intolerances" that Garzón has argued before. Forst also believes that for tolerance to be reasonable it needs to be surrounded by a fence of intolerances, e.g. determined limits. And these limits are marked by the reasons we have to reject which, following Forst, can be of two kinds. The first one "lies between the normative realm of the practices and beliefs one agrees with, and the realm of the tolerable practices and beliefs that one finds wrong but still can accept in a certain way."[5] The second lies between the realm of tolerable practices and the realm of the intolerable, which is strictly rejected; these are, strictly speaking, the limits of toleration.

Forst stresses that the reasons we might have to reject do not have to be identical to the ones we had to object. We might ethically or aesthetically disapprove of something (*objection*) and after a critical examination we can finish reinforcing our judgment with moral reasons (*rejection*). Both, *rejection* and *acceptance* are the results of critical scrutiny made to our *objections*. In this sense, Forst shares Garzón's process of *moralizing* the convictions from which the objections are raised. But before we enter in the discussion of Forst's justificatory scheme it is necessary to make a brief revision of the conception of tolerance that he defends.

Forst is very careful in saying that these conceptions of toleration should not be understood as a linear historical development of tolerance, nor considered regimes of toleration located in different social or historical circumstances. He outlines four conceptions which can be found at any moment and within any society and they could be present simultaneously. In fact, for Forst this last possibility is the one that helps us to explain the conflicts between the different ways for understanding tolerance. These four conceptions are: *the permission conception, the co-existence conception, the esteem conception, and the respect conception.*[6]

This last conception is the one that Forst indeed favors. Under this conception tolerance is conceived as a moral attitude based on the recognition of all individuals as citizens of the State with equal legal and political status. Forst conceives this conception as the practical capacity of respecting each other as moral-political equals, "even though, they hold incompatible ethical beliefs about the good and right way of life, and differ greatly in their cultural practices."[7] They treat each other as equals in the sense that all of them share a "common framework of social life that is guided by norms that all parties can equally accept, and that do not favour one specific 'ethical community'."[8]

Forst speaks of two different models of the *respect* conception: one, guided by a 'formal equality,' and another referred to as a 'qualitative equality.' The former operates with a strict distinction between the political and the private realm, attaching to the private realm all the ethical differences among citizens and eliminating them from the political or public one. Forst believes that this conception's strategy is to narrow the scope of ethical beliefs defending them through a pure understanding of equal subjective rights. The problem is that there can be ethical cultural communities that require a certain public presence that other forms of life do not need. In that sense, Forst claims that the formal equality conception can be intolerant towards those forms of life. This problem is solved by the 'qualitative equality' conception. Under this conception "persons respect each other as political equals with distinct ethical-cultural identities that must be tolerated as (a) especially important for a person and (b) providing good reasons for certain exceptions from or changes to existing legal and social structures, in order to promote material and not just formal equality. Social and political equality and integration are thus seen to be compatible with cultural difference—within certain (moral) limits of reciprocity."[9]

Forst argues that the conception of tolerance as respect for others as autonomous and equal citizens "presupposes the capacity and the willingness to differentiate between: (a) the realm of those values and practices that one fully affirms, (b) the realm of beliefs and practices one judges to be ethically bad but that one still tolerates because one cannot judge them to be morally wrong in a generally justifiable sense, and (c) the realm of what cannot be tolerated, judged on the basis of norms and principles that are justifiable to all citizens and not determined by only one party."[10]

The amalgam between practices that are accepted, ethically disapproved yet tolerable, and ethically disapproved and intolerable can only be explained through his structure of practical reason. This takes me to the next stage of Forst analysis of toleration: the *justificatory* analysis.

## TOLERANCE AS A VIRTUE OF JUSTICE

Forst's deontological conception of practical reason is a very interesting and complex one. In it we can find an undeniable Kantian trait as well as features of many other neo-Kantian philosophers such as John Rawls and Jürgen Habermas. We have already discussed some features of the Kantian influence in this type of liberal thinkers, mainly regarding the normative force and the universal character he attaches to moral norms.[11] In what follows I will complete the picture of Forst's conception of practical reason and relate it to his understanding of tolerance.

In several works Forst has claimed that tolerance is a virtue of justice. For him justice differs from other normative realms such as the ethical, political or legal realms. Justice claims priority over other normative spheres, universal validity and distinctive justifying methods, features that make it a different normative realm than the other three. For these reasons, Forst defends the idea according to which these different normative spheres must be understood as different "contexts of justification" that require different normative treatment.

Still, aside from these differences between those "contexts of justification," there is one problem that Forst thinks liberalism has failed to see, namely that a complete theory of justice (in the way he understands it) needs to attend the many and different ways in which these "contexts of justification" connect with each other. Instead of seeing these different realms only in a vertical simplistic way in which they are not connected and they have sharp borders between each other, we must look at them also in a horizontal way. This more complex but complete perspective will, in fact, allow us to recognize the connection between the legal, ethical, political and the moral identities of a person. In this sense, Forst says:

> The vertical perspective helps clarify certain misunderstandings of the debate, but neither this nor the horizontal perspective can claim to gather all the arguments into a comprehensive synthesis. It permits the possibility of bringing the two sides—*Sittlichkeit* and morality, the good and the just—in a manner that connects the recognition of the ethical identity and collective forms of life as well as substantive determinations of social justice with the validity of individual rights, discursive procedures, universal moral principles; and it does so on the bases of *one* conception of communicative-practical reason and in consideration of *different* normative contexts.[12]

As it is possible to see, the normative interconnection proposed by Forst does not remove the priority character that he gives to moral norms over the rest of the normative realms. What he is basically claiming is to make adjustments as to get these other contexts in tune with the realm of moral universal principles:

> Within different normative contexts, one has to distinguish various conceptions of the individual, collective, or moral "formal" good that enjoy "priority" wherever it is a matter of ethical questions; in contexts, however, in which no shared ethical convictions provide convincing answers there is a need for norms that can be justified in a different (but also) intersubjective way. [13]

The conception of practical reason that Forst defends has to be understood as a constructivist conception according to which moral norms are not justified by any ethical or natural criteria but by an intersubjective procedure. In the absence of objective transcendental moral truths, the only way to achieve moral validity is through a discursive conception of practical reason directed to achieve reasonable agreements that cannot be rejected with *general* and *reciprocal* reasons.

Tim Heysse has said that Forst develops two different understandings of *reciprocity*: 'reciprocity of content' and 'reciprocity of reasons.'[14] Following Heysse's distinction it is possible to say that the former kind of *reciprocity* means "that 'A' cannot claim a right or a resource she denies to 'B'" (of content), and that according to the latter it means "that the formulation of the claim and the reasons given must be open to questioning and not to be determined by one party" (of reasons).[15] On its part, *generality* for Forst means that "the reasons that are sufficient to support the validity of norms should not just be acceptable to, say, two dominant parties in a society but to every person and party involved."[16] Hence, the criterion of *reciprocity* responds to a broad, still deep, sense of impartiality as the one claimed by Garzón (among others), and the one of *generality* responds to the universal character that deontological authors claim for moral norms. Both criteria give content to what Forst has called the *principle of justification*.[17] The *principle of justification* in Forst's work constitutes an a priori moral right which has to be granted to all human beings understanding them as *justificatory beings.*

Norms that are justified under these criteria of the principle of justification claim to have a *categorical* and *unconditional* binding valid force. "The force of moral validity claim is that nobody has good reasons to question the validity of such norms; any person can in principle demand that any other person should follow them."[18] The categorical and unconditional force that moral norms adopt by way of the principle of justification (*reciprocal* and *general*) is not shared by any other kind of norms. Assuming that moral norms are categorical means that we cannot have "reasonable moral grounds [. . .] to bear against them. With ethical answers, that is not the case; they can be ethically justified and binding for one person or community even on reasonable grounds—ethical or moral—can still be brought to bear against them."[19]

As it was discussed in chapter I, for some philosophers the idea of different spheres (ethical, political, legal or moral) from which different practical questions stem has led them to believe in the fragmentation of practical reason, context in which no single correct answer exists. To this problem there have been several type of answers: (1) Some claim that moral questions can only be answered on ethical bases, (2) Others say that there is a distinction between moral and ethical problems, morality nonetheless must be anchored on some conception of the good, (3) A third group has argued that moral norms must be reasonably justified in accordance with principles which are independent of any conception of the good. This third possibility is the one that deontological philosophers such as Forst have chosen. For him, the separation of practical reason between spheres of: "what is 'good' for me," "what is commanded by law," "what is politically justified 'for us'," and "what is morally right 'for all'," assumes an autonomy between them and a differentiation in the practical answers that they require.[20] Given the differences between these levels, the answers will not necessarily be in agreement with one another. Same practical questions raised at different levels might conflict with one another. Still, Forst believes that an 'objective' criterion found in a *formal* or *procedural* way can give good reasons to answer all these practical questions in one only correct way.

This perspective leads him to claim that if tolerance is taken to be a virtue of justice then it must be justified in a *reciprocal* and *general* way. If "the *objection* is based on one's particular ethical (or religious) views; the *acceptance*, however, is based on a moral consideration of whether they qualify for being generally enforceable. If they turn out to be sufficient for a negative *ethical* judgment, but not for negative *moral* judgment of certain practices or beliefs, the case for toleration arises; for then one has to see that one's ethical judgment does not justify a generally shareable moral condemnation and a rejection."[21]

Thus, Heysse is right when he says that for Forst tolerance stems from a reflection on our beliefs and on their chances of being generally accepted by the supporters of the different religious, philosophical or ethical views present in society.[22] Putting things this way, the acceptance of the principle of justification means that we are not legitimated to impose our relevant convictions to anyone else if these do not pass the threshold of reciprocity and generality. If we accept this principle, according to Forst, we will be also able to define the limits of toleration.

It is possible to compare Forst's conception of being tolerant with Rawls's conception of reasonableness. Both claims, to more or less the same degree, require the capability of bracketing our own ethical, religious or philosophical views when these cannot be generally claimed or publicly enforced. For Forst toleration also includes both the normative and the epistemological elements that we can find in Rawls's sense of justice.

Forst defines the normative element as the principle that "stipulates that moral norms which legitimize the use of force or, more broadly speaking, a morally relevant interference with the actions of other persons, must be based on reasons" that are general and reciprocal; that is, respecting everyone's right to justification.[23] Rawls, for his part, defines the basic aspects of being reasonable in the following way: "reasonable persons, we say, are not moved by the general good as such but desire for its own sake a social world in which they, as free and equal, can cooperate with others on terms all can accept. They insist that reciprocity should hold within that world so that each benefits along with others."[24] Both terms emphasize the idea that the only way for individuals to show respect and consideration to others is by providing reasons that can justify their actions and interventions.

The case of the epistemological element of being reasonable consists in an insight into the finitude of both theoretical and practical reason in finding 'final' answers to the questions of the good that all can agree on. This element is close enough to Rawls's "burdens of judgment"[25] or Ackerman's skepticism about the possibility to find the correct ways of life.[26] The burdens of judgment for Rawls are a second basic aspect of reasonableness which takes into account the sources, or causes, of disagreement between reasonable persons.[27] What the idea of the finitude of reason or the burdens of judgment prevents, in both theories for Rawls and Forst, is that people stop interfering in other people's lives following their particular conceptions of the good.

Taking into consideration the aforementioned we can see: (1) why under Forst's perspective tolerance is understood as a reasonable attitude, as a virtue of justice, and (2) why he believes that the respect conception of tolerance is more justified than the rest. Tolerance, in this sense, is considered a practice and an attitude that considers others as free and equal persons that deserve moral recognition.

The basic idea found in the deontological perspectives, according to which only impartial moral reasons (reciprocal and general) are ultimate (categorical) and the only ones capable of justifying acts of tolerance, related to the idea that objections can be different from those of a moral type, creates a series of problems which are very difficult to face by this type of moral philosophy. Apparently deontological authors accept the idea of including other type of objections besides those of a moral nature because, otherwise, tolerance will be snared in a world of dilemmas. Before it was argued that deontological moral theories, in general, reject the existence of this type of conflict, some proposals such as Forst's still accept the possibility of their existence, though he sustains that they are solvable. Still, which are the normative possibilities that objections based on ethical or aesthetic values can survive if they contradict moral categorical norms? These are some of the problems that I will discuss in the next chapters.

## NOTES

1. Forst, "Toleration, Justice," 72.
2. Tim Heysse, "Toleration and Political Conflict. A Comment on Rainer Forst's Analysis of Toleration," *Bijdragen. International Journal in Philosophy and Theology*, 4 (2010): 391.
3. Forst, "Toleration, Justice," 72.
4. Forst, "Toleration, Justice," 72. (Emphasis added)
5. Forst, "Toleration, Justice," 72.
6. Rainer Forst, "Toleration," *Stanford Encyclopedia of Philosophy* (2007), accessed January 22, 2015; Rainer Forst, "Toleration, justice," 71–85.
7. Forst, "Toleration, Justice," 74.
8. Forst, "Toleration, Justice," 74.
9. Forst, "Toleration, Justice," 75.
10. Forst, "A Critical Theory of Multicultural Toleration," in *The Right to Justification*, 141.
11. We can find Forst's defense of a Kantian framework of practical reason in his "Practical Reason and Justifying Reasons: On the Foundation of Morality," "Moral Autonomy and the Autonomy of Morality: Towards a Theory of Normativity after Kant," and "Ethics and Morality," all in *The Right to Justification*.
12. Forst, *Contexts*, 230–231.
13. Forst, *Contexts*, 232.
14. Heysse, "Toleration," 398.
15. Forst, "Toleration, Justice," 76.
16. Forst, "Toleration, Justice," 76.
17. This has been one of the biggest contributions of Forst's philosophy and it has been defended in several papers and books, however, two of them are particularly representative on this issue, *Contexts of Justice, op. cit.*, and his most recent book, *The Right to Justification, op. cit.*
18. Forst, "Moral Autonomy," 49.
19. Rainer Forst, "Practical Reasons and Justifying Reasons. On the Foundation of Morality," in *The Right to Justification*, 17.
20. Forst, *Contexts*, 244–245.
21. Forst, "A Critical Theory," 148.
22. Heysse, "Toleration," 396.
23. Heysse, "Toleration," 398; Forst, "Toleration, Justice," 81.
24. Rawls, *Political*, 50.
25. Rawls, *Political*, 54–58.
26. Ackerman, *Social Justice*, 141.
27. Rawls, *Political*, 55.

# TEN

# Tolerance and the Moral System

According to what has been presented so far, it seems that there are still many doubts regarding the deontological mechanism of justification of tolerance, and particularly, regarding the connection that deontological authors suggest between the basic normative system (which contain our ethical, religious, philosophical and aesthetic values) and the justificatory normative system of *moral norms*. This is, between the tendency to prohibit an objected act and the balancing of reasons that favor the permission or the acceptance and/or the prohibition or the rejection of the act in question.

It is from the principles that rule the interaction between these two normative systems that this proposal drowns in multiple problems that are difficult to discern at a first glance but that make a very hostile environment for tolerance as I will argue in the next chapters. There I will be arguing that deontological liberalism faces two kinds of problems. The first one is related to the interaction of the two normative systems, namely, the systems that hold non-moral values and the moral system. This interaction in the case of tolerance, hosts two types of conflict: one between the conflicts which arise between non-moral values (ethical, aesthetic or philosophical) and the moral norms of the justificatory system, and another between the moral norms themselves which is the one that constitutes the so call "moral paradox of tolerance": the practical situation where the agent is torn by two equally valid moral claims.

The second set of problems refers to the limits of tolerance. Under the deontological structure of practical reason analyzed so far, the limits of tolerance are settled by the moral principles that we use in order to reject our ethical objections towards certain acts or practices. Deontological theories assume the idea that once we reject our intention to prohibit certain acts or practices that injure one of our relevant convictions the normative system from which our objection arises is moralized, in the sense that we realize that there are no moral reasons for us to impose such a belief upon others. It will be argued that this structure of reasoning assumes that every act of tolerance strengthens the circle of intolerances until tolerance becomes unnecessary or irrelevant.

Hence, according to this the interaction of the basic normative systems and the justificatory one using the terms of Ernesto Garzón, or between the Rational and the Reasonable using Rawls's, creates several tensions between tolerance and the deontological structure of practical reason. Before we enter into the arguments that sustain the existence of these tensions, I find it useful to recall two things from the proposals we have already analyzed:

The first is that Rainer Forst and Ernesto Garzón affirmed that tolerance is not something that involves uniquely moral objections; quite the opposite. Garzón affirms that the list of prohibited (yet potentially tolerable) acts also includes things that arouse *dislike* or *distaste* within us, and that it would be too radical to exclude them from the scope of the (in)tolerable.[1] Forst on his part says that "it would be inappropriate to exclude other forms of normative critique, such as, for instance, aesthetic critique."[2]

This stance is associated with the distinction already analyzed between the two types of rejection: *dislike* and *disapproval*. I have explained that Peter Nicholson understands *dislike* as a non-moral matter of irrational or a-rational feelings, while *disapproval* as a matter sustained by moral reasons.[3]

As I have sustained before in chapters 4 and 5, this distinction has divided moral philosophers into two seemingly irreconcilable groups. We can say that while one includes those who consider that tolerance should only include *disapproval* as part of its conceptual scope (Peter Nicholson, D. D. Raphael and John Horton for example), the other sustains that both types of objections are legitimate to find within the scope of tolerance (as is the case of Mary Warnock, Annette Schmitt, and though in a very different way, also Ernesto Garzón and Rainer Forst). These two stances are the ones that I have denominated as the *narrow* and the *wide* thesis of the concept of tolerance.

When Nicholson distinguishes between convictions that are based on reasons and those that are not, I have argued that in fact what he highlights is the rationality that underlies each and every kind of conviction and the types of reasons given to support them.[4] This is the criterion I think deontological liberals such as Garzón and Forst have in mind when they include other convictions different from the ethical and moral ones into the realm of tolerance.

In the case of Garzón this may now be noted with the distinction he draws between *reasonable* and *unreasonable tolerance*. In the case of this distinction, it is sufficient to recall that the difference resided in the quality of the reasons in which an act of tolerance was sustained. It should also be borne in mind that the most adequate criterion for Garzón "in order to establish a line of demarcation between both types of reasons"[5] is the criterion of impartiality.

On Forst's side, we must remember that the objection component "must be normatively substantive, but is not necessarily restricted to 'moral' reasons,"[6] "the term 'objection' needs to be normatively justified (though not generally sharable) in some sense, and must not be based on mere prejudice."[7] Thus, the main characteristic that Forst requires for a conviction to be a candidate for tolerance is its normative justification, this is, it should be backed up by reasons.

Then, being based on reasons is the minimum requirement to consider convictions as legitimate candidates for tolerance. In other words, the difference drawn is between convictions that can provide reasons and convictions that cannot lay the difference between rational and completely irrational or arational convictions. Although this perspective seems more plausible than that of Nicholson, I have argued that defining the convictions for tolerance only as the rational ones is insufficient even for deontological liberals. It was discussed that convictions that can be candidates for tolerance must include other important characteristic: the *relevancy* of the conviction. The *relevancy* criterion takes into consideration the importance that certain convictions have within what Bernard Williams has called the *ground project*.[8] I have underlined the idea that a conviction should not be irrelevant or contingent for an individual's plan of life but important for a person's project of life and relevant for his/her understanding of what constitutes a good life.

This brings me to the second issue that I want to address before delving into the specific complications that the relation between tolerance and modern liberal deontologism presents. This other issue is twofold: on the one hand, there is the fact that although deontological authors accept the distinction between *moral* and *non-moral* convictions, they do not exclude *dislikes* from the scope of what is tolerable and, on the other, the compatibility that this acceptance may have with one of the principles of their moral system: mainly, the principle of the supreme character of morality, i.e. with the "supremacy" of the justificatory normative system. Specifically, I am referring to the type of conflict that could be generated between both types of normative systems.

Let us recall the general stance that the deontological moral system adopts with regard to tolerance. According to what I have been saying so far, deontological philosophers, in more or less the same fashion argue that the mechanism of tolerance is triggered when prohibitions founded on reasons (moral, religious, political, scientific, aesthetic, etc.) have been violated by an act X and the agent's reaction would be to act according to his/her prohibition, but for specific *moral reason* he/she refrains from doing so, either because he/she "eliminates" the said prohibition or because he/she "raises" it.

Under these circumstances, tolerance is characterized as the practice of deliberately allowing something of which one *disapproves* or *dislikes* on the basis of moral reasons.

If this is the case, as I said before, both perspectives face two types of conflicts. The first is when a rule and/or a morally justified principle has been affected. Here the problem is deep, because this is generated when one of these principles enters into conflict with another that is part of the justificatory moral system. These are the kinds of problems that the "moral paradox" refers to. The depth of this problem lies in the fact that it can give way to a genuine moral dilemmas, which deontological moral systems are not equipped to accept or to face.

The second conflict arises in the cases of non-moral rules and/or principles that have been affected and in order for us to know whether we can interfere against the act in question, we must submit those norms to the critical scrutiny of the moral principles found in the justificatory system. Here the problem is rooted in a theoretical conflict of lesser depth than the previous one but still very puzzling.

The contradiction between these two types of norms is less profound because, if we recall, according to the deontological moral system, moral reasons are ultimate reasons. For example, Garzón will say that "there are no reasons that can be imposed upon morality."[9] Forst in the same vein would say that "the force of moral validity claim is that nobody has good reasons to question the validity of such norms,"[10] and Rawls will state that "the Reasonable subordinates the Rational because its principles limit, and in a Kantian doctrine limit absolutely, the final ends that can be pursued."[11] If this is the case, then what is the point of making them 'compete' with non-moral convictions? And, above all, what chance would they have of being reinforced after being critically scrutinized by the moral system? These questions are the ones that I will address in the following chapters.

## NOTES

1. Garzón, "No pongas," 188.
2. Forst, "Toleration, Justice," 72.
3. Nicholson, "Toleration as a Moral Ideal," 160.
4. Nicholson, "Toleration as a Moral Ideal," 160.
5. Garzón, "No pongas," 197.
6. Forst, "Toleration, Justice," 72.
7. Forst, "Toleration, Justice," 82 note 3.
8. Williams, "Persons, character," 12–13.
9. Garzón, "La Alternativa del Disenso," 479.
10. Forst, "Moral Autonomy," 49.
11. Rawls, "Kantian Constructivism," 317.

*IV*

# The Moral Paradox of Tolerance

# ELEVEN

## The Limits of Tolerance

Setting limits on tolerance is one of the most difficult philosophical tasks for any moral and political theory. Which are the limits that a tolerant person must reach for either not becoming utterly permissible or obstinately recalcitrant, is far from being clear. In the particular case of liberalism, this uncertainty is due to the existence of three main circumstances. The first one relates to the disparities within liberalism in the way to approach and interpret the principles of political morality. Liberalism is far from being a univocal linear political and moral doctrine. This heterogeneity of conceptions brings uncertainty regarding which are the criteria that can be used to justify an act of tolerance. The second is tolerance's substantial vacuity. Tolerance so understood is an empty vase which cannot provide the substantive character of the reasons for objection, acceptance, and rejection. This means that tolerance belongs to what Rainer Forst has called *normatively dependent concepts*.[1] Forst defends the idea that this vacuity can be filled by recurring to a specific conception of *justice* which has to be in accordance with a notion of practical reason.

This means that any set of limits put on tolerance depends specifically on the perspective of justice and the scheme of practical reason that is adopted by a particular liberal stance. Liberal philosophers attached to deontological liberalism like Rainer Forst for example, have tried to settle a more or less determined frame of limitations based on the priority of the right thesis (among others), while other liberal philosophers who reject this priority thesis, depend strongly on some substantive ethical structures or on some kind of virtue ethics.[2] This being the case, the limits of toleration depend mostly on the moral or ethical background hold by the different moral-political approaches to liberalism.

The third circumstance is the dependence of tolerance on particular circumstances and contexts of conflict. One thesis that I will defend in the last chapter is that in order for tolerance to avoid the 'conceptual paradox' and for not becoming a *suicidal concept* it needs to be understood as a *context dependent concept* as well. This means that if tolerance is constrained by a determined deontological set of rules (in which cases is it always justified to tolerate and in which cases is it never justified) tolerance loses all of its meaning, flexibility, and moral relevancy. Under this consideration tolerance cannot be based exclusively on the *relevant characteristics* considered as a norm (as generalists and universalist pretend) but has to pay attention to what, following Jonathan Dancy, will be called *salient features* which make each case of tolerance different from the other despite the *relevant characteristics* they share.[3] The justification of this third claim of the context dependency of tolerance, as said before, will be left for the last chapter where I will argue that tolerance as an aretaic base concept requires a structure of practical reason closely related to moral particularism; this will be called the 'contextual response.'

For the moment, let us focus on the normative dependence advanced by Forst. Following what has been said so far, it makes sense to think that relativists and skeptics will set very loose normative barriers for limiting tolerance under the premise that morality depends on the eye of the beholder or in each single culture or that there are no valid reasons to support the idea that one course of action is justified while another is not. In the same way, minimalist objectivists (or non-cognitivists) will be less relaxed and will offer a more rigid set of limits based on principles of justice or morality while, robust objectivists (or moral cognitivists) will be by far the most rigid of all considering the existence of certain criteria for the objective knowledge of the good. However we must consider that these are mainly abstract assumptions that later need to be contrasted with concrete theoretical propositions.

Tolerance's substantial vacuity does not mean impossibility to consider some basic a priori limits that some versions of liberalism, according to their own structures, have to defend in the name of coherence. Some of these can be deduced from the premises of each theoretical proposal and also from the same conceptual structure of tolerance.

Before entering in the discussion of those possibilities, we must consider that within modern deontological liberalism there are two limitations of tolerance that derive from its own interpretation of the first and the second circumstances of tolerance: (1) only rational and relevant convictions can raise questions about tolerance, and (2) it is only possible to tolerate those things that we can (physically and normatively) stop, deter or detain.

What we have discussed throughout the previous chapter is that the limits imposed by these two conceptual conditions for tolerance reach all the different versions of liberalism. If liberalism does not want tolerance to fall under what Leslie Green has called "vicious toleration"[4] then it has to be based on relevant and rational convictions and not on prejudice, hatred or superstition, on one side, or on trivial, non-relevant and contingent convictions, on the other. In the same direction, if liberalism does not want to confuse tolerance with other attitudes such as patience, submissiveness or resignation it has to accept that the tolerator must have at his/her disposition the (factual or normative) possibility to repress that which he/she disapproves. No doubt, it can be objected that these two considerations are also subjected to several interpretations.

Facing the idea that tolerance cannot be practiced among equals and that we need the 'power' or the 'competency' to stop or forbid an act that we disapprove of as a necessary condition of tolerance can still be put into doubt.

It can be argued that in plural societies we can find several examples of people that cannot stop the things they say to tolerate. This would imply that for describing an act of tolerance there is no need to take into account the 'power' or the 'competence' to stop, deter or forbid those acts that individuals disapproved of but still tolerate.

Let us think of someone who is extremely attached to his religious beliefs and that he strongly believes that homosexuality is wrong. Every year the gay pride parade crosses in front of his home, and he develops a series of acts just with the idea of ruining the parade: he plays loud extremist music, slaps the people around him who participate in the parade, displays offensive signs against gay people on his balcony, etc. Regularly this kind of behavior will be described as intolerant even though he apparently does not have prima facie any kind 'power' or 'competency' to detain or to forbid the gay pride parade.[5]

No doubt cases like this are recurrent in plural and democratic societies. However, it is very important to pay close attention to their surrounding features. Following the conceptual frame that has been argued before, the first thing we must ask ourselves is if this person is against homosexuality per se or if he is against the public disclosure of homosexuality. We must be sure about what he disapproves of. Second, we must take into account the two different conceptual considerations: a) if the conviction upon which his disapproval is based on is *rational* and *relevant*, and b) if so, if he has any possibility to stop, deter or forbid what he disapproves.

Regarding the first possibility, if we respect both conceptually imposed limits, we could say that actually he cannot tolerate them because he cannot do anything about their homosexuality. He cannot stop it, or forbid it. To say the contrary will be as much as to say that he can tolerate and earthquake or that he tolerates the fact that some people are 1.90 meters tall. Still under this first perspective of the case, the most important of all are the reasons why he disapproves of homosexuality. In chapter 5 I drew the difference between a *reasonable believer* and a *fanatic believer*. If we stick to the above example, we are talking about an intolerant attitude which is, as it has been argued previously, the reaction of a *fanatic believer*. This is someone who holds an unwavering religious stance and truly believes that anyone who thinks differently is doomed to perdition and, therefore, he/she seeks to use any kind of social repression to ensure the dominance of his own conception of the good in the name of salvation. In such a case we can argue that such an individual has situated himself/herself outside of the realm of tolerance. He/she is no longer acting within a rational discourse, therefore, we are not asking this individual to be tolerant, what are we asking him/her in fact is to get rid of his/her most deep-seated prejudices. As Bernard Williams has argued:

> if one group simply hates another, as with a clan vendetta or cases of sheer racism, it is not really toleration that is needed: the people involved need rather to lose their hatred, their prejudice, or their implacable memories. If we are asking people to be tolerant, we are asking for something more complicated than this. They will indeed have to lose something, their desire to suppress or drive out the rival belief.[6]

Considering this example, it is important to take into account that religious toleration is only possible for the reasonable believer, for the one who adopts a more modest position facing his religious doctrine or set of beliefs and is willing to respect other people's ways of life by bracketing his or her beliefs when judging the life of others.

The second possibility is more promising as a counter-argument than the first one discussed above. The idea that what he/she morally disapproves of any homosexual public disclosure, such as the gay pride parade, requires us to pay attention to the possibilities that he/she has to stop or to forbid such kind of behaviors. This must be done in order to realize if he/she is really immersed in a discussion about tolerance and that he/she is not, in fact, practicing any other attitude such as patience or resignation.

If we assume that he/she lives in a democratic society then we can also assume that he/she has plenty of resources to which he can appeal if he/she wants to stop, deter or forbid this kind of conduct. His range of options can vary from lawsuits to parliament lobbying, organizing social pressure with other supporters of his cause, or moving out of the neighborhood or the locality. Though, there is the possibility that he cannot appeal to any of these different resources. In that case, then, and according to the conceptual frame of tolerance, this individual is in fact not immersed in a conflict of tolerance, but rather he is being just intransigent or unyielding.

My arguments in previous chapters, though, have been directed to analyze the roots of such disagreements and to settle some of them. In this sense, the 'rational and relevant' criterion is intended to reconcile both the wide and the narrow theses concerning the idea of *relevant convictions* mainly, through the interpretation of the conceptual premises posed by deontological authors.

The same goes for the *power* and *competence* thesis which, as stated before, has been something accepted in a more peaceful way by different authors, thus it answers the claim of Williams about only considering "physical strength" in the concept of tolerance.[7] In that case, even Ernesto Garzón who sustains the existence of tolerance among equals will agree on this particular point.

Nevertheless, the two limits mentioned above are not the only ones. We should consider them as two limitations of general application. Still, as argued before, we can find others in a deductive way. These other limits are to be found, as Rainer Forst has suggested, within the different conceptions of justice and their structures of practical reason.

Take, for instance, the case of a liberal version that holds consequentialist tendencies. We know the radical differences that we can find between deontologism and consequentialism: while the former understands correct actions as those that *respect* moral values, the latter claims that correct actions are those that *maximize* the good. Still, what is important is to see at this moment are only the different scopes that this type of liberalism grants to tolerance. Consequentialist theories start from the claim that there is something intrinsically valuable, and argue in favor of the actions and practices that maximize the realization of that specific value. This means that the most important feature for this moral standpoint is that the consequences carried by certain actions increase in one way or another such a value. Making the maximizing outlook its strongest tenet, tolerance is allowed in all cases where its result can be seen as a benefit for such a value. Take for instance the next example: if the value of peace is the one considered by one consequentialist theory as the intrinsic value to maximize, then a consequentialist willingly would accept to wage a war if he/she believes that such war will end all wars. Why refuse combat—he/she would adduce—if I can promote the value of stable peace? I know many innocents will die, but more will be the innocents that will live peacefully once this battle is over. The same argument goes for tolerance. The limits are to be found in the calculus that the tolerator makes between the valuable options he/she faces and computing the benefits that a tolerating attitude could achieve for one of them. In a way, under such moral standpoint there are no fixed limitations for tolerance. These are tied to the probable results that an action can produce. In this case Susan Mendus's opinion is that consequentialist theories face one main problem "it does not in itself explain what is wrong with intolerance, but only suggests why intolerance is not expedient [and] it draws no moral limits on toleration but implies that anything must be tolerated provided that it will promote (relative) peace."[8]

This last perspective, together with deontological liberalism, differs in many ways from a third kind of liberalism that we can consider: perfectionist liberalism. Perfectionist political morality is committed, regularly, to four claims: "(1) that some ideals of human flourishing are sound and can be known to be sound; (2) that the state is presumptively justified in favoring these ideals; (3) that a sound account of political morality will be informed by sound ideals of human flourishing; and (4) that there is no general moral principle that forbids the state from favoring sound ideals of human flourishing, as well as enforcing conceptions of political morality informed by them."[9] Perfectionism then implies a fuller and more demanding notion of toleration. Under a perfectionist stance it is not enough for citizens to consider themselves as carriers of the same rights and freedoms to be worthy of tolerance, but it is necessary for them to consider the other styles of life as ethically valuable and held with good reasons. If a perfectionist tolerator finds a way of life that is not attractive he or she can only find reasons to refrain him or herself in thinking that even though it is an unattractive way of life still, it is ethically worthwhile.[10] The principles that limit tolerance under this perspective are related to ideas of human perfection, values that allow humans to flourish and to construct their lives in ways that are considered virtuous. Anything that falls outside of the realm of this conception of the good cannot be an object of tolerance. This perspective, in general terms and with different levels of strength, is defended by philosophers such as Joseph Raz, Thomas Hurka, George Sher and Steven Wall, among others.[11]

Another perspective that can be considered to exemplify our point is moral relativism. Relativism has been permanently present in the history of tolerance. In a way, popular culture often assumes that toleration is, almost by definition, equal to a moral relativist stance. Under this level of analysis there are several misunderstandings that tend to interconnect pluralism and tolerance with relativism.[12] But it is also true that in specialized literature it is not so strange to find this kind of arguments as well. Regularly, the moral relativist stance is based on the idea the "that there are no neutral moral standards by means of which to adjudicate between competing moral beliefs or practices."[13] The grounds on which moral relativists base this position is as follows: "they all sustain that, that which is morally good or bad cannot be definitely established, it all "depends": for some, it depends on what one *person* accepts as ethical criteria for *themselves*, it is therefore sustained that no one can judge another (due to the absence of neutral moral standards), in other words, there cannot be any interpersonal moral evaluation."[14]

Tolerance, from a relativist point of view, is usually used as an argument serving to protect the diversity of ethical stances that precisely, because they depend on what each person considers good or bad, are not subject to an external moral standard. They claim that these ways of life are incommensurable and that they cannot be subject of any objective evaluation thus, in order to respect them, as we should, the practice of tolerance becomes necessary. In this way, relativists pretend to provide an answer to the question: why should we have to tolerate the beliefs and conducts of others?, by stating that it is "because in matters of morality everything is relative"[15] 'nobody has the power to tell us how to live or how to choose our life,' and 'when it comes to matters of morality, it is incorrect to legislate for others.'[16]

Considering the answers provided by a moral relativism stance, only in this practical sense, the problem to establish limits on tolerance is not resolved. In fact, relativist cannot provide any kind of limits on toleration if, at least, they assume that as any other type of theory they must commit themselves to some minimal requirements of coherence and consistency. Of course, we can find stronger arguments coming from moral relativists. Such is the case of Geoffrey Harrison in *Relativism and Tolerance*.[17] Harrison's main idea is that the relativist stance must only be understood as a "meta-ethical" theory and not as a normative one.[18] According to him, relativism seen in this meta-ethical way supersedes the flaws that normative relativism finds in its relationship with tolerance.

Until now it has been argued that the problem of settling limits on tolerance is equally related to conceptual, normative factors as to empirical factors. This makes the problem of the limits of tolerance to look like a great puzzle in which some of the pieces do not always fit. It is almost obvious that an instrumental conception of toleration will find a perfect match within consequentialist moral theories. But, can we say the same if we try to match it with deontologism? The answer also appears obvious: the rejection that deontological moral theories make to attribute moral relevancy to the results of our actions makes these two pieces appear incompatible. What has been explained before about moral relativism, could lead us to think that tolerance understood as a moral ideal becomes incoherent under its theoretical premises. But can we say the same about the match of tolerance as a moral ideal with moral deontologism?

If we interpret some of its main tenets we can deduce that besides the two abovementioned limits (the *rationality* and *relevancy* criterion that convictions have to cover in order to be considered as candidates for toleration and the *power* and *competence* to stop, detain or dissuade the tolerated act), this kind of liberalism sustains other important limits: the ones imposed by individual rights and the principles of justice. These kinds of limits occupied our attention during previous chapters. Nevertheless, it has been argued that one of the main ideas surrounding this liberal perspective is that in the public realm, what should guide the conducts of all individuals are moral universal norms that can be accepted by any reasonable person, independent of his or her conception of the good. Following this construction, the limits of tolerance are imposed by the normative realm of the 'right,' in the sense that a person must tolerate the acts of others that do not infringe any moral norm independent of what his/her ethical values dictate. In its general bases this perspective is the one defended by philosophers such as John Rawls, Ernesto Garzón Valdés and Rainer Forst.

At the end of chapter 10, I argued that deontological liberalism encounters two types of problems regarding this scheme of practical reasoning. One of them was qualified as 'profound' because it represented the idea of moral dilemmas. I will deal with these kinds of conflicts in chapter 13 "Tolerance as a Moral Dilemma." The other kind of conflict was considered to be 'less profound,' because it refers to the conflicts generated between non-moral values (ethical, aesthetical, social, etc.) and the moral norms of a justificatory system. These conflicts, as argued before, emerge from the limits that the realm of the 'right' imposes on the realm of the 'good.' These conflicts are the ones related to the limits that deontological liberalism puts on tolerance within the private realm. We will deal with these conflicts in the next chapter: "Tolerance and the Conceptions of the Good."

## NOTES

1. Forst, "Toleration, Justice," 75.
2. This is the case, for example of Glen Newey and Joseph Raz: Newey, *Virtue*, Chapter 3, and Joseph Raz, *The Morality of Freedom* (Oxford, Clarendon Press, 1985).
3. Jonathan Dancy, *Moral Reasons* (Oxford-Cambridge, Blackwell, 1993), 112–116.
4. Leslie Green, "On Being Tolerated," (paper presented at "The Legacy of HLA Hart" Seminar, Cambridge Forum for Legal and Political Philosophy, July 28, 2007): 4.
5. I owe this example to Professor Raf Geenens who has challenged in many ways the arguments I have defended against the possibility of tolerance among equals. I am profoundly thankful for this comment as for the many others that he has given to my work in general.
6. Bernard Williams, "Toleration: An Impossible Virtue?," in *Toleration*, ed. David Heyd, 19.
7. Bernard Williams, "Toleration, a Political or Moral Question?," in *In the Beginning was the Deed: Realism and Moralism in Political Argument*, ed. Geoffrey Hawthorn (Princeton University Press, 2005), 128–138.
8. Susan Mendus, "Introduction," in *On Toleration*, ed. Susan Mendus and David Edwards, 5.
9. Wall, *Liberalism, Perfectionism*, 8.
10. Raz, *The Morality*, 402. Raz considers that even in such cases sometimes one can tolerate out of mercy.
11. Joseph Raz, *Ethics in the Public Domain: Essays in the Morality of Law and Politics* (Oxford, Clarendon Press, 1995); Thomas Hurka, *Perfectionism* (Oxford University Press, 1993); George Sher, *Beyond Neutrality*; Wall, *Liberalism, Perfectionism*.
12. Newey, *Virtue*, 124–127, 132–133.
13. Timothy Mosteller, *Relativism: A Guide for the Perplexed* (New York, Continuum, 2008), 55.
14. Ruth Zimmerling, *El Concepto de Influencia y otros Ensayos* (México, Fontamara, 1993), 67–68. I will discuss this point in greater detail in chapter VI.
15. Zimmerling, *El Concepto*, 68.
16. Newey, *Virtue*, 132.
17. Geoffrey Harrison, "Relativism and Tolerance," *Ethics*, 86, 2, (1976): 122–135.
18. Harrison, "Relativism," 132.

# TWELVE

# Tolerance and the Conceptions of the Good

So far I have only considered problems related to settling limits on tolerance and showing some of the tensions that these problems create within different conceptions of justice and structures of practical reason. Now I will consider in specific terms one of the problems that tolerance creates within a deontological structure of practical reason. These conflicts in particular are the kind of conflicts that a person can experience when he or she displays an act of tolerance and they assume a deontological perspective of morality.

Previous chapters highlighted some of the main theses that deontological philosophers, such as John Rawls, Ernesto Garzón and Rainer Forst as representative authors of this current, sustain. Some of these theses are important for the matter I will address now, and broadly speaking we can summarize them in: (1) the acceptance of non-moral convictions (ethical, aesthetic, social, etc.) as part of the scope of the (in)tolerable, (2) the conceptual requirement to balance, in *case of conflict*, the convictions of the basic normative systems (BNS) with the moral norms of a justificatory normative system (JNS), and (3) the categorical status of moral norms and their priority over any other kind of normative considerations. Now that these three matters have been articulated, it seems to me that they encapsulate some of the high-interest problems.

If we accept that the mechanism of tolerance suggested by the *DMS* consists basically in the potential conflict between principles or convictions of the basic system and the norms of the justificatory system, then what happens in the case of convictions that are not moral (ethical, philosophical, aesthetic), though they are rational and relevant? What opportunity to survive are we granting to these convictions when they are forced to compete with moral principles? How much space are we giving

129

tolerance to be a *dispositional property* or a 'recurrent attitude of a virtuous agent'? It should also be noted that if we do not take this balancing of reasons seriously, it is because we are implicitly speaking of a type of 'conflict' between non-moral, *subjective* values or ethical norms and universal moral norms.

We should not lose sight that the difference between these type of norms and values, that has been highlighted before, is based on the idea that while the norms and values that I have been calling *subjective* are understood as those based on the values that serve to guide our own life, they answer questions regarding the good "for me," yet do not operate as universal guidelines of conduct. The moral norms are precisely those presented in the previous parts of this book as norms that stem from an impartial perspective, claim universal validity and require different justificatory methods. Garzón defines them as those which "take into account the interests of others as autonomous beings capable of formulating respectable life plans insofar as they do not violate the principle of harm."[1] But it is possible to find this same difference between moral norms and ethical values, in Rainer Forst's work. He sustains that ethical values can be justified in a *three-dimensional* way: the subjective, the intersubjective, and the objective. Still, they are not general and categorical in the way moral norms are.[2]

With this in mind, we have to ask ourselves: what type of normative conclusion could result from the inter-systemic process of balancing like the one suggested by the deontological philosophers? Could a deliberation, in a situation where aesthetic or fashion objections are involved, result in a general norm that imposes on us a moral duty to dress well?

Let us think of that situation: an act that is prohibited by a rule and/or principle of our aesthetic basic normative system is continuously being affected by other individuals. First, we must ask ourselves, how relevant would it be to commit a *crime of fashion* under the view of moral norms? In second place, we must consider whether it makes any sense at all to speak of a balancing between these two types of norms—moral and aesthetic. And if there is a balancing operation, how does it work?

Perhaps, deontologists might accept that this is possible, still during a deliberation process we will wonder what kind of a conflict can be generated by these two type of norms. In other words, under a deontological perspective of morality do we genuinely have a problem in deciding which one of two norms to follow: the one that is morally based—recall that we are also sustaining a principle that dictates the priority of moral norms—and the other that although subjectively justified by reasons and considered relevant for the agent is not moral.

It is important not to lose sight of the fact that although the mechanism of tolerance is triggered by the act of a stranger, the conflicts that concern us in this moment are the conflicts faced by one single participant. Unlike the conflicts that are regularly of the interest of moral philosophers: conflicts in which what matters is finding the solution to a dis-agreement between two people or groups of people, the type of conflict I am concerned with here only involves one person. A person who, in principle, sustains two contradictory norms: one that tells him that he must act against an action X (*objection*) and another that tells him that he must not act against X. Although the problem is faced by a single agent it definitely relates the possibility of interfering in someone else's life (the tolerated one), but the conflict that I am referring to is precisely directed to the problem of how to solve this situation.

Seemingly, in order to resolve this kind of conflict one must choose between one of the norms in question. However, when confronted with the cases I have been considering, we must ask ourselves to what extent it is possible to say that we actually have a genuine *conflict* in our hands. What should be considered is not only the fact that there is a subjective value that contradicts a moral norm, but also if there is an actual problem in deciding which one of these norms should be chosen.

It is important to keep in mind that qualifying a case as a *case of conflict* depends on a number of variables, but also that the gravity or intensity of each conflict varies depending on the structure of practical reason that one adopts, such as for example deontological, utilitarian, relativist, etc.

It should be remembered that the road chosen by deontological liberal philosophers is a process in which the 'right' has priority over the 'good.' This is achieved by recognizing the kind of reasons that justify moral norms and the ones that justify other kind of non-general values. In Forst's view "the essence of the distinction between ethics and morality lies in the fact that, in practical conflicts calling norms that delimit what is strictly required or forbidden among human beings, the threshold of jus-tification increases and reciprocally and generally specifiable reasons are required."[3]

Bearing this in mind, let us now consider an example. Suppose that a university professor is always concerned with being well dressed: sup-pose he is a sartorialist. And due to these sorts of aesthetic likes and dislikes, he deeply hates shirts with ruffles, fundamentally because these types of shirts are so passé, because he thinks that they are not elegant, and because he thinks that they do not flatter anyone.

And now he is at a crossroads. He has been invited to a faculty dinner and his wife is going to wear a ruffled shirt that she just bought. Here, if he wants to be tolerant, the deontological structure of practical reason would induce him to submit his prohibition to a moral justificatory trial: to the scrutiny of the moral criteria of *reciprocity* and *generality*. Hence, he must ask himself if it is morally correct to prohibit his wife (and thereby all those who fall under the same assumption due to the universalizabil-ity criteria of morality) from wearing ruffled shirts.

Leaving aside the question over whether the professor has the 'com-petence' or 'power' that allows him to prohibit his wife (or any other person) to wear ruffled shirts (which is, in itself, a serious problem in the face of these cases due to the considerable lack of rationality that entails wanting something that one knows one cannot achieve), it is difficult to see what kind of normative conclusion could be derived from a scrutiny such as this one.

Let us say that, in the event that he decides to 'tolerate' his 'poorly' dressed wife, it would be, according to the *DMS*, because after balancing his rule of fashion against a moral norm, he resolved that it is morally permissible to allow other people to dress in a way they like. Or, in the event he decided 'not to tolerate' his wife's shirt, it would be because he believes that it is legitimate to think that there is a duty (a moral duty) to dress in a certain way.

If we leave things on the level of fashion, it seems to me that both conclusions are counterintuitive to say the least. I do not see how the rule that 'ruffled shirts are prohibited under a strictly aesthetic sense' could come into 'conflict' with some other norm of the justificatory system. There is no possibility of finding a contradiction between the reasons that underlie this aesthetic prescription and the moral reasons provided by a justificatory system.

Furthermore, I do not see the possibility of an effective normative balance of reasons, and above all, I do not see the possibility of arriving at a reasonable answer. Can we derive normatively speaking a moral duty of 'dressing correctly' from this reflective critical scrutiny? Leaving aside the question of what 'dressing correctly' means, or how one would go about deciding something like this, in either case, the conclusion would be a moral-aesthetic hybrid that few would be willing to accept. It is clear then that the core of the matter is whether it is actually relevant to include these types of values within the scope of tolerance; whether it is appropriate to speak of tolerance in cases such as those that do not involve moral norms.

A moral philosopher like John Horton says that there are at least two different routes to know when it is inappropriate to act against something:

> The most obvious and widely recognized way is when what is being permitted should properly be prevented. The second way is more oblique but not less important. Here restraint is inappropriate because it should not be necessary. One should not need to restraint one's desire to seriously impede some action or practice, because one should not have that desire in the first place.[4]

Certainly, to think that to legitimately—or appropriately—restrict the freedom of others requires something more than merely thinking that what that person is doing, thinking or wearing is something that we dislike, represents bad taste, or is just not pretty.

Richard Hare follows the same line of thought as Horton does. Someone like Hare would say that if the professor actually believes he is in a conflict, what he has to do, instead of balancing these two rules and arriving at "such a principle [that] would be a hybrid monster, both moral and aesthetic and neither,"[5] is to leave both his aesthetic and moral principles intact and act in favor of the moral principle. That is: *respect* or *accept*.

Adopting a more condescending stance to the likes of others is necessary because I cannot justifiably impose my own, however desirable that may be. By saying this, we are distinguishing between *condescendence* and *tolerance* which, as stated in previous chapters, by definition are not the same.

No doubt, there might be cases that present similar characteristics, in which the tolerator would have reasons to sustain an aesthetic prohibition of the same nature and after the scrutiny with the JNS acts according to it. Thus it is possible to say that when the deontological conceptions of tolerance as those analyzed above accept these types of convictions within the ambit of the (in)tolerable, it is because they have other ideas in mind.

It is possible to say that the university professor had some reasons to sustain such a conviction but it was not *relevant* for his life. Possibly, if instead of being a university professor he were a famous fashion designer who was invited to a designer's gala the situation of his wife wearing a ruffled shirt could suppose a direct harm of his interests, and of his desires, because his prestige might be at risk, because he considers that the crowd will mock him, or because the press would give his work a negative review.

There has been much discussion as to what we must understand by the term *harm*. Undoubtedly, the term relates the famous *principle of harm* of J. S. Mill. Since I do not mean to detain myself in this ample debate, for the moment, it will be sufficient to say that some interpreters of J. S. Mill, such as J. C. Rees, John Horton or Richard Hare have for example affirmed that the actions protected by Mill with his principle were those self-referring acts that "do not harm *the interests* of others."

I am aware of the many philosophical problems that this interpretation of the "harm principle" of Stuart Mill may generate. Especially, if we take into consideration the many varied stances that have been stated in its respect. For example, some authors claim that the only thing Mill meant to say with the principle of harm was that the self-referring acts that only affect the agent and do not have a *direct* effect on others should be neither condemned nor prohibited. However, other authors such as J. C. Rees criticize this interpretation arguing that Mill actually wanted to say that the principle of harm only covered those self-referring acts that did not affect the *interests* of others. Philosophers such as C. L. Ten affirm that the interpretation of authors such as Rees suffer from vagueness, fundamentally because the term 'interests' denotes so many aspects that it would eventually cover everything. Ten argues that when Mill spoke of 'interests,' he was actually referring to happiness. Therefore, all of the self-referring acts protected by his principle were those that did not directly affect the happiness of others. It is clear that when Ten swapped the term *interests* for the term *happiness* he did not fix the problem of vagueness. However, especially with this change, the even more important problem, mentioned by John Horton, weighs in. He argues that if we interpret Mill's principle in terms of happiness we would be circumscribing said principle to a unique moral theory: utilitarianism. Under a very different perspective we find authors who are much more radical, such as Alan Ryan, who argue that Mill's principle can only be understood as an ethical limitation of acts that are not self-referring because, in reality, for Mill these do not belong to the realm of morality. [6]

Certainly, the expression 'harming the interests of another' is not a specific one. However, for the case in hand, I will be using the interpretation posed by Richard Hare. Hare, in a work entitled *Wrongness and Harm,* argues that the analysis of the concept of *harm* can be carried out in terms of the affectation of interests and the affectation of interests in terms of the frustration of the desires.

In other words, for Hare, "to harm somebody is to act against his interests" and "the notion of interests is conceptually linked to that of desires, or that of wanting."[7] Hare says that it is "evident from the fact that it would be scarcely intelligible to claim that a certain thing was a man's interest, although he neither wanted it nor had ever wanted it, nor would ever want it, nor anything that it was a necessary or sufficient means to, nor might any of these things be the case."[8]

What I wish to conclude from the example of the ruffled shirt is that the scenario would not be the same if I were a professor or if I were a famous fashion designer. This scenario changes because the interests of both change based on their 'roles' and 'circumstances,' and it is exactly because of their 'roles' that an effective and objective damage of interests can be suffered.

From this perspective, it could be said that one of my interests as a fashion designer is for my wife and I to always be well-dressed (my professional reputation depends on it, for example), and that my wife, by wearing an aesthetically 'incorrect' shirt, is acting against those interests thus she can inflict harm to my career and reputation.

To tolerate that my wife wears a ruffled shirt to a gala night, despite my declared aversion to those shirts, may possibly be due to moral reasons. If we recall, for example, the case that David Ross presents in *The Right and the Good*, he accepts that his wife goes to a dinner poorly dressed, because he resolves that telling her that she looks bad could hurt her feelings.[9] And as no one has a right to hurt anyone, it is better to go to a dinner with a happy yet poorly dressed wife.

Let us not lose sight of the fact that even if the designer were to adopt Ross's point of view, he would still not discard his aesthetic conviction. The problem for him is not, *strictu sensu,* whether his wife wears a shirt that he does not like, but rather that her doing so may cause him harm. The idea I am attempting to transmit has nothing to do with the relativity that might exist between the different types of desires; rather, the target toward which the argument presented here is directed, is the one which shows that the stances of both individuals, in our case the professor and the designer, are based on clearly different perspectives, and that deontological liberalism by obviating the contextual differences cannot give a plausible answer to the conflict in question.

According to my analysis, in the first case there are no reasons that support the prohibition, while in the second case apparently there are. For this reason, in the case of the professor, it would not be appropriate — in the sense that I have been using this term — to sustain that he 'does not tolerate' his wife's shirt, given that he has no reasons upon which to base his dislike. He knows, for example, that attending these dinners properly dressed holds no admirable value nor it is an act that directly affects his personal interests (his career, his prestige, his friendships, etc.). On the contrary, in the case of the designer, there do seem to be reasons that support his direct interest in having his wife attend the gala dressed a certain way, such as his professional reputation.

Let me recall that in this case I am leaving aside the question of whether a husband has the 'competence' to tolerate a poorly dressed wife, because what I am interested in analyzing is up to what extent is it important to include the *likes* and *inclinations* as part of the scope of the (in)tolerable.

This is important, because it could be counter-argued that, according to what has been said, I am not claiming anything different from what has been argued by Mary Warnock to refute the distinction between *dislikes* and *disapprovals*. However, I do not think this is the case.

In the case of the professor, I do not consider that there is enough room for him to properly speak of tolerance, but rather of indifference or respect towards the likes of others. And, this is so, because his dislike, his prohibition of certain kinds of shirts, is not based on quality reasons or on legitimate reasons to interfere in the freedom of others. While, in the case of the designer, as I have stated, he seems to have reasons that justify making such a prohibition, yet it could still be the case that after putting himself in his wife's place he would nonetheless decide to tolerate her act.

It is possible that he also thinks that his wife might be the mockery of the crowd for wearing that shirt, or that she could feel bad for not being properly dressed for the occasion and have a lousy time. In spite of these reasons, he decides to tolerate the shirt because he thinks that telling his wife that she is poorly dressed could hurt her feelings, since she put so much effort into looking nice.

Unlike in the other case, here the designer is also considering his professional interests, which, depending on the circumstances of the case, can be affected. Then, the critique that the argument is not very different from the one presented by Warnock is now refuted, especially because there is a difference between the two types of injuries which makes it easier for us to locate them within their respective normative systems.

The above follows because of the circumstances that have been considered: we can clearly see that in this case, tolerance is not based on an aesthetic choice, but is rather a moral choice. The aesthetic convictions of the designer have actually remained intact, just as Hare suggested for the professor.

This conviction remains intact because the designer continues to think that these types of shirts are aesthetically horrendous. However, that is not the actual fact that mattered to him. This element did not come into play during his deliberation, but rather the calculation he carried out fluctuated between getting a bad review in the press and his wife's feelings. There are two different traditions in moral philosophy that will accept that this decision is morally oriented, such as the view supported by utilitarian or particularist moral philosophers for example.

This however is an argument that Garzón's perspective, in particular, and deontological philosophers in general, would not be willing to accept. It seems to me that this is fundamentally because of the type of deliberation used by the designer. For Garzón:

> To the extent in which we do not autonomously adopt the reasons of the supreme justificatory system, tolerance could be interpreted as a close relative of hypocrisy: we still consider the behavior that resulted in the prohibition as reprehensible, and we could even internally despise the 'tolerated' author, yet we assume tolerance under a mere cost-benefit calculation: for prudential reasons, for enforcing the rules of courtesy or due to *political correctness.* [10]

From Garzón's perspective, the designer is not being tolerant, but rather hypocritical. He is a hypocrite, because he maintains the prohibition on the ruffled shirts, yet solely based on prudential reasons, refrains from making it effective. And he is also being hypocritical to his wife because he is not telling her just how much he dislikes her shirt or because he does not entirely accept her use of these types of shirts. [11]

Now let us suppose that the designer has internally adopted the principle of 'never harming a loved one.' With this, if one does not want to fall into the supposed hypocrisy, the solution can only take two routes: either, in accordance with this last principle he will have to 'eliminate' the other that requires him to avoid unfavorable professional reviews—in this case he would be acting tolerantly—or, he could otherwise disregard the said principle, maintain the other, and act accordingly: not tolerating his wife's shirt, hurting her feelings, and avoiding the possible bad reviews.

But this second solution would, no doubt, be qualified by Garzón as a clear symptom of irrationality, due to its deliberate violation of an autonomously accepted moral norm. Similarly, taking the first solution (tolerating his wife's shirt despite the fact that he has always tried to avoid bad reviews) could also, according to Garzón, mean the complete abandonment of the system that sustains his aesthetic rule, in other words, this means: "throwing overboard his entire aesthetical [sic] value system, renouncing to an essential element of his orientation in the world, something that, *prima facie*, is not morally demandable."[12] Besides, also according to Garzón, this would render his tolerance *unreasonable* according to his own life plan.

Deontological philosophers would argue that the aesthetic principle must be derogated or must be reaffirmed, and that this process, according to the justificatory structure, involves the *moralization* of the system to which the norms or values belong.

Along these lines, we can coincide with the theses sustained by authors such as Hare and Horton, which state that if people actually submitted each of their likes to moral scrutiny every time someone committed an act that they disliked, we would not only be living in a sort of a moral inferno, but our normative systems would become an unintelligible mixture of hybrid rules with no practical meaning whatsoever.[13]

It can be objected that so far our discussion has only considered conflicts that relate aesthetic or fashion convictions that, in the end, are probably not so relevant in someone's life. Then, it is important to consider what would happen in the case of ethical values. Could ethical values have a better chance to survive the critical scrutiny of the moral justificatory system in comparison with the aesthetic ones?

Rainer Forst has discussed this point at length. No doubt that Forst accepts the possibility of conflicts between ethical values and moral norms. For example, in his *Ethics and Morality* he considers problems that can relate both ethical values and moral norms such as the problems of abortion, euthanasia or genetic manipulation. His standing facing those kinds of problems is quite clear. Forst says that "in such cases there is obviously agreement on the fact that moral arguments have more weight that the ethical ones. And with the help of the formal criteria for moral arguments, it can be concretely examined whether the respective claims of the participants bringing forward arguments are actually justifiable."[14]

Forst's claim is that different normative dimensions—ethical and moral in this case—must be brought together within a person's practical deliberation. This stand, as we have seen before, represents a particular characteristic of deontological moral perspectives, namely the idea of the *unity of practical reason*. Carlos S. Nino, another deontological liberal philosopher, explains this by saying that "the moral discourse would not be able to fulfill its function of guiding conduct, if the principles for action accepted by it were not going to have any kind of hierarchical status in front of other kind of reasons"[15] such as, prudential reasons or religious beliefs. Those other reasons and values can justify actions when there are no moral considerations in play. As soon as moral reasons come into play, all other kinds of reasons cannot provide any kind of justificatory criterion. Any philosopher that adheres to the so-called unity of practical reason thesis would agree on this hierarchical accommodation of practical reasons.

The idea behind this criterion is that there must not be a practical discontinuity in the identity of people. With this theoretical assumption deontological authors try to avoid what can be called a practical "schizophrenia"[16] where our ethical values contradict the universal requirements of morality. Then, the solution resides in the "ability to interconnect these roles and contexts in justifiable ways,"[17] for Forst this "assumes, therefore, that one knows which reasons are appropriate in which contexts and what one 'owes' to whom and for what reasons. That which is morally required remains thereby an independent normative sphere, which becomes part of a person's character by way of being conscious as a moral person of having the unconditional duty to justification."[18] To this input Forst adds in *Toleration, Justice and Reason* that: "it is *morally* required and right to tolerate what you find *ethically* disagreeable and wrong within the limits of reasonableness and reciprocity that all have to accept."[19]

In brief, what deontological authors suggest is that our ethical values only serve to answer questions that involve "me," and not to answer questions and problems that involve "us." In such cases we need to be morally conscious either by not applying those ethical values to the case in question or by submitting our ethical values to the scrutiny of the *principle of justification*. In the case that they 'pass' the threshold of *reciprocity* and *generality*, we must not consider them anymore as merely ethical values but as moral norms. This is also considered by Rawls's "reflective equilibrium" where reasonable agents confront their ethical judgments with the principles of justice so they can be adjusted in such a way that both coincide. This process is considered by Rawls as the best representation of having a "sense of justice."[20]

In the case of tolerance the structure presented by this rational procedure could lead to three conclusions regarding the normative status of our ethical values: (1) either after a critical scrutiny with the *principle of justification* we realize that all the time we were holding a moral norm and not an ethical value, (2) or we realize that we were holding a value that at the end was contrary to morality, or (3) we realize that there are equally valid moral reasons that simultaneously uphold both the *accep-*

*tance* and the *rejection* of certain ethical value on which the *objection* rests.[21]

In the first two cases tolerance turns out *irrelevant* and in the third one it becomes *recalcitrant*. In the first case it becomes irrelevant because if the conviction that I thought is an ethical value turns out to be a morally grounded norm, then, I do not have any more restrains that impede me from imposing it on others. In the second case it is because if the ethical value turns out to be morally incorrect, under a deontological system, what I have to do is to eliminate such value from one of my systems of values: in that case, at the point where my initial ethical objection disappears I stop having any reason to be tolerant.

These two first situations are the ones that constitute the idea I have been referring to as tolerance becoming a 'suicidal concept.' The term 'suicidal' needs a further explanation as any other metaphorical term used within a philosophical discourse. Metaphors can shed light when they are not understood in a literal but in a figurative way. As when Mario, the main character in Antonio Skármeta's *Burning Patience*[22], says to Pablo Neruda that the smile of Beatriz (his platonic love) resembles a butterfly. This expression taken in a literal way would lead us to think that Beatriz is a deformed creature that does not deserve any of our attention, while, understanding it in a figurative way, the metaphor describes a beautiful and charming smile which is difficult to resist. Metaphors taken in this way can be taken as extensions of the thought that tend to satisfy the needs of a speaker who wants to go beyond the plain descriptive use of language. Metaphors can then be understood as a good component of language and thought instead of a superfluous ornamental element. In her *The Sovereignty of Good* Iris Murdoch has defended the use of metaphors in philosophical discourse not only by saying that they help but rather by saying that they are necessary: "The development of consciousness in human beings is inseparably connected with the use of metaphor. Metaphors are not merely peripheral decorations or even useful models, they are fundamental forms of our awareness of our condition."[23]

It is in this sense in which the term 'suicidal' must be taken. The main idea I am expressing with it is another 'paradox' into which tolerance falls while being hosted by a deontological structure of practical reason. This paradox can be qualified as a 'conceptual paradox' that embraces tolerance under the rigid structure of deontological rules and principles. Mainly, because under such a structure, tolerance loses all of its nature and moral flexibility which are concomitant to the idea of tolerance as a dispositional property of moral agents. As it has been described above, one of the consequences that a tolerant agent can face by adopting a deontological structure of practical reason is to reduce every time more and more the scope of acts that can be candidates for tolerance. In this sense, tolerance becomes suicidal. Every act of tolerance is a step towards its elimination. In a deontological sense, a tolerant agent is tolerant in as much his/her expectations are that one day he/she would stop being tolerant.

The abovementioned paradox consists in what has been called the "the chronological problem of tolerance."[24] This criticism specifically refers to a situation that is generated by the interaction of two normative systems proposed by deontological authors. This interaction tends to widen the fence of intolerance every time that there is an act of tolerance. In that sense, it appears that under a deontological structure every act of tolerance is a step towards intolerance.

We can represent this with the triadic formula of tolerance proposed by deontological philosophers such as Garzón and Forst. If we remember, both of them stated that tolerance can be formulated under these terms *aTbX c , t1* , this implies that *Ph X* in *Cn Bsa (t0)*, which according to them does not reflect the conflict between the BNS and the JNS. In order to account for his statement we must formulate the following scheme:

$$aTbX_{c, t1} \rightarrow Ph\ X \in Cn_{Bsa(t0)}\ \&\ P\ X \in Cn_{Bsa(t2)}$$

That is, before the act of tolerance, at t0, the act was prohibited in the basic system, after an act has fallen under this prescription but thus tolerated, now, at t2 the same act is permitted. Therefore, the chronology of tolerance can be resumed as follows: at time t0 X is prohibited in the Bs (BNS) of *a*, at time t1 *a* tolerates X and this results in the derogation of the prohibition X in Bs (BNS) based on t1. If the result of the derogation of a prohibition is a permissive norm or express permission then *b* acquires a right to X and it would not follow to affirm—based on the t1 + n—that *a* tolerates X.[25]

That is to say, tolerance would be exhausted in one single act. According to this scheme, if someone decides to tolerate something on Monday then he/she cannot say that he/she tolerates it on Tuesday. If this happens, then a statement that says that someone tolerates, *every time that act X takes place*, would no longer be true. Because the tolerator, in accordance with this scheme, would have then *moralized* or eliminated the conviction from where the *objection* arose, and under this panorama the tolerated would have acquired a right (in the public sphere) or a strong permission (in the private one).

The central problem in this strategy is that if the result of the balancing that deontological authors are referring to is the creation of rights (or strong permits) or the confirmation (moralization) of a prohibition, when enough time has passed—sufficient enough as to have submitted all our convictions to the critical scrutiny of the moral system—there will be nothing left within the scope of what is tolerable, and it will all be part of the scope of the intolerable. In this sense, it would seem that tolerance tends to disappear. Under this structure of practical reason, tolerance becomes "suicidal."

The third case becomes recalcitrant because it rises what has been called the moral paradox of tolerance which in moral philosophical debates is said to be able to qualify as a genuine moral dilemma. This last case leads me to the next problem in question, which I have called "profound."

## NOTES

1. Garzón, "No pongas," 197–198.
2. Forst, "Ethics and Morality," 65.
3. Forst, "Ethics and Morality," 67.
4. Horton, "Toleration as a Virtue," 38.
5. Richard M. Hare, *Freedom and Reason* (Oxford, Clarendon Press, 1964), 168.
6. For this discussion, see, J. C. Rees, "A Re-Reading of Mill on Liberty," *Political Studies*, 8 (1960): 113-129; C. L. Ten, "Mill on Self-Regarding Actions," *Philosophy*, 43, 163 (1968): 29–37; Alan Ryan "Mr. McCloskey on Mill's Liberalism," *The Philosophical Quarterly*, 14, 56 (1964): 253–260.
7. Richard M. Hare, "Wrongness and harm," in *Essays on Moral Concepts*, Richard M. Hare (London, 1972), 97.
8. Hare, "Wrongness," 98.
9. Ross, *The Right*, 19–21.
10. Garzón, "El sentido actual," 26.
11. Garzón, "El sentido actual," 26.
12. Garzón, "No pongas," 193.
13. Hare, "Wrongness"; Horton, "Toleration"; Williams in *Moral Luck* affirms something similar to this. Williams says that "we are sometimes guided by the notion that it would be the best of worlds in which morality were universally respected and all men were in a disposition to affirm it, we have in fact deep persistent reasons to be grateful that that is not the world we have". Bernard Williams, "Moral Luck," in *Moral Luck*, 23.
14. Forst, "Ethics and Morality," 68.
15. Nino, *Ética y Derechos Humanos*, 111–115.
16. Forst, "Ethics and Morality," 71.
17. Forst, "Ethics and Morality," 72.
18. Forst, "Ethics and Morality," 72.
19. Forst, "Tolerantion, Justice," 81.
20. Rawls, *A Theory*, 42.
21. Heysse, "Toleration," 405.
22. This book was later brought to the screen under the direction of Michael Radford and with the title *Il Postino*.
23. Iris Murdoch, *The Sovereignty of Good* (London, Routledge Classics, 2002), 75.
24. Navarro, "Relfexiones," 280.
25. Navarro, "Relfexiones," 280.

# THIRTEEN

## Tolerance as a Moral Dilemma

Tolerance understood as a moral ideal entails a problem that contemporary moral philosophy has qualified as "paradoxical." D. D. Raphael illustrates this situation as follows:

> Toleration is the practice of deliberately allowing or permitting a thing of which one disapproves. [. . .] This means that your inclination to disallow must not be the result of a mere whim or arbitrary dislike; it has to be reasonably grounded disapproval which you can expect to be shared by others. To disapprove of something is to judge it to be wrong. Such a judgment does not express a purely subjective preference. It claims universality; it claims to be the view of any rational agent.[1]

Under this perspective there is something important that we should ask ourselves: if our disapproval is morally grounded—as Raphael, among others, presumes—then why should we go against it? Why should we tolerate? In other words, why is toleration conceived as a virtue or a moral duty? Why is it correct? Let us use the following analogy to exemplify this situation: tolerance, in this case, is very similar to extortion, in the sense that extortion tends, much like tolerance, to create a situation of "moral confinement":[2] "If I don't accept what is demanded then I stand to lose something I value, yet if I accept, I encourage future extortion." Under this perspective, one can only come out from the conflict through a morally prohibited path. In the light of this and with reference to a case of tolerance where two moral norms conflict, if I tolerate, I suppress myself from acting in a way that I consider to be morally valuable, whereas if I do not tolerate, I suppress myself from acting according to a value that I believe to be equally valuable (which could also be a moral duty to tolerate).

When confronted with such a situation, the question that comes to mind, intuitively at least, is: How do we respond to this problem? In the case of tolerance the answer is easily predictable, and it even has a sort of Shakespearian flair, because we are left with two possibilities: *to be tolerant* or *not to be*. However, even when we accept that the answer does not represent a major difficulty, the problem remains. In other words, this is the problem, not its solution. The dilemma is resolved if we know how to arrive at one of these two apparently simple answers.

Strictly speaking, it is a situation where we harbor two morally contradictory judgments: the injured moral conviction that urges us to act against the action that injured it and the moral reasons of equal value that impose on us the duty not to intervene. Let us not forget that we are operating under the assumption that the agent is convinced that both judgments hold equal moral importance—in other words, they are incommensurable or equally valid—that is, undefeatable.

This situation would then qualify as a typical case of a *moral dilemma*. Christopher W. Gowans defines this type of dilemmatic situations as those in which "an agent S morally ought to do A and morally ought to do B but cannot do both, either because B is just not-doing A [which leads it to incompatible results] or because some contingent feature of the world prevents doing both."[3]

Another author who has delved into the philosophical nature of tragic conflicts or moral dilemmas in extenso is Guillermo Lariguet. According to him, from this concept of a moral dilemma, we can derive certain practical consequences: "i) the conflict does not have a possible rational solution, for example, because the values or containing principles are considered as mutually incomparable or undefeatable, or ii) the conflict could be resolved by choosing one of the principles, but the choice would entail a sacrifice or moral loss."[4]

The types of conflicts I am referring to are generated by the inconsistency between two moral rules or principles and the possible ways in which we can rationally solve them. When I say "means of rational solution" I refer to the capacity to provide reasons of weight (moral weight, in the liberal fashion) that justify the choice between one of the principles in conflict. It seems to me that methods based on chance such as tossing the coin, are not methods that are anywhere near the reach of the idea of moral rational solution that I have in mind. Jon Elster has eloquently argued that these types of decision-making methods, based on chance, can actually turn out to be a good way of resolving these types of practical conflicts, especially because we are granting the same winning odds to both principles in conflict (50% and 50%). Although I agree with Elster's observation, the problem at issue here is the search for a *moral* solution to the conflict, and not merely a viable solution.[5]

So, the first question that we must address is: what types of conflict does tolerance represent? Do they really qualify as true moral dilemmas?

In principle, this matter is of utmost relevance, because it could be argued that the types of conflicts harbored by tolerance are not 'true dilemmas,' but rather 'false dilemmas' or 'apparent dilemmas.' An argument that has been used to classify dilemmas as false or apparent is the one that states that one of the options at stake is in fact insignificant.[6] However, the conceptual construction that was previously presented and sustained would defeat this argument by saying that tolerance also involves *morally relevant convictions*: not only does the tolerator consider that his/her moral disapproval represents a relevant conviction of his/her normative system, but also that he/she considers it to be justified, and indeed morally justified. I have not yet said much about the criteria that we must take into account in order to know which convictions are really morally justified and which are not. Undoubtedly it is not enough that the tolerator considers them to be morally justified. We must follow another type of objective criterion that classifies them as such.

Nonetheless, for the time being and for our present purposes, it is not necessary to deal with these types of problems. For the moment it is sufficient to assume that the convictions at play are morally justified. If we assume that the convictions are justified, then the cases of tolerance are cases that have already crossed the "threshold" of *generality* and *reciprocity*,[7] as Rainer Forst would say, or the test of objectivity or justifiability and we can therefore affirm that what we have before us is a conflict that could be a dilemma. And if it is a dilemma it is because what is at stake is already meaningful or very meaningful. If we presume that the moral justification for the rejections is based upon moral disapproval, then, we could conclude that the conflicts that surround the acts of tolerance are potentially dilemmatic.

These types of conflict faced by tolerance strongly resemble the collisions between principles or rights. Legal theorists have adopted different kinds of argumentative formulae that try to withstand these types of conflict. Consider, for instance, two of the most representative philosophers in that field: Alexy and Dworkin. Both of them believe that there are correct rational answers to these kinds of conflict. In order to arrive at this answer, they propose a set of rules of rationality that are aimed at deciding which of the values in conflict *wins* in the particular situation. The "weight formula" proposed by Alexy and the interpretativist conception of Dworkin are clear examples.[8] This kind of criterion is not exclusive to legal philosophy. Consider, for example, the lexicographic order of the principles of justice proposed by John Rawls.[9] In that sense, both philosophers—Robert Alexy and John Rawls—propose the same kind of lexicographic order of values: both defend a "cardinal" order of values. In other words, from their perspectives the "weight" of a principle is determined by a quasi-mathematical formula (the "weight formula" of Alexy and the "Principle of the Reasonable" of Rawls).[10] This kind of ordering principles and values differs from the kind of models proposed by other philosophers such as Dworkin, who has in mind an "ordinal" order of values and principles. For Dworkin, the weight of the principles or values is related to their intrinsic moral value and not to any other kind of criteria.[11]

According to these models presented and defended within liberal thinking, the establishment of a lexicographical order of the values at stake will help to reject the existence of these practical quagmires. Fundamentally, these rational schemes are directed at the resolution of conflicts by favoring one of the conflicting principles. Indeed, one of the ways in which these problems can be resolved is found within the rational possibilities of favoring one of the two principles in conflict. Other models are dedicated to the search for rational means that may favor both, albeit not "completely" but at least in a rationally acceptable measure. One way of resolving dilemmas is the one that Lariguet, among others, calls the "third way." This perspective is based on the idea introduced by Isaiah Berlin according to which in the face of conflicts of values—tragic he said—we sometimes hope to achieve certain "mutual cession," "basic commitment" or "partial consensus" among the stances adopted by the value in conflict.[12]

This second possibility, from a deontological stance, is actually a sort of idealistic utopia in the case of moral dilemmas, mainly, because these by definition push the moral agent to decide between one of the conflicting principles and since both cannot be satisfied one of them will have to be sacrificed in the name of the other. It is at this point, precisely, where most of the problems reside: how can we decide in favor of one of the principles in conflict when both of them are considered to be morally relevant and eventually incommensurable?[13] Similarly, if the case is solved by any rational means, we must inquire what has been the moral loss or sacrifice implied by such a solution. What is the moral cost carried by such method?

Regarding the subject of the 'paradox' or 'dilemma' of tolerance, we can essentially find three kinds of answers that have been proposed by different authors who have written on this topic. All of these answers have been designed to solve this matter,[14] still only one of them is related to deontological liberalism. The first one argues that the idea of tolerance implies the absence of objective moral values; therefore, there are no real moral conflicts and we must tolerate any kind of moral standpoint. The second type, which is endorsed by deontological authors, relies on the idea that there is an external objective criterion which helps us to solve any kind of moral conflict. The third and last classical answer argues against the value of tolerance as a whole. According to this last answer, tolerance is only a mechanism to impose a certain way of life on the masses. Since only the second of these answers is to be found within the type of liberal thought I am interested in, I will not address any criticism of the other two proposals. This is fundamentally due to the fact that the third model response is committed to the thesis that tolerance does not embody any particular value,[15] and the first one is related to moral relativism. The former stance claims that tolerance is an evil that must be discarded from our political and moral discourses. This is the stance that has been advocated mainly by liberalism's detractors, such as many philosophical traditions derived from the Marxist thought. This model tends to be adopted by those thinkers who do not identify any fair and organized way of resolving social conflicts within the liberal political doctrine or the liberal ideology. Fundamentally, they think that an "open," "diverse" and "plural" society is not the best solution; quite the opposite, for them it is a symptom of disorder and chaos. Instead, what we should be looking for, according to this current of thought, is a "closed" and "unified" society.[16] Precisely because of this, philosophers such as Herbert Marcuse or Slavoj Zizek affirm that tolerance does not bring anything good with it; on the contrary, tolerating diversity is condemning communal unity to failure and disorder. Authors that belong to this school of critical thought understand liberal tolerance as the philosophy of "anything goes," and it is because of this that for Marcuse tolerance becomes repressive and for Zizek, it is nothing more than a rhetorical resource that serves to oppress the masses.[17]

We have discussed before some of the problems that a relativist stance face. Still, developing the case further, let us take into account the above situations, which, in the face of tolerance, tell us that there is only room for some possible solutions:

(a) To renounce the idea that *moral disapproval* is part of the concept of tolerance, and thus better limit it to cases of *dislike*;
(b) To argue in favor of the existence of another external means of justification that dissolves the conflict;
(c) To deny the existence of such kind of conflict and relate to it the idea of a deficient practical reasoning; or
(d) To argue that no good is derived from tolerance: this is the strategy of those non-liberal theories such as critical or Marxist theories.[18]

Based on this, it can be assumed that these dilemmatic situations are more intense, less intense or even nonexistent, depending on the type of moral theory we adopt. For example, ethical relativism is a posture which is normally associated with the first solution offered above. If we declare ourselves to be supporters of this kind of ethical theory then it would seem logical that the conflict of tolerance should never appear. If we adopt a consequentialist posture, normally associated with the second solution, there may be an answer to the conflict, but at a very high moral cost. If we embrace a critical theory associated with the fourth solution, such as a Marxist stance, the conflict comes to a speedy resolution because it does not exist and tolerance is not good, since it does not have nor will it acquire any value. Liberal deontologism, in its part, will be related to b) and c).

Not all schemes of practical reason are prepared to deal with this problem. Still, not all of these theories accept the existence of this type of dilemmatic conflict. This is the case of deontological moral theories. Some consequentialist theories do not deny the existence of dilemmatic conflicts, but they think of them as resolvable. Richard Hare is known for proposing a sui generis utilitarian theory called "prescriptivism," under which moral dilemmas are defined as *apparent* conflicts to which agents *feel trapped* due to their ignorance or to a special psychological state of mind that does not allow them the possibility to find the most plausible and rational way out.[19] Hare would say that the rational way out is to submit our basic or intuitive level of beliefs to our critical scrutiny in order to find a way out of the supposed dilemma. This is due, mainly, to the idea that in an intuitive or basic level our believes are thought to be primitive or unfinished, hence they require a reflective criticism to acquire their final shape.

By considering these philosophical reactions and normative strategies the only purpose pursued is to support two claims advanced before that will be constantly assumed in my argument. The first is related to the *context dependence* thesis of tolerance. If tolerance as a moral ideal has the tendency to generate dilemmatic situation, this means, that its limits are constrained by the context in which it develops and that this context pushes moral theories into a trap. In this sense I defend an ontological existence of dilemmatic conflicts. In other words, I do not understand them only as epistemological problems. The second is related to Forst's "normative dependence thesis," which explains that the intensity or the anxiety that these types of conflicts inflict on us is mainly due to the moral stance adopted by the person who is facing them and not to the idea that there are tragic conflicts or moral dilemmas with different ontological degrees of intensity, as once argued by E. J. Lemmon.[20]

Taking into account these considerations and knowing what tolerance qua a moral ideal means and requires we can address some of the problems that deontological liberalism faces with the "moral paradox of tolerance." This is the question that I shall try to answer in the following pages.

## MORAL DILEMMAS AND DEONTOLOGICAL MORAL THEORY

As stated before, moral dilemmatic situations have put legal and moral theories in a bind. There are philosophers dedicated to this topic and concerned with the structures of practical reason who have not rushed to define any stance but, in many cases, some have gone so far as to deny their existence. For authors such as Alexy and Dworkin these types of conflicts are products of the imagination of cabinet philosophers. An author like Richard Hare qualifies these types of conflicts as tales written by "fiction writers," while other authors such as Isaiah Berlin and Bernard Williams for example, sustain the existence of these types of conflicts and, therefore, assert that a good moral theory must contemplate them and know their consequences.

Hence, there are philosophers who sustain that moral and legal theories must be dilemma free, if they have the purpose of guiding the conduct of people, while other philosophers assure that a correct moral or legal theory must acknowledge the existence of moral dilemmas in order to know how to resolve them.[21] In the case of deontological moral theories, moral dilemmas are taken to be a sort of epistemological deficit. For these types of theories, moral dilemmas do not exist. In fact, according to them the agent who thinks to be under a tragic clash of values is in this situation because he or she has not made a correct diagnosis of the situation. Kantians rely on two principles which help them to deny the 'real' existence of this kind of conflicts: (I) "ought implies can," and (II) the principle of agglomeration and conjunction.[22] According to the first one Kantians sustain that if a person is obliged to do $A$, then he/she can do $A$. Related to this principle, the principle of agglomeration establishes that if an agent is obliged to do $A$ and he/she is obliged to do $B$, then it follows that he/she is obliged to do both things (OA & OB). This is exactly the situation that dilemmatic conflicts do not allow, either because normatively speaking $A$ and $B$ are incompatible, or because from them we arrive at contradictory conclusions, or because the circumstances do not allow us to satisfy both requirements.

Deontological moral theories also deny the existence of any kind of dilemmatic conflict based on two philosophical assumptions, one epistemic and another normative: (III) the epistemic is related to the way they idealized the construction of normative systems. Deontological normative systems are based on the idea of *consistency*. This does not only refer to the idea of a *complete* system of rules, but also to the logical denial of the idea of *inconsistent* (contradictory) rules within a normative system.[23] The normative assumption (IV) is related to the known priority of the right over the good thesis. For deontological moral theories conflicts generated by cases of tolerance are between ethical believes and moral norms. In such cases, according to this thesis the moral norm will defeat the ethical consideration if we are to act correctly and committed with a sense of justice.[24]

In this sense a liberal deontological approach holds the following thesis:

> (1) Acting correctly means acting in accordance with our moral duties, duties that are self-imposed (autonomously accepted) and rationally created (without considering the agent's relative reasons) norms.

(2) Obeying moral norms does not imply considering the (beneficial or prejudicial) consequences that could be generated through such action. This leads deontological authors to reject utilitarianism as a stance for guiding moral action as well as the reject moral egoism.

(3) Normative systems have to be *complete* and *consistent*. This claim leads deontological moral theories to hold a monistic normative system that can avoid *incoherence* and *inconsistency* problems. This is achieved by basing their entire system on one governing principle or in a principle of principles.

(4) Moral norms are undefeatable. If we want to act morally, there cannot be any other kind of values or principles distinct from the moral ones that can defeat the moral norms. A moral agent is categorically bound by the norms of morality.

Having defined deontological moral theories as such, we may suppose that for deontological authors these types of conflicts are products of a systemic pathology. It is however not enough to reject these kinds of conflicts. On the contrary, we should focus on the reasons why they do not accept them—that is to say, why do they consider them as pathological—and understand which consequences this stance entails in cases of tolerance. With these characteristics of a deontological perspective of practical reason in mind we can consider now the arguments they proposed and to which I will formulate some critics.

## THE ARGUMENT OF THE LOGICAL CONSISTENCY AND NORMATIVE COHERENCE

Deontological authors currently sustain that to affirm the existence of moral dilemmas is the product of a normative pathology. From a general point of view, we must first locate the disease. Many authors who deny the existence of moral dilemmas, among whom we find Kantanian authors, usually argue that these types of problems are located on an epistemic level and not on an ontological level. They would then say that if a person claims to find himself or herself in a dilemmatic situation it is because his/her system of principles is either poorly organized or because he/she has failed to see that, in reality, the circumstances of the case do not require him/her to do anything that could be considered as morally contradictory.

These arguments find their roots in two abovementioned basic principles of the deontic logic: the principle of consistency and the principle according to which *ought* implies *can*. An interpretation of the latter would state that moral systems cannot morally force us to perform two contradictory conducts. If in one case, two norms prescribe conducts which are incompatible under the same circumstances, then due to the physical impossibility of the case, from a logical point of view, one of the norms in conflict must be invalid. This type of argument tends to free the agent from the responsibility of not complying with one of his/her moral duties. Hence, the option he or she chooses will not entail any kind of immoral consequence. According to the first principle, coming face to face with a dilemmatic situation suggests a sort of inconsistency that emerges from our principles. This supposition is derived from the idea that monistic normative systems cannot generate dilemmatic situations, such as the ones that could be generated by a pluralist normative system. How are we to accept the notion that two different norms in the very same situation can morally oblige us to do *A* and to not do *A*, while at the same time accepting that both norms are valid or concordant under the terms of our system's governing principle? Modern deontological liberals resolve this type of inconsistency—as we have seen—by using the "broom of logic" discarding one of the discordant principles. But, as I will explain later, despite these kinds of answers that monist moral philosophers have given, there are other philosophers, like Ruth Marcus, who think that pluralist systems are not the only ones that can harbor conflicts of this nature, and that systems based on a sole principle, like the Kantian system, can also generate these types of conflicts. [25]

Clearly, these are the cases that show why deontological authors introduce the requirement that tolerance must be based on two different normative systems. The distinction between 'ethics' and 'morals' erases the possibility of finding tolerance dilemmas.[26] This solution is well known by those who deny the possibility of the existence of dilemmas by alluding to a superior normative system, such as is the case of authors like Richard Hare. This explains the fact that if a normative system contains two discordant norms, one that requires $p$ and another that requires $Mp$, the solution to the conflict will be found within the critical or justificatory normative system and not within the system in question.

The answer that Garzón gives to Rainer Forst's critique can give us a clue of the importance that he grants the justificatory normative system. Forst argues that "in the case in which both the components of the rejection as well as those of the acceptance are based on reasons of the same type, it results in a paradox that directly guides us to the center of the problem of tolerance because those reasons seem to demand rejection as well as acceptance. This can be resolved by establishing, for example, a framework of religious fundaments, a hierarchy of reasons...."[27] Garzón responds to this by saying that: "obviously when something seems to be *P, and after a careful examination of the case* it turns out that it is not *P*, it can be concluded, without further examination that it was never *P*, that is to say, that here the paradox adduced does not exist."[28]

In fact though, Garzón's answer to the problem is not satisfactory. The difference between Garzón and Forst appears to be that while Garzón rejects the idea of 'genuine moral dilemmas' Forst does not. According to Forst, who as we have seen also sustains the difference between two realms of normativity and gives priority to the realm of the 'right,' cases as this one are highly possible. He does not only accept the idea of tragic conflicts between moral reasons but also between moral norms and the different normative levels. That is to say, conflicts between the different "contexts of justification."[29] Though, for him these conflicts flow from rejecting the idea that there is 'objective' criterion that makes all values compatible. In this sense, he believes that a *formal* (proceduralist) criterion can provide 'good' reasons to answer practical questions as such in a moral way. Thus, Forst accepts the existence of dilemmas at an ontological level, but he thinks that these can be solved through morally intersubjective reasons which provide one "correct answer" to the problem.[30]

Despite the differences, what is latent in both perspectives is that the tools used to examine such kind of practical questions do not derive from the same normative system that generates the conflict in the beginning. This is due to a common deontological idea according to which basic normative systems are not *self-sufficient*. The supposed inconsistency is resolved by eliminating the norms that contradict those norms which are morally justified. Strictly speaking, this is why Garzón refers to conflicts of an *inter-systemic* nature as opposed to a *intra-systemic* conflicts. We have seen that Forst accepts both *inter-systemic* (between different "contexts of justification") and *intra-systemic* (between moral norms themselves), but still the method to solve this kind of dilemmatic situations responds to the same structure of reasoning.

In the face of cases such as these, as we have seen, the rationale that deontological authors such as Garzón and Frost provide for tolerance is: when a BNS norm has been injured and we, by not being sure of its validity, have to place it under the critical scrutiny of the JNS. Certainly this formula seeks, under some notion of consistency, to evaluate the reasons that sustain the injured conviction and consequently resolve the problem at hand. If this is how it is, then there are only four possible logical solutions for the case of tolerance:

> (1) If the norm of the BNS prescribes that in circumstance A, $p$ is the case, and the JNS, on the contrary, stipulates that $Mp$, then due to the superior status of the JNS, $p$ is set aside.
>
> (2) If the norm of the BNS says that in the circumstance A $Mp$, and the JNS prescribes the opposite, that is to say, $p$, then the norm that dictates $Mp$ is set aside.
>
> (3) If the norm of the BNS says that in the circumstance A, $p$ is the case, and the JNS confirms the prescription, then the BNS norm is confirmed and moralized.
>
> (4) If the norm of the BNS says that in the circumstance A, it is not the case that $p$, and the JNS confirms said denial, then the norm is also confirmed and the system is moralized.

Whatever the situation may be, the important point is that, apparently, under a deontological scheme, tolerance implies a systemic cleaning process. According to what has been sustained, under this perspective tolerance plays the role of a process of deliberation through which the possible *elimination* or possible *confirmation* of the norm of the basic system in question is considered. In other words, it is a process that keeps the basic normative systems actualized (Rawls's 'reflective equilibrium' follows the same procedure of adjustments). It should be noted that this procedure relies on the idea of consistency. This solution intends to prevent the moral agent facing the disjunctive from having to choose between two contradictory norms that are considered relevant. In brief, it prevents the tolerator from experiencing a situation of moral *vertigo* by assuring him or her that his normative system would effectively serve as a guide of conduct.[31]

Aside from the purposes that the deontological strategy has, it is still uncertain whether it can eliminate the possibility of *vertigo* that some cases of tolerance may present. Authors such as Bernard Williams, as we will see in chapter 15, would say that setting aside one of the norms in question is not a solution that will help us to avoid this type of *vertigo*. Setting aside a norm that we consider relevant may leave a "remainder"[32] or a "moral residue." In other words, similar decisions may be accompanied by feelings of guilt, remorse or regret which let us know that, whatever the reasons may have been for doing what we did, we have done wrong.

Although a stance like Williams' could be debated under Garzón's scheme, if having stated that we thought a norm was 'true' it turns out that, after examination, it was not true then this situation cannot cause a "moral residue." There cannot be any feeling of regret for not complying with a norm that, at the end, we concluded was 'false.' However the long tradition that this archetypal Kantian response has, it should not be concluded to be valid until we have examined it in a more comprehensive way.

Let us, for example, think of the case of a mother with a strong liberal orientation who also happens to be a vegetarian for moral reasons. Should she tolerate the fact that her underage son is a lover of hamburgers? In either of the two cases, tolerating or not tolerating her son's inclination for red meat, according to the deontological scheme, would nonetheless require her to disregard a principle that she considers to be morally relevant. It seems that the same deontic *impasse* in which the fashion designer from the earlier example found himself would take place. If she tolerates the fact that her son eats red meat, she would have to throw overboard her moral principle which favors the life of animals. If she does not tolerate her son's habits, then she has to let go one of the principles that are important to her liberalism e.g., the free development of personality.

In this case, it seems that whatever decision is made will entail a sort of "moral residue" or "moral loss." In the end, both not tolerating and tolerating will have some moral cost. What is true is that the deontological scheme considers all acts of tolerance as a sort of *zero coordinate* that gives the agent the opportunity to actualize his/her normative systems in accordance with his/her morally justifying principles. For this reason, in the case of Garzón specifically, it is assured that within the genealogy of individual rights, as well as social rights, it is convenient to distinguish the acts of tolerance (which are the grandparents) from the strong permissions, authorizations or, better put, the individual rights (which can be considered as the grandchildren).[33]

In this vein, it would appear that Garzón claims that the only principles an agent should be willing to accept internally are the principles of the JNS. This seems to be the same in the case of Forst when he says that "the intersubjective character of moral reasons is fundamental and cannot be reduced to the ethical perspective of what is good "for me,"[34] and the case of Rawls when he sustains that a reasonable person who has a sense of justice will make possible, through reflective equilibrium, that his/her conception of the good would be compatible with the public conception of justice.[35] But this being the case, what importance does the deontological perspective attribute to particular conceptions of the good?

The truth is that if we accept that individuals internally accept the norms of their BNS, even though we have found them to be morally unjustified, then requiring them to be set aside would imply a moral cost. Therefore, I do not think that this strategy can easily rid itself of objections such as the one made by Williams.

As it has been noted above, from such a perspective deontological theories understand tolerance as a situation that places individuals in a *zero coordinate* from where they can either create new permissions or depart from old prohibitions avoiding, through the delicate process of balancing, conflicts that in the future can qualify as tragic.

Note that under this perspective the possibility of reiteratively *lifting* a prohibition is somewhat diluted. In the case of the vegetarian mother, for example, discovering that her son is a hamburger lover has pulled her in different directions by two principles that have equal moral weight: one related to her liberal conviction to protect her son's 'freedom of personal development' and another, related to the moral considerations she sustains on the consumption of animal products and the life of animals. The conflict that she faces amounts basically to whether or not she should soften up the normative force of the rule she holds, which states that it is 'prohibited to eat meat' and protecting her son's freedom to develop his own personality, or by prohibiting him to eat hamburgers (and therefore injuring that principle) and maintain her vegetarianism intact. I have argued that the conflict becomes recalcitrant due to the moral residue or loss that results from whichever choice she makes, either if she chooses to respect her son's personal development, or to forbid him to eat hamburgers. Any decision would suppose sacrificing something (morally) important within her system of values.

## THE ARGUMENT OF ONE SUPRA-VALUE

Unlike the previous argument, the argument of one supra-value is constructed under the thesis of moral monism which has an ample acceptance within deontological liberalism. Commonly, this stance is associated with an objective view of morality as being universal and normatively consistent. Nowadays, for example, one of the more usual arguments of a theoretical monistic stance is that individuals are autonomous beings capable of directing the course of their own lives.[36] Respecting this principle assumes that one is acting in a morally correct manner when allowing others to dictate their own actions, including when these same actions are disapproved. Certainly, tolerance does not play merely the role of a virtue, but also that of a duty held by the tolerator. The most relevant characteristic of this moral point of view is that the autonomy principle marks the limits of tolerance: everything that does not violate this principle enters into the realm of the tolerable, and anything that violates it enters into the realm of the non-tolerable or of the intolerable. However, the monist moral theories that base their systems on the autonomy principle are not the only kind of monism. There are many other varieties which embrace other values as primary values. Consider for example utilitarianism, which bases the whole justification of moral actions on their capacity to maximize the happiness or the well-being of the greatest number of people.[37]

Certainly, when we speak of personal autonomy, we are mainly referring to the moral theories of a Kantian linage. In these kinds of theories personal autonomy plays the role of a criterion for systematizing moral norms. Still, as it has been argued, Kantian moral theories face a very specific problem when referring to tolerance as a moral ideal, and in particular related to moral dilemmas. We must bear in mind however, that this kind of 'weakness' when facing the dilemma of tolerance is not exclusive to the Kantian theories of morality. Indeed this problem is faced by all moral theories of a monistic nature or by those types of moral theories that impose a primary value or principle as the governing criterion of the entire moral system.[38] In this sense, Kantianism is as monistic (assuming the value of personal autonomy as its highest governing value) as utilitarianism (establishing the principle of maximization of happiness for the greatest number of people as their governing criteria for the resolution of conflicts).

John Kekes in his *The Morality of Pluralism* defines moral monism as the version of ethics that accepts the existence of an ideal standard against which we can compare reasonably all the different moral values.[39] Actually this mechanism, the main purpose of which is to systematize moral (and/or legal) norms, has a long tradition within Western philosophical thought. It is sufficient to note the criteria that have been invoked by thinkers such as Plato (and his "Form" or "Idea of the

Good"), Kant (with his "Categorical Imperative"), Rawls (with his principle of "The Reasonable"), or Hans Kelsen (with his "Grundnorm").[40] The idea surrounding the existence of a super-value or of a super-norm that plays the role of an all-encompassing source within the moral (or legal) realm is quite appealing, especially because within its virtues we find a logically solid way of eliminating the possibilities of conflicts. Fundamentally, it can eliminate the types of conflicts that I have been referring to so far, namely conflicts between two principles or values of a normative system. In a strict sense, we can understand these types of conflicts as conflicts between two or more norms that belong to the same system. If there is a super-value that grants coherence and consistency to the entire normative universe then, according to the rules of deontic logic, the direct consequence is that it would be incoherent and inconsistent to conclude that there could be two or more norms that emanate from this super-value that were also contradictory. How can two norms that belong to the same source contradict each other? Equally important, how can a norm contradict its source? In spite of the appeal of this stance, some contemporary liberal philosophers have criticized it harshly, starting with one of the champions of modern liberalism, Isaiah Berlin.

In *Two Concepts of Liberty*, Berlin classifies as erroneous the idea of one value capable of systematizing and granting coherence to the entire universe of values that we may find within modern liberal societies. Specifically, Berlin says, "it seems to me that the belief that some single formula can in principle be found whereby all the diverse ends of men can be harmoniously realized is demonstrably false."[41] And then he continues: "It is as if I were to say: 'I have a wound in my leg. There are two methods of freeing myself from pain. One is to heal the wound. But if the cure is too difficult or uncertain, there is another method. I can get rid of the wound by cutting off my leg. If I train myself to want nothing to which the possession of my leg is indispensable, I shall not feel the lack of it'."[42]

Certainly, the stance adopted by the monists is normally regarded as the most elegant way of rejecting the existence of tragic conflicts. Nevertheless, considered under a stronger magnifying glass than that used by deontic logic, monism's strategy appears to be less plausible. My argument is that through the prism of tolerance, two arguments can account for this by exposing monism's theoretical inability to harbor a moral concept of tolerance.

The first of these reasons is that, as a result of the rules of the deontic logic that this posture imposes upon itself in order to avoid normative conflicts (such as *obligationes non colliduntur*, the principle of universality or under models such as the Kelsenian idea of "chains of validity"),[43] when the time comes to decide what to do or how to act, it seems that these systems are more committed to what is logically valid than to what is morally correct or adequate. This is due to the fact that, among other things, the monist system is designed in such a way that when one principle enters into conflict with another, one of them necessarily has to abandon the normative system to which it belongs (*obligationes non colliduntur*). This normative consequence is derived fundamentally from one of the basic presuppositions of moral monism, according to which the umbrella provided by the super-value (personal autonomy or any other meta-value) does not have space for two contradicting convictions. The conclusion from this fact is that one of the conflicting principles necessarily contradicts the content of the meta-value. Within the framework of Kantian monism, this situation is considered to be an inter-systemic pathology that needs to be cleaned up with the broom of logic. This means that ordinary people must place systemic consistency above their attachment to certain beliefs and moral interests.

However, one of the projects of monism is to eradicate the possibility of conflict from within the deliberative scenario. Ruth Marcus has argued that moral systems based on a unique principle could also harbor normative conflicts.[44] If the argument of Marcus is right, as I believe it is, then monism's second most important reason is also flawed. The argument of Marcus is the following: it is not necessary to have two conflicting principles in order to preach the possibility of a conflict. "It is enough for there to be incompatible actions that emerge from one same source"[45] in order for a conflict to take place. The example used by Marcus is that of a person who, in good faith, makes two promises at a given time and has sufficient grounds to presume that they will not conflict with each other. However, due to unforeseeable circumstances that were outside his/her control, they end up conflicting each other. We can illustrate this by imagining an individual who promises a friend (who lives far away) that when he visits the country where he lives, he will show him around. The day finally arrives, and the friend calls to say that he is in town. However, our individual has also promised to attend his best friend's wedding that very same day. In this case, both promises were made in good faith, but the circumstances do not allow for both to be fulfilled at the same time.

However, from the perspective of tolerance, the strategy of Marcus does not tell us anything new. Consider a situation where what is at stake is the autonomy of the person who tolerates as well as the autonomy of the person who is being tolerated. In such a case, how would the monistic systems respond? Even when it has been demonstrated that conflicts of this sort can be generated under one monistic system, the tools that these types of systems provide (such as coherence and logical consistency) are not sufficient in order to resolve the types of conflicts that have been stated. However, the argument of Marcus yields two important lessons. The first one is, of course, the false presumption that conflicts cannot emerge from one value or principle. The second one is that circumstances are, more often than not, what triggers these kinds of conflicts. Therefore, and in accordance with these two perspectives, the proposal made by moral monism has only contemplated what could be called in abstracto conflicts, forgetting the possibility that certain circumstances can generate a conflict of incompatibility with an empirical root, which could be termed in concreto conflicts.[46] In my opinion, these are precisely the types of conflicts that are present in the cases of tolerance. In these situations, the values of an agent do not enter into conflict until they are tested by the actions of a third party. Let us consider, once again, the vegetarian mother. It is possible that she would have never arrived at the conclusion—in abstracto—that by adopting a conviction which required her to respect personal autonomy and the free development of personality, simultaneously with a conviction that prohibits the killing of animals for consumption; at any given time they would come to be inconsistent. It was not until her son decided to become a lover of hamburgers that this inconsistency emerged.

Out of the arguments put forward by the monistic theories, there are two ideas that should also be analyzed from the perspective of the moral ideal of tolerance. These two ideas have been recurring themes throughout this study. The first one is: the thesis of the universality of moral judgments as the supreme criterion for their justification. The second deals with the denial or failure of this theoretical posture with regard to the consideration of the moral consequences that an agent may suffer, from having to decide in dilemmatic conflicts such as those generated by acts of tolerance. I am specifically referring to the idea that these types of conflicts commonly, whatever their resolution may end up being, tend to entail some sort of sacrifice or moral loss. These are the points towards which I will direct my attention in the pages of the last chapters.

## NOTES

1. Raphael, "The Intolerable," 139.
2. Georg Henrik von Wright, *An Essay in Deontic Logic and the General Theory of Action* (Amsterdam, North-Holland, 1968), 80.
3. Christopher W. Gowans, "Introduction: The Debate on Moral Dilemmas," in *Moral Dilemmas*, ed. Christopher W. Gowans (Oxford University Press, 1987), 3–33.
4. Guillermo Lariguet, "Conflictos trágicos y Derecho. Posibles Desafíos," *Doxa. Cuadrernos de Filosofía de Derecho*, 27 (2004): 318–319.
5. Jon Elster, *Taming Chance: Randomization in Individual and Social Decisions* (The Tanner Lectures on Human Rights, Utah University Press, IX, 1988).
6. Guillermo Lariguet, *Encrucijadas Morales: Una aproximación a los Dilemas y su Impacto en el razonamiento Práctico* (Madrid/México, Theoria cum Praxi, 2011), 50.
7. Forst, "Toleration, Justice," 77.
8. Alexy, *Teoría de la Argumentación*, 364-374; Dworkin, *Taking Rights*, 279–290; Ronald Dworkin, *A Matter of Principle* (Cambridge Massachusetts, Harvard University Press, 1985), 119-145; Ronald Dworkin, "Do Liberal Values Conflict?," in *The Legacy of Isaiah Berlin*, ed. Mark Lilla, Ronald Dworkin and Robert B. Silvers (eds.) (New York Review of Books, 2001), 73–90.
9. Rawls, *A theory*, 214.

10. Alexy, *Teoría de la Argumentación*, 349-374; Rawls, *A Theory*, 27, 56.

11. Dworkin, *Taking Rights*, 285; Dworkin, "Do Liberal Values Conflict?," 89–90.

12. Lariguet, *Encrucijadas*, 34.

13. I am using the terms *incomparable* and *incommensurable* interchangeably, as I am also using the terms *moral dilemma* and *tragic conflict*.

14. Mendus, "Introduction," in *Justifying Toleration*, S. Mendus, 4.

15. Slavoj Zizek, *Defensa de la intolerancia* (Madrid, Sequitur, 2007), 55–62.

16. Mendus, *Toleration*, 69.

17. Marcuse, "Repressive Tolerance," 81-123; Zizek, *Defensa*, 55–62.

18. Mendus, "Introduction," 4.

19. Richard M. Hare, "Moral Conflicts" (*The Tanner Lectures on Human Values*, The Utah State University, October 1978).

20. E. J. Lemmon, "Moral Dilemmas," *The Philosophical Review*, 71, 2 (1962): 139–158.

21. Ragnar Ohlsson, "Who Can Accept Moral Dilemmas?," *The Journal of Philosophy*, 90, 8 (August 1993): 405–415.

22. Gowans, "Introduction," 20-22; Guillermo Lariguet, *Dilemas y Conflictos Trágicos: Una Investigación Conceptual* (Lima-Bogota, Temis-Palestra, 2008), 61.

23. Carlos Alchourrón, Eugenio Bulygin, *Introducción a la Metodología de las Ciencias Jurídicas y Sociales* (Buenos Áires, Astrea,1987), Chapter X.

24. Forst, "Toleration, Justice," 81.

25. Ruth Barcan Marcus, "Moral Dilemmas and Consistency," *The Journal of Philosophy*, 77, 3 (1980): 121–136, 122.

26. Heysse, B. Segaert, "Perplexities," 355.

27. Rainer Forst, *Toleranz im Konflikt* (Francfort del Meno, Suhrkamp, 2003), 35.

28. Garzón, "El sentido actual," 15. Emphasis added.

29. Forst, *Contexts*, 244.

30. Forst, *Contexts*, 245.

31. Guillermo Lariguet, "Conflictos trágicos genuinos, ponderación y límites de la racionalidad jurídica. En torno a algunas ideas de Manuel Atienza," *Isonomía. Revista de Teoría y Filosofía del Derecho*, 24 (2006): 102.

32. Bernard Williams, "Conflict of Values," in *Moral Luck*, 72.

33. Garzón, "El sentido actual," 40; Garzón, "Algunas reflexiones," 425.

34. Forst, *Contexts*, 245.

35. Rawls, "Justice as Fairness," 406; Thomas Pogge, *John Rawls: His Life and Theory of Justice* (Oxford University Press, 2007), 166–167.

36. John Stuart Mill, *On Liberty*, in *On Liberty in Focus*, ed. John Gray and G. W. Smith (London/New York, Routledge, 1996), 23-128; Mendus, *Tolerance*; Raphael, "The Intolerable"; Vázquez, *Liberalismo*; Horton, "Toleration"; Scanlon, "The Difficulty," among others.

37. J. J. C. Smart and Bernard Williams, *Utilitarianism: For and against* (Cambridge University Press, 1973), 4.

38. John Kekes, *The Morality of Pluralism* (Princeton University Press, 1993), 63–75.

39. Kekes, *The Morality*, 67.

40. Plato, *The Republic* (London, Penguin Classics, 2003), 226; Kant, *Groundwork*, 40–41; Rawls, *A Theory*; Hans Kelsen, *Teoría Pura del Derecho* (Universidad Nacional Autónoma de México, 1976; this version is the Spanish translation of Hans Kelsen, *Reine Rechtslehre*, Auflage, Wein, 1960).

41. Isaiah Berlin, "Two Concepts of Liberty," in *The Proper Study of Mankind: An Anthology of Essays*, Isaiah Berlin (New York, Farrar, Straus and Giroux, 2000), 239.

42. Berlin, "Two Concepts," 207.

43. Joseph Raz, *The Concept of a Legal System: An Introduction to the Theory of Legal System* (Oxford, Clarendon Press, 1980), 105.

44. Marcus, "Moral Dilemmas," 125.

45. Marcus, "Moral Dilemmas," 125.

46. Lariguet, *Dilemas y Conflictos*, 18.

# FOURTEEN

## Tolerance in the Moral System

I have raised several criticisms and objections to the deontological moral system. The main purpose of this has been to show the impossibility of a deontological moral system to host tolerance understood as a moral ideal. In this last part I will make explicit which are the three features that make impossible this relationship. Under the above perspective, the three features I am referring to are: (1) the priority of the 'right' over the 'good,' (2) the universal character of moral norms, and (3) the impartiality thesis.

According to what has been argued so far, these three features are the ones that make it extremely difficult, if not impossible, for deontological liberalism to take the moral ideal of tolerance as part of its normative repertoire. In brief, what has been argued in the pages above is that the priority of the right thesis gives little importance to the value and the place that the conceptions of the good have in people's lives, that the universal character of morality neglects the importance that different contexts and circumstances have when someone is submerged in questions related to tolerance, and that the impartiality thesis pushes individuals into taking practical decisions that not always honor their specific moral and ethical beliefs.

Regarding the first feature—the priority of the 'right' over the 'good'—deontological liberalism assumes that, conceptually speaking, tolerance is a moral ideal or a virtue of justice, and as such tolerance implies the distinction between 'ethics' and 'morality.' This affirmation derives mainly from the third circumstance of tolerance which tells us that in order to tolerate it is necessary to scrutinize critically, through a reflective equilibrium, the weight and value of the conviction that has been injured by the act or practice of a third party. This reflexive exercise consists in the moral evaluation of the conviction in question. Therefore, in order to speak of tolerance we must accept: (a) that the convictions

161

considered as candidates for tolerance belong to what we call a conception of the good (religious, ideological, philosophical or moral), (b) which under the light of morality are understood as a system of rules and principles that are not self-sufficient or that are subject to the "burdens of judgment," and (c) that if they want to be considered as 'reasonable' they must coincide with the moral norms.

Hence, giving priority to the 'right' over the 'good' is thought to provide enough good reasons that invite us to tolerate an act that injured one of our most relevant convictions. Although the priority thesis is a strategy of practical reason exclusively related to deontological liberalism, the idea of a double level morality can be found with the same purposes in other moral perspectives. For example, for utilitarian authors such as R. M. Hare all individuals are equipped with a certain amount of knowledge as to what is good and what is bad—knowledge that helps us resolve certain moral disagreements or make decisions in certain moral situations. However, for Hare, this knowledge is found within the basic level of reasoning, a level that he calls "intuitive."[1] But how can we determine whether the intuitions that we hold in the face of a disagreement are the correct ones? Hare's answer, when confronted with these types of problems, is to appeal to a higher level of moral thought, to a level that can criticize the prima facie intuitions; a "critical" level, in which we can consider diverse opposing intuitions and chose the best of them, be it from the same person or from different people, and judge them, so as to elucidate which one is better.[2]

Another utilitarian author who argues something similar to what Hare does is Eduardo Rivera López, who speaks of a higher "epistemic" plane that is very close to a sort of moral skepticism. However, as he forewarns us, this level of thought must not be confused with a dogmatic skepticism, or with a fanatically cynical posture. On the contrary, we are dealing with a *fallibilistic* level, which consists of each "rational individual who, therefore, seriously takes into account the difficulties of judging, and will hold a position of wavering certainty in the epistemological level. In other words, he will be a *fallibilist* in moral matters. Why? Because we have no reason to think that these difficulties will only reach the doctrines *of the others*."[3]

Ernesto Garzón Valdés, following Rawls, argues explicitly the insufficiency of the basic normative systems saying that if agents pretend to be reasonable they must submit their conceptions of the good to a superior normative system—a system that provides the necessary tools required to face the kind of conflicts generated by the basic normative system.[4]

For some moral theories, such as the ones I have been referring to, the acceptance of a second normative level, that is superior to the basic or intuitive one, is an affliction that has been widely accepted. This idea, in fact, has been even transplanted within the theory of legal reasoning. Consider for instance legal theories that argue the existence of a different level of norms which is superior to that of the mandatory rules. This other level is the level of principles, and it is the kind of level that assures the path to settle normative conflicts within the law. In contemporary legal philosophy, the distinction between *rules* and *principles* has been also widely accepted.[5]

The important thing that we should keep in mind is that deontological liberalism is not alone in considering a double level morality. Still, it stands alone in defending the priority of the 'right' over the 'good' in terms that the 'right' is independently justified and not related to the 'good.' What liberals of this sort argue is that tolerance has to be backed by this type of structure that not only distinguishes between two levels of practical deliberation, but that also establishes a sharp definition and distinction between what is 'ethics' and what is 'morality' and gives priority to the later over the former as a mechanism that serves to avoid all the conceptual and justificatory problems that regularly surround an act of tolerance. Then the main objections have been directed to the priority of the 'right' over the 'good' thesis based on the independence of the former regarding the later, but not to the idea of a double level structure of practical reason.

In the case, regarding the universal character of moral norms, it was Kant who determined with greatest force which criteria should constitute the *formal* bases for the evaluation of moral judgments. *Universality* and the *non-conditioning* of moral judgments have been some of the most recurring tools used by deontological theories as the basic lines of moral reasoning.[6] Nonetheless, what does the claim that a moral judgment should be universal actually mean? In general terms, we could say that the advocates of moral universalism claim that there are two ways of viewing it. One of them states that "if we admit that someone can *justify* their actions and attitudes upon the basis of a certain principle that is applicable to the case, then any potential participant in the moral discourse may also justify his actions and attitudes on the basis of that very same principle, as long as his case does not differ from the other with respect to the properties that the same principle regards as relevant."[7] This is the version of the Kantian universalism. It is not that the other way of viewing this criterion differs much from the previous one but rather that the act of shifting the perspective from its previous viewpoint also changes its practical consequences. This other way of looking at the principle of universality is borne out of the semantic equivalence that authors such as Richard Hare, for instance, claim exists between a universal descriptive proposition and a prescriptive proposition.[8] The way this is to be approached is as follows: "any moral judgment enounced by the speaker within a determined set of circumstances forces him to sustain that same moral judgment in any other circumstances, whose universal properties that characterize it are similar in all relevant aspects, for the mere logical character of the terms being used, since from the prescriptive universalizable propositions, a singular imperative directed towards the speaker himself, is *logically* implied."[9]

One of the main objections against the deontological structure of practical reason is related to the principle of universality. It has been argued that one the main problems that this principle raises in the case of tolerance is that if a person has reasons to tolerate an act $X$ which has been committed by $Y$ in specific circumstances $C$ at a time $T1$, consequently, according to these criteria of moral reasoning, the tolerator is morally *bind* to tolerate *all* acts that fall into the category of $X$ which have been committed during circumstances $C,'$ $C''...$ $Cn$ which contain the same relevant characteristics than '$X$' at times '$T2,'$ '$T3,'$ '$T4'...'Tn.'$ This way of reasoning generates great tensions with the idea that tolerance may be tested during reiterated circumstances.

This situation is also an evidence of the internal contradiction that exists within those moral theories that sustain the principle of universality and, at the same time sustain the thesis that tolerance is a moral ideal. However, as I have argued, this contradiction can only be objected in the cases of private tolerance. This is because, in the public sphere, the mechanism of rationality imposed by the principle of universality has served to *recognize* many institutions, laws, values, and ways of life that exist within liberal and democratic societies, taking them outside the realm of tolerable things, e.g., they are non-negotiable.[10] This is the main reason why, within the deontological liberal perspective, it does not make much sense to say that tolerance is an attitude adopted by public institutions.

Nonetheless, it is important to note that this criterion, along with the non-conditioning of moral judgments, intensifies the so-called 'dilemma of tolerance.' This is because the principle of universality does not only exclude the possibility that tolerance may be practiced in reiterated circumstances when is confronted with an injury that presents similar characteristics in different times and circumstances, but it also corners the tolerator into having to discard one of his/her relevant convictions. This situation, as has been argued, that it places the tolerator in a sort of moral *impasse* that generates a feeling of *vertigo*. Philosophers such as von Wright understand this moral "impasse" as an idea according to which there are situations where the options that are placed before an individual when deciding which course of action he/she should take are morally prohibited. Von Wright says that in those cases, our duty lies in choosing the least bad thing. These situations can generate the sensation of moral *vertigo*: a sensation which is produced by the fact that our normative systems have given up, and find themselves to be standing on a boundary from where they can no longer offer a correct practical answer that does not entail some form of loss or moral sacrifice.[11]

The same fate is experienced by the criteria of the *non-conditional* nature of moral judgments, which is another of the great tools that has been defended by those moral theories that belong to what Bernard Williams has called the "moral system."[12] The non-conditional status of moral judgments, or what in deontological terms can be denominated as their *categorical* sense, sustains that moral judgments cannot be considered valid if they have been formulated by taking into account the personal interests or desires of the agent formulating them. In other words, agent-specific reasons cannot be considered as 'good' reasons for justifying a moral judgment.[13] Some of my critiques have been directed towards this particular point of view and I will return to them in brief.

The third feature, sustaining why deontological moral systems cannot host tolerance as a moral ideal, is related to the "impartiality thesis." Although this perspective is directly indebted to the universality principle, it is worth distinguishing it from that principle for analytical reasons. Philosophers such as Ernesto Garzón Valdés, Rodolfo Vázquez, D.D. Raphael, and Peter Nicholson, to name just a few, sustain the thesis according to which an *ethics of tolerance is an ethics of impartiality*. This means that the only sources of good reasons to justify tolerance are those that belong to an *impartial perspective* or to the so called *moral point of view*. This is the kind of perspective that obliges moral agents to make decisions that are detached from any self-interests or desires. The kind of impartiality that I am referring to is the one that derives from the universalistic claim that all moral judgments have to be independent from any particular or individual point of view; this is, moral norms must be constructed independently from any conception of the good.[14] What these philosophers mean by proposing this third person perspective[15] is that moral norms should be formulated without being influenced by any contaminating ethical biases or subjective prejudices that tend to be attached in some particular conceptions of the good.[16] In order to avoid this personal perspective and to achieve some kind of objectivism, philosophers such as Richard Hare and John Rawls have developed a kind of heuristic formulas that help them to attain this kind of impartiality. I am referring specifically to the "archangel" which, according to Hare, is an ideal reasoner, immune to logical fallacy or inference mistakes, has superhuman powers of thought and knowledge, and has no human weaknesses. Also, I'm thinking of John Rawls's "veil of ignorance," which implies a kind of blindness that regular human beings suffer from such that they cannot know who they are, what their economic situation is, to which social group they belong, etc., and all this ignorance will help them make the most impartial decision.[17] The idea of an *ideal observer* is a very common philosophical tool directed towards achieving this kind of objectivity.[18]

I will not argue against the impartiality thesis. On the contrary, I will sustain that impartiality is a very important tool for moral reasoning, and mainly when we use it as a test for justice.[19] What I have in mind is that sometimes impartiality cannot be the only way to achieve correctness in our moral reasoning. This claim derives from the fact that the impartiality enthusiasts often leave aside matters that are considered important to certain conceptions of the good. Oversight ethical claims can have damaging results to the mere idea of living a life that is thought to be worth of living. According to deontological liberalism, tolerance is a virtue of justice; hence tolerance is understood as a practical response to conflict that must be guided by impartial reasons. But this conception of tolerance, as it will be argued in the last section, tends to leave aside the relevancy that ethical beliefs have for the individual's plans of life turning into either a tyrannical moral mechanism or an irrational way of conduct.

## NOTES

1. Hare, *Moral Conflicts* , 177.
2. Hare, *Moral Conflicts* , 178–179.
3. Eduardo Rivera López, *Ensayos sobre Liberalismo y Comunitarismo* (México, Fontamara, BEFDP, 58, 1999), 22.
4. Garzón, "No Pongas," 190; Garzón, "¿Puede la razonabilidad," 257.
5. Take for instance Ronald Dworkin *Taking Rights Seriously*; Robert Alexy, *Teoría de la Argumentación Jurídica*; Neil MacCormik *Legal Reasoning and Legal Theory* (Oxford, Clarendon Law Series, 1994); Luc J. Wintgens, *Droit, Principes et Théories: Pour un Positivisme Critique* (Bruxelles, Bruylant, 2000).
6. Since the appearing of John Rawls *A theory of justice*, these two criteria have been recurrent in the moral-political discussion. Rawls with the original position and the veil of ignorance, tries to fulfill these requirements of the Kantian moral philosophy. See Chapter II; Rawls, *A Theory* , 118 and ss.
7. Nino, *Ética*, 110–111.
8. Philippe Gerard, *Droit et Démocratie : Réflexions sur la Légitimité du Droit dan la Société Démocratique* (Bruxells, Publications des Facultés Universitaires Saint-Louis, 1995), 18 and ss.
9. Hare, *Freedom*, Chapter 2; Osvaldo Guariglia, *Moralidad: Ética Universalista y Sujeto Moral* (México, Fondo de Cultura Económica, 1996), 94.
10. The thesis that a catalogue of basic goods that are not bound to political negotiations—in the sense that thay should be taken out of the realm of political decisions made by a majority—should exist within democratic and constitutional (liberal) societies has been broadly discussed by deontological philosophers such as John Rawls in his *A Theory of Justice* and in his *Political Liberalism* on the Anglo-Saxon front; by Ernesto Garzón Valdés in "Representación y democracia," *Doxa. Cuadernos de filosofía del derecho*, for Latin-American philosophers; and by Luigi Ferrajoli in *Derechos y Garantías: La Ley del más fuerte* (Madrid, Trotta, 1999), to name only a few examples.
11. Georg Henrik von Wright, *An Essay in Deontic Logic and the General Theory of Action* (Amsterdam, 1968), 80.
12. Williams, *Ethics*, Chapter 10.
13. Gerard, *Droit et Démocratie*, 25.
14. I use both ideas, the *moral point of view* and the *ideal observer,* interchangeably. I am referring to philosophers such as Immanuel Kant, Richard Hare, John Rawls, Roderick Firth, among others.
15. Daniel Markovits, "The Architecture of Integrity," in *Reading Bernard Williams,* ed. Daniel Callcut (London/New York, Routledge, 2009), 110–111.
16. Rawls, *Political*, 23; Hare, *Freedom*, Chapter 2; Williams, "Persons, character," 2–5.
17. Richard Hare, *Moral Thinking* (Oxford University Press, 1989), 44; Rawls, *A Theory*, 118–123 and in *Political*, 23–28.
18. Roderick Firth, "Ethical Absolutism and the Ideal Observer," *Philosophy and Phenomenological Research,* 12, 3 (Mar, 1952): 317–345.

19. Williams, *Ethics*, 63–64.

*V*

# The Aretaic Turn

# FIFTEEN

# The Practical Impossibility of Tolerance

The general idea that has been defended in part IV is that tolerance understood as a moral ideal is incompatible with the logical requirements imposed by a deontological structure of practical reason. This claim has been reinforced by showing how the Deontological Moral System cannot give plausible answers to the two main problems generated by the normative nature of tolerance: (1) the problem regarding the value of the conceptions of the good, and (2) the problem of the 'moral dilemma' of tolerance. In this sense, three main arguments have been presented so far.

The first one is that the structure of practical reason held by the deontological system of morality neglects the value that people attach to their ethical beliefs and to their conceptions of the good. The normative power that deontological philosophers give to universal moral norms is so strong that it manages to remove the entire relevancy that ethical values can have within a practical deliberation. This scheme makes out of tolerance a tyrannical tool of morality.

A second argument that has been presented refers to the tensions created by the conceptual claims that tolerance imposes and the structure of the Deontological Moral System. It has been said that the principal characteristics of the deontological moral system and the way it conceives moral norms make out of tolerance a 'suicidal concept.' Here I make specific reference to the three main characteristics of the deontological structures of morality. These are: (1) the distinction between two levels of normativity: the 'ethical' level to which our conceptions of the good belong (some authors refer to that level as the 'intuitive' or 'basic level' of moral reasoning) and the level of 'morality,' which is considered as a justificatory level superior to the ethical level, (2) the universal character as the non-conditioning criterion of moral norms, and (3) the impartiality thesis which, together with the universal character, are the most important criteria for the justification of moral norms.

A third argument has been directed toward the problems related to the moral dilemma of tolerance. In this case, it has been argued, that deontological authors suffer from two incapacities: (1) that they reject the idea of dilemmas as a whole, therefore, for them the so called 'dilemma' or 'paradox' of tolerance is an imaginary scenario produced by 'cabinet philosophers,' rendering the problem to an 'epistemic deficiency' of the tolerator, and (2) when some deontological philosopher grants the possibility for the existence of tragic conflicts of values (dilemmatic), the same logical requirements of the Deontological Moral System neglect the results that an act of tolerance might have within the life of an agent. In that sense, if we accept that tolerance as a moral ideal incarnates dilemmatic conflicts then the solutions proposed by the Deontological Moral System can be so damaging to the ethical system of an agent that it turns the mere idea of tolerance into an irrational way of conduct.

Taking these objections into account, my main purposes in this last part of the book is to argue that if tolerance is to be understood as a moral ideal, then it has to rely in a structure of practical reason that trusts the moral intuition of rational agents, who are aware that different *circumstances* and different *contexts* create different moral scenarios that require the skills and the rational intuition to be solved in the best way possible. This means that agents take care and protect what seems to be vitally and simply important to them (beliefs, interests, personal attachments, etc.) without damaging the important matters of someone else's life. Tolerance understood in this way, turns into an ethical resource necessary for not becoming utterly permissible or obstinately recalcitrant in democratic societies, which are characterized by a plurality of different and, sometimes, incompatible conceptions of the good.

Part of this argument has been already proposed, yet not fully developed, and it refers to the idea that tolerance is not only a *normative dependent concept*,[1] but also a *context dependent concept*. The good reasons for tolerance are to be found not only in deductive systems of norms but also in an inductive way through the specific contexts of toleration. Following the contextual dependence thesis the two problems of tolerance will soften up: the moral dilemma and the problem of settling the limits. Chapters 16 and 17 will be dedicated to arguing this possibility and to defend the idea that tolerance is a contextual dependent concept, and that, therefore, conceptually it requires a structure of practical reason which is sensitive enough to the important role that 'contexts' play in our moral deliberations.

The arguments that I will present in this last part are directed toward reinforcing the two main claims that I have defended throughout this book:

(1) That the characteristics of the 'right' developed by deontological philosophers (*universal* and *prior*) make out of tolerance a suicidal concept.

(2) That the negligence that deontological liberalism professes towards ethical values (mainly through the *impartiality* requirement) makes out of tolerance an irrational attitude rather than a moral virtue.

These claims are concomitant with a more general claim that has been defended in a less explicit way throughout this work. This general claim sustains: (3) the impossibility of talking about tolerance as a moral ideal under a liberal deontological structure of practical reason.

In this chapter and in the next two I will argue that these tensions, which I have claimed to be unsolvable , are created because tolerance is a n ethical concept which is difficult to be managed by a deontological framework of practical reason. Tolerance, understood in that sense, requires another kind of normative framework than the one offered by the legalistic (deontological, and we can also include consequentialist) moral theories .[2]

The normative framework in which tolerance can develop itself as a moral ideal has to be a substantive one. Namely, a theory related to virtues ethics, which is the kind of theory that precisely would be sensitive enough to the *contextual dependence thesis* defended above, due to its relation with particularism. In that sense, I take virtue ethics as a genuine rival perspective to all legalistic conceptions of morality.

Tolerance understood in this way is not only a matter of following rules as deontologists' claim but it also rather depends on the agent's practical wisdom ( *phronesis*). Accordingly, it would be argued that tolerance requires an agent-centered moral theory rather than an exclusively action-centered one. The general bases for this twist of perspective will be given according to Bernard Williams's account of tolerance and his critiques of the way in which deontological moral theories have treated this concept.

## TOLERANCE AND THE 'MORAL SYSTEM': BERNARD WILLIAMS'S CRITICS

The importance of taking into consideration the approach of Williams for defending the idea about the impossibility of talking about tolerance within a deontological moral system rests on the kind of criticism that he has made to this type of philosophical structure. For Williams, deontological practical reasoning is wrong in many ways, for example for him the distinction between *ethics* and *morality* is an unfortunate result of an artificial theoretical construction that has little to do with the way in which individuals think and decide in their moral everyday life.[3] In fact, in chapter 10 of his famous *Ethics and the Limits of Philosophy*, Williams suggests that the special system to which contemporary moral philosophers refer to as *morality* is something that in fact "we would be better off without it."[4]

The following pages will explain the reasons that justify why Williams endorses such a strong thesis vis-à-vis the 'moral system' or 'morality.' Considering this, it is possible to say that Williams's criticisms do not only intend to show the weaker points of the 'moral system' theories but also why this approach to ethics fails completely. One claim that will be made about the work of Williams is that in it we can find the germs of the idea about tolerance that I want to defend: in order to understand tolerance as a moral ideal it is necessary to embrace a soft particularist approach to practical reason that recognizes the value that people give to their own ethical beliefs in their everyday life and the importance they attach to their own conceptions of the good, and to recognize the role that *contexts* and *circumstances* have in our moral deliberations.

One of Williams's most important claims against the authors of the 'moral system' is the little attention they pay to all kind of 'ethical beliefs' or to the 'individual conceptions of the good.' This claim has been addressed in fact by many other philosophers. For instance, this is one of Sandel's criticisms of the deontological doctrine, specially related to the one of Rawls, when he says that for this doctrine the good is something seen as the "indiscriminate satisfaction of arbitrarily given preferences, regardless of worth."[5] Williams in this sense, has "argued powerfully that if ethical norms are to have authority, then they must integrate into a life worth living [...] [mainly, because] too much ethical theory was too a-historical, too utopian, and too abstracted from concrete human life to provide intelligent guidance."[6] Then, the criticism raised to the 'moral system,' in general, and to the deontological doctrine in particular, is directed to show the negligence they have had towards the importance that personal ethical beliefs about the good have in people's everyday lives.

By 'moral system' Williams understands all moral theories that can be described through the next nine characteristics:

> 1) The 'moral system' is essentially practical; my moral obligations always contain things that I can do.
> 2) Moral obligations cannot (actually) enter into conflict.
> 3) All particular moral obligations need the logical support of another general moral obligation.
> 4) All moral obligations are inescapable: moral obligations are *peremptory* considerations for action.
> 5) All considerations we believe to be important from a practical standpoint must be presented as moral obligations.
> 6) If, on the strength of these considerations, some cannot take on the form of moral obligations, it is because, at the end, they were not so important.

7) The 'moral system' as it is presented (for example, through Kantian or utilitarian theories) does not accept the so-called *moral luck*. Williams calls this the "purity of morality."

8) Culpability is the main characteristic reaction of the 'moral system.' And that guilt is directly related to the agent's will.

9) The 'moral system' and all that it represents, is impersonal.[7]

Williams has taken the time to formulate at least one commentary against each one of the theses held by the so-called "moral systems." For example, let us examine the case of the first and the second theses, which also take on a meaningful prominence with regard to the idea of tolerance that will be defended.

According to these two theses, the 'moral system' is something primordially practical, and secondly, the conclusion that derives from it cannot require me to do something that is not practically possible. Both theses entail two famous traditional ideas of deontological philosophy that we have previously debated, namely: (1) *"ought* implies *can,"* and (2) moral obligations cannot enter into conflict *(obligationes non colliduntur)*.

Behind Williams's lenses, both ideas are incorrect. The practical impossibility that the first thesis tries to avoid directly entails two ideas: first, that moral obligations cannot require me to do something that is either physically impossible or factually impossible and second, denying the idea that two particular obligations which enter into conflict can be derived from one general moral obligation.

In accordance with the first idea expressed by Williams, I do not think there is a conflict or criticism. Any person, not necessarily a professional in logic or a philosopher, would agree with this no questions asked. This is a matter of common sense, if you will.

As for the second idea, the authors of the 'moral system' would say that if our deliberation, based on a general moral obligation, cornered me into accepting that *A* is obligatory and *B* is obligatory, although *A* and *B* are incompatible and incommensurable and therefore cannot apply at the same time, then what we have to do is to deliberate once again. This point has been made clear in chapter 13 'Tolerance as a Moral Dilemma.' However, philosophers like Williams argue that there are cases in which the contextual circumstances can corner our deliberation thus, once again, taking us down the same road: towards the same two conflicting obligations. Therefore, the answer provided by these moral perspectives is not an answer at all.

But even so, authors of the 'moral system' would argue that one of these obligations does not actually apply to the case in question or that one of them has to be rejected. The arguments used by certain authors of the 'moral system' would very much resemble those presented by W. D. Ross, meaning that one of the *oughts* was only prima facie. Alternatively, they can resemble arguments such as those presented by Shelly Kagan, by saying that the decision to choose between both obligations must be made according to pro tanto reasons.[8]

According to Williams however, these types of answers suffer from poor moral visibility. They are a falsification of ordinary moral thought: "[it] does not mean they do not both (actually) *apply* to the situation; or that I was in some way mistaken in thinking that these were both things that I ought to do."[9]

To make stronger this same argument, Williams includes to the claim the notion of *moral regret*: "Regret necessarily involves a wish that things had been otherwise, for instance that one had not had to act as one did."[10] In other words:

> There are two sides to action, that of deliberation and that of result, and there is a necessary gap between them. Regret must be governed, in good part, by results that go beyond intention. Sometimes regret can focus simply on the outside circumstances that made the action go wrong, and the thought is: I acted and deliberated as well as I could, and it is sad that it turned out that way.[11]

Let us recall Chappell's paradigmatic example in order to illustrate Williams's point.[12] The example refers to a cruise ship officer who has been shipwrecked in the middle of the Atlantic. Our officer leads a group of passengers he managed to rescue from the catastrophe to shore in a lifeboat. The lifeboat is full and if another person gets on, it runs the risk of sinking. But many other survivors, who are still in the water fighting for their lives, try to get on the lifeboat in a desperate attempt to survive. The officer, who holds the general obligation of always trying to help people in danger, is, at this moment, caught between two contradictory particular obligations: a) saving the life of those who are inside the lifeboat, or b) trying to save the life of all. The officer decides and strikes the hands of the men who are trying to get on the lifeboat with one of the oars, knowing well that by doing this, those men will drown.

For Williams, the authors of the 'moral system' would argue something like this: *actually, the officer did not have the obligation to save the lives of the men who were in the water. His real obligation is towards the men who were on the lifeboat, and, therefore, he did not act in an immoral manner when he struck their hands with one of the oars.* According to the perspective of the 'moral system' the officer did not act immorally, in such a case Williams would ask: what does the officer have to do in order to get rid of the feeling of loss and regret that overwhelms him? Should he tell the families of the men who lost their lives that he had no obligation to save them?[13] This example is just a glimpse into the kinds of critiques and problems that Williams is interested in analyzing.

It is important to note that under Williams's perspective, the 'moral system' is mainly represented by Kantian and utilitarian moral theories. This does not mean that Williams does not include, within his catalogue of 'enemies,' other currents or theories that contain similar features to those presented by deontologism and consequentialism. But undoubtedly, the ones that are his main targets are Kant (and all of his allies who range from Rawls and Habermas all the way to authors such as Rainer Forst and Ernesto Garzón) and the consequentialists *in genere* (which range from Jeremy Bentham and J. S. Mill all the way to Richard Hare and Joseph Raz).

The critiques that Williams directs against the 'moral system' can be seen more directly when contrasted with some of the problems that tolerance has generated for contemporary moral thinking. Though, before entering into the arguments that Williams might give to prove the impossibility of justifying tolerant attitudes through the lens of the 'moral system' it is important to consider some problems that he sees in the concept of tolerance.

## THE IMPOSSIBILITY OF TOLERANCE AS A MORAL ATTITUDE

Williams's skeptical realism towards the attempts of moral theorization is proportional to that which he professes about the idea of tolerance qua moral ideal. In his 1996 essay *Toleration, a Political or Moral Question?* he starts by saying:

> There is something obscure about the nature of toleration, at least when it is regarded as an attitude or a personal principle. Indeed, the problem about the nature of toleration is severe enough for us to raise the question whether, in a strict sense, it is possible at all. Perhaps, rather, it contains some contradiction or paradox which means that practices of toleration, when they exist, must rest on something other than the attitude of toleration as that has been classically described by liberal theory.[14]

From this paragraph we can infer some important features of Williams's understanding of tolerance. The first lies in the distinction between the *attitude* and the *practice* of tolerance. For Williams, there are two ways of understanding tolerance, and according to him these are the two different forms in which classical liberalism (so denominated by Williams himself) used the concept. The second important matter is that for Williams, one of the ways of understanding it— i.e. concretely *the practice of tolerance*—rests or is based on diverse tolerant *attitudes*. The third is that he finds that the *moral attitude* of tolerance is almost impossible to achieve.[15]

Williams's conception of the *practice* of tolerance is constructed as a general representation of what we regularly understand about this concept. He says that: "the sphere of toleration has to be one in which the agent has some very strong view on a certain matter; thinks that people with conflicting views are wrong; and thinks at the same time that, in some sense, those others should be allowed to have and express those views."[16]

Seeing things in such a broad and general way, allows Williams to recognize several *practices* of tolerance that have been displayed throughout history. For example, he reflects on Europe in the sixteenth and seventeenth centuries, the times of the bloody religious wars. During those years, we could say that, for example, Holland was much more tolerant than Spain and that England had more tendencies to be tolerant than Italy or Germany. Although these judgments can be made by considering the practices of these countries, and although all these practices were similar in a way, all of them were based upon diverse attitudes and not upon one single moral attitude. For this reason, Williams urges us to distinguish between different attitudes of toleration that explain a lot more than the mere practice of tolerance.[17]

To exemplify this, Williams takes the skeptical attitude developed by some groups during the religious wars. And he says that this attitude was adopted mainly because skeptical individuals believed that there was less to know about our divine destiny than what the warring parties supposed. In fact, those who adopted the skeptical perspective towards religious beliefs started to think that there was no truth, or at least not a truth to which human beings could acquiesce, upon which they could base the validity of one creed against another. Another of Williams's examples is the attitude of indifference adopted by the broad Anglican Church, which affirmed that the precise substance of the Christian faith did not matter as much as people had supposed, and that what was at stake was less than what was thought by the Christian church.

These examples are important for realizing the deepness of Williams's distinction: he takes the *practice* of tolerance as something that has certain continuity in history, the changes in understanding tolerance are not to be found in the practice but in the *attitudes* that underline such *practices*. Williams names several attitudes of tolerance: *mutual cooperation* (that maintains a Hobbesian equilibrium), *shared understanding* (which is based on a common political sense),[18] a *skeptical stance* (which is based on principles of instrumental rationality, very close to the way Karl Popper or Mill conceptualize it),[19] and the *moral attitude*. Nevertheless, this last one is the one of our concern now: firstly, because as it has been argued it is the one adopted by deontological liberals and secondly, because Williams's most profound skepticism towards the possibility of tolerance is in regard to this attitude. In his *Tolerating the Intolerable* Williams begins by saying that:

> The difficulty with toleration is that it seems to be at once necessary and impossible. It is necessary where different groups have conflicting beliefs—moral, political, or religious—and realize that there is no alternative to living together, that is to say, no alternative except armed

conflict which will not resolve their disagreements and will impose continuous suffering. These are the circumstances in which toleration is necessary. Yet in those same circumstances it may well seem impossible.[20]

Hence, Williams says that tolerance understood in that strict sense "requires us to accept people and permit their practices even when we strongly disapprove of them; but skepticism and indifference mean that people no longer strongly disapprove of the beliefs in question, and their attitude is not, in a strict sense, that of toleration."[21]

When we say that a person morally disapproves of something, we are likewise saying that, if a person allows or permits the practice that he/she morally disapproves of, it is because that person is being tolerant. However, as Williams argues, this is not enough to qualify that practice as tolerant in the moral sense. We need to know which attitude underlies that practice. Williams recognizes that in order for tolerance to be understood as a moral attitude, we need to realize which kind of attitude underlies the practice. In the case of tolerance as a moral attitude the reasons to tolerate must belong to that rank. It is because of this that tolerance so understood can neither be based on attitudes of indifference or skepticism, nor on a Hobbesian calculation. On the contrary, the attitude must be based on moral principles.

Tolerance understood in this sense requires to be based on moral grounds so the practice of restraint can become morally relevant in particularly rough situations and not be confused with political toleration. According to Williams, this difference can be seen if we consider Thomas Nagel's formulation regarding the relation between toleration and liberalism. Nagel says:

> Yet liberalism purports to be a view that justifies religious toleration not only to religious skeptics but to the devout, and sexual toleration not only to libertines but to those who believe extramarital sex is sinful. It distinguishes between the values a person can appeal to in conducting his own life and those he can appeal to in justifying the exercise of political power.[22]

For Williams, the scenario presented by Nagel's passage is not as clear-cut as liberal authors claim it to be. Nagel's formulation represents the liberal outlook, popularized by Rawls in which liberalism is not seen as 'just a sectarian doctrine.' The central idea of Nagel is already familiar to us; his position adopts the deontological perspective of stating that the principle of tolerance should not be founded on any particular ethical perspective but on moral reasons. In this sense, tolerance should be the moral practice that allows the fact of reasonable pluralism.[23] It is conceived similarly in the schemes defended by philosophers such as Dworkin, Rawls, Nagel, Garzón and Forst, among others. According to Williams, the maneuver made by these perspectives puts them in tension:

on the one side, they say that certain conduct or a certain way of life is sinful, but, on the other, they argue that such conduct or way of life should not be suppressed by state power.

Following the nature of this tension, Williams says that Nagel's passage, then, has at least two different readings: the first one is expressed by the following reasoning:

> "This other agent has a sinful and disgusting way of life and engages in sinful disgusting practices. However, it is nobody's business to make him, force him, induce him, or (perhaps) even persuade him to take another course. It is up to him — his morality is in his own hands."[24]

The political consequence of this type of reasoning is that the political power should not be used to constrain the practices or lifestyles chosen by the individuals. According to Williams, this perspective expresses a particular moral doctrine, a moral doctrine which adopts, as a moral ideal, the value of personal autonomy. Certainly, this moral doctrine may accidentally entail certain political consequences (such as not utilizing the coactive power of the State). However, this does not mean that behind this way of thinking a particular moral doctrine will cease to exist.

The second interpretation offered by Williams is expressed through this other reasoning: "This person's way of life is sinful and disgusting. Indeed we should do everything we decently can to persuade him to change his ways and to discourage other people from living like him. We may appropriately warn our children not to consort with his children, not to share his social life, and discourage as many people as we can from thinking well of him as long as he lives in this way. However it is not appropriate that the power of the state be used in this way."[25] Contrary to the previous argument, this one — according to Williams — expresses a political stance. Williams warns us that this other (political) stance may be rooted in a moral criterion regarding the nature of the State. However, even if this were the case, the political conclusion that is derived from the argument cannot be taken as a direct consequence of this particular moral doctrine as in the first one.

Hence, in the first reading of Nagel's passage we encounter the question posed by Williams: what moral value can ground this kind of tolerant attitude? And the answer is the value of *personal autonomy*. Autonomy understood in the same way as it has been understood by many philosophers of liberalism to justify tolerance. For example, consider the place that this value has taken in Rainer Forst's or Ernesto Garzón's structures of practical reason (understanding it as the source of normativity). Also consider the place it has in other deontological theories such as those developed by John Rawls and Thomas Nagel for example.[26] However, it is in this case that Williams's response seems to be devastating. Williams says that tolerance based on autonomy abdicates its role; it becomes impossible to achieve: "All toleration involves difficulties, but it is the virtue that especially threatens to involve conceptual impossibility."[27]

To defend the conceptual impossibility thesis, Williams argues the existence of two problems derived from the first reading of Nagel's quotation: (1) any political stance that justifies tolerance under the value of autonomy cannot claim to be different than 'another sectarian doctrine,' and (2) that according to this perspective someone who does not believe in the value of autonomy can thereby affirm that tolerance is an unattainable value. This second argument is centered on the limits presented by the tolerator when he/she expresses his/her disapproval towards something. These limits are set by the autonomy of the tolerated agent who, according to Williams, restrains the tolerator from being intolerant.

The first problem refers to the idea of founding tolerance on the value of personal autonomy. According to Williams, if liberalism does this it cannot escape the idea of being just another sectarian doctrine. To avoid this outcome it must found tolerance in other non-substantive criteria. According to Williams, "it is very difficult both to claim that the value of autonomy is the foundation of the liberal belief in toleration, and at the same time to hold, as Nagel and Rawls and other liberals hold, that liberalism is not just another sectarian doctrine."[28] It can be argued that in the specific case of Rawls 'full autonomy' is distinguished form rational autonomy and that full autonomy is considered a political and not an ethical value.

Nevertheless, Rawls's attempt to detach autonomy from an ethical conception is far from being clear and sound. Rawls conceives 'full autonomy' as "the recognition and informed application of the principles of justice in [the citizens'] political life, and as their effective sense of justice."[29] By conceiving autonomy in this way Rawls gets trapped by his own scheme: the principles of practical reason are justified, according to Rawls, because they come from us; they represent full autonomy. Then practical reason finds its own foundations in the autonomy of individuals that find themselves in the original position. A first reading of Rawls's formulation will lead us to the idea that his structure of practical reason only rests on formal criteria, but it is not like this: it also relies in substantive notions such as the idea of reciprocity as a constitutive element of the reasonable. What Rawls sustains is that the principle of reasonableness derives from the existing political culture and from specific social traditions, that is, they are externally imposed upon individuals found in the original position and not autonomously exercised. This, however, clearly contradicts the idea a 'freestanding' conception of justice. Rawls's liberalism "no longer seems committed to a philosophical account of the human self, but only to a historic-sociological description of the way we live now."[30] Then, if he maintains the idea that autonomy requires the acceptance of existing public culture *via* the reasonable, he cannot support the thesis of a 'freestanding' conception of justice and leaves the door open to the objections made by Michael Sandel and Richard Rorty, among others, or if he rejects this possibility then he starts embracing a full Kantian account of autonomy. In both cases, Rawls fails to maintain the idea of a 'political conception of justice.'

The second argument that I previously referred to is based on the following reasoning given by Williams with regard to tolerance's moral attitude. Williams says: "the agent who disapproves of other's values should refrain from any untoward pressure on the other to change his outlook. There is, of course, the question of what 'untoward' will mean, but it is essential that the account of the liberal outlook, that the idea of such untoward pressure goes wider that merely the matter of direct political interference."[31] And he continues with the following idea:

> But if the agent who disapproves of the other's values and is committed to the attitude of toleration is cut off from all such expressions, it becomes increasingly unclear what room is left for the agent genuinely and strongly to disapprove the other's values. The idea of a strong, moral disapproval which can be expressed only in (something like) a rational argument, and is otherwise required by the demands of toleration to remain private, seems too thin and feeble to satisfy what has been agreed to be the requirement of the tolerant attitude, namely that the agent does in fact strongly disapprove of the practices about which he is being tolerant.[32]

This is another way of presenting tolerance's 'paradox' or 'dilemma.' Indeed, if someone morally disapproves of a practice, which is the reaction expected by the tolerator? How can this person act without being told that he has ceased to be tolerant and starting to become intolerant, how can a tolerant person react without affecting the autonomy of the tolerated? The central idea of Williams's argument is schematized in two questions: (1) What types of influences or social pressures can be taken as violations of another's personal autonomy?, and (2) Which are the means of expression available to moral agents so that they can be seen as individuals who seriously disapprove of the conduct and values of another and engage in a tolerant attitude?

The answers of both questions do not necessarily have to coincide. As we can see, the first question is directed towards one of the basic features of the concept of personal autonomy: in order for a person to be *autonomous* or to make *autonomous* decisions the minimum requisite is that he/she must be free from external compulsion. If the tolerator applies pressure (or any other measure) while expressing his/her moral disapproval, and achieves through that the change of mind of the tolerated, it is possible to say that in such a case autonomy has not been respected and that, thereby, the choice has not been autonomous.

The second question presented by Williams, although related to the first one, is different in nature. Here the matter at stake is how much or through what means can the tolerator express his/her disapproval without harming the other person's autonomy or without being considered as intolerant. Where is the point in-between expressing one's disapproval and becoming intolerant? In this sense, when tolerance is understood as a moral ideal that protects personal autonomy, it gets trapped by its own net: we cannot express our feelings towards something we disapprove either (1) because we may possibly harm the autonomy of another, or (2) because we can become intolerant.

In such cases there is the possibility of adopting other existing attitudes that do not harm the autonomy of the other and that make tolerance—as a practice—possible. This other attitude could be 'indifference.' However, as Williams acknowledges, indifference becomes logically incompatible when we include in the equation the idea of a moral agent that *firmly and genuinely disapproves* of the values or practices of another individual.

## THE DEONTOLOGICAL FAILURE TO JUSTIFY TOLERANCE

It is easy to imagine which could be Williams's critiques to the structure of deontological liberalism when it is used to justify tolerance as a moral attitude. These critics can be guided by Williams's actual objections to the 'moral system.' Although Williams never applied these objections particularly to the justification of tolerance, we can infer their shape.

One of the main objections raised to the deontological theory in the previous chapters was that when this theory faces the problems of the 'limits' and of the 'moral paradox' of tolerance its structure cannot come from a logical and from a moral point of view with plausible answers.

In the earlier chapters some of the reasons that show this difficulty were enumerated. These include one difficulty of the great relevance, namely the difficulty that deontological theories have, as those configured by John Rawls, Ernesto Garzón and Rainer Forst, in 'waning,' 'stopping' or 'softening' for a given period of time a prohibition hold by the basic normative systems, this without having to eliminate or to moralize such a prohibition. The problems found in this way of reasoning were two: first of all, neither of these practical conclusions—eliminating or moralizing—allow future acts of tolerance towards conducts and practices that share the same relevant characteristics. In second place, this kind of reasoning makes out of tolerance a 'suicidal' concept due to the idea that every act of tolerance results in a bigger and wider realm of 'intolerances.'

It must be remembered that this difficulty is mainly rooted in the idea that all of the moral obligations come from a super-value or a super-principle, which in the Kantian scheme defended by deontological authors is the personal autonomy. Such a structure is fundamentally compromised by two logical elements: (1) coherent systematization of moral norms, and thereof (2) dispelling the possibility that two or more norms are at the same time valid; this is, obligation cannot enter into conflict.

Williams offers a detailed critique to both ideas hold by the 'moral systems' in his book *Ethics and the Limits of Philosophy*. Specifically in the chapter "Morality: The Peculiar Institution," Williams explains the core idea that rules the structure of the 'moral systems.' This idea is constituted by a logical commitment found in the principle that he calls: the *obligation-out, obligation-in* principle. The idea that Williams expresses throughout this principle is framed by the shared belief that all practical conclusions—derived from a rational deliberation—must be treated as *particular moral obligations* that supposedly are supported by one *general moral obligation*.[33]

Conceived in this way, anyone who accepts the perspective of morality offered by the 'moral system,'—mainly related to Kantian moral philosophy—will feel morally constrained by the system itself to think that if an individual X has a particular obligation in circumstances C to do ø, it is because X has a general obligation to do ø in all the situations that contain the same relevant characteristics than C. As I have noted before, the assumption held by this perspective—of morality guided by the logical rules of a system—create great tensions between the moral ideal of tolerance and the deontological structure of practical reason.

Williams believes that most of our practical deliberations are doomed to run into problems once we embark on the journey of searching for the general obligations that support our particular practical conclusions. These problems do not only pertain to matters of philosophical character, such as which is the general obligation that supports one particular obligation, but they also relate to burdens of conscience created by leaving things aside that we considered *important* but do not find their place within the structure of obligations.

"Important" things understood in the way that Williams does, should not be taken as something that is 'important to the universe' or that is 'important for human beings.' Important matters in Williams sense are something taken to be, "simply, important." In Williams's words:

> It does not matter for the present discussion that this notion [importance] is poorly understood. I need only three things of it. One is that there is such a notion. Another is that if something is important in the relative sense to somebody, this does not necessarily imply that he or she thinks it is, simply, important. It may be of the greatest importance to Henry that his stamp collection be completed with a certain stamp, but even Henry may see that it is not, simply, important a number of things that are, simply, important as well as many things that are not, and they should be able to tell the difference between them.[34]

Now, if we relate the notion of importance to the principle of a general obligation, then, we will be able to grasp Williams's idea about the philosophical and conscientious troubles. These are created because the deontological system, on the one hand, does not grant moral validity to things that seem irrelevant under its prism but are important to us. According to the deontological scheme, in order for something to be justified, it must be supported by a general moral obligation on the one hand and, on the other hand, the logical principle that rules out the structure drives individuals into letting go things and convictions that are considered *important* for the individual.

This reduction of morality (reduction in a double sense: (1) all practical conclusions, if they are important, have to be moral—theses fifth and sixth from the above mentioned–, and (2) all convictions held by a person must conform to the requirements of generality and coherence imposed by the 'moral system'—theses second and third) is what makes Williams say that the claims imposed by this perspective of morality are highly demanding and therefore practically unacceptable.

Within the context of tolerance, it is this conception of moral obligations that impeded the liberal-vegetarian mother (from the example described in the previous chapters) to decide whether or not she could tolerate the fact that her son was a hamburger lover.

Because of the constraints created by the deontological structure of practical reason, in this situation she felt compelled to choose between two different scenarios: (1) either freeing herself from the obligation which imposed on her the need to respect the free development of her son's personality (which would entail her letting go of an important part of her liberal ideology) or, (2) disembarrass the conviction that it is morally repugnant to kill animals for consumption (which would entail letting go an *important* conviction that gives meaning to her life).

Having established matters in this way, it would seem that Williams is right. The position in which the mother is placed is highly demanding. Philosophers such as Williams and Martha Nussbaum, for example, would not hesitate to say that morality cannot actually require us to abandon one of the two conflicting convictions.[35]

If we pay attention, the element that is implicitly intensifying the gravity of this situation is one of the three pillars of the deontological system, i.e. the *universality principle*. The Kantian version of the universality principle, which is the one adopted by other deontologist philosophers such as Garzón and Forst, states that we should "act on no other maxim than that which can also have as an object itself as a universal law."[36] From the deontological perspective, this principle encapsulates the procedure that helps us decide whether an act is morally justified or not. When someone is deliberating upon which action to take, what he/she has to do is ask himself/herself which rule he/she must comply with, and from there start asking himself/herself whether he/she would be willing to apply such a rule to all the cases that share the same relevant characteristics of the case that originally raised the question. If the answer is yes, then the rule must be obeyed and the act should be understood as morally justified.

If, for example, the vegetarian mother were to choose to tolerate the fact that her son eats hamburgers, the practical conclusion of her deliberation would then be that she must *accept* that any other person at any other given time can also eat hamburgers.

However, if the requirements of the deontological system were to be taken seriously, then the mother would be aware that whichever decision she makes from this perspective will entail unpleasant consequences for her and for those around her. For example, let us suppose that she does not tolerate her son eating hamburgers. She knows that through this prohibition she is not only interfering with the free development of her son's personality (his autonomy), but also that her relationship with him may deteriorate. But if she tolerates him eating hamburgers, which would eventually — due to the universality principle — impose on her the obligation to *accept* anyone who eats meat, then this would no doubt end up causing serious damage to the way she sees the world in general and her life in particular.

Having reached this point, we can appreciate that many of the problems generated by the principle of "obligation-out obligation-in," are reduced to placing the mother in a situation where she has to either *accept* or *reject*. Yet it should be noted that the position in which the mother is placed is a direct consequence of the procedure that is the driving force behind this principle: in order to make moral decisions the agent must abstract himself/herself from his/her own life, from the attachments that bind him/her to the people that surround him/her and from the entire framework of the *important* things in his/her life (such as loving relationships with family and friends, personal projects and interests, etc.) so as to be able to comply with the requirements of the general moral obligations.

This detachment from the ethical beliefs that constitutes the *self* [37] according to Williams, is one of the main features that have been traditionally defended by deontological moral theories. Many contemporary philosophers have adopted the same theoretical stances that abdicated the importance of ethical beliefs in the moral every day of individuals. For instance, John Rawls demands that the moral norms should be chosen by people who are unaware of who they are and ignorant of the relevant characteristics of their personalities and of their immediate life.

This is precisely the core idea that, according to deontological authors, should guide any type of deliberative procedure. This idea is regularly called the 'moral point of view.' Those who accept the deontological perspective say that due to the procedural rules that constitute it, it can be clearly distinguished from a non-moral viewpoint or, what is essentially identical, from a self-interested point of view. If this is so, then the configuration of the so-called moral point of view prohibits us qua moral agents, from making decisions that are biased or decisions that entail personal benefits.

If we return to the example we are using, it is possible to see that the convictions held by the liberal-vegetarian mother do not only serve as a guide of conduct, but also play a very *important* role in defining her place in the world, in defining her as a person. It is these kinds of convictions that, Williams says, create our *character*. Or belong to what Williams calls the *ground projects*. They are those types of convictions that provide a driving force propelling her towards the future and give her reasons to live.[38]

For Williams, a person has *character* in the sense of having projects and categorical desires with which that person is identified. The categorical qualifier alludes to the notion that in the life of a person, or in a fragment of their life, there are certain projects or desires which constitute what Williams calls the *ground project* (or set of projects), which are closely related to his existence and which to a significant degree give a meaning to his life.

Considering things in such a way, we can conclude that the mother is indeed facing a *tragic* or *dilemmatic* situation. Still, as we have seen before, deontological philosophers sustain that these types of situations are only apparent. They are the product of an epistemic deficiency. According to this perspective, if the mother were to adopt an impartial perspective, she would have to decide which of the two conflicting convictions imposes a *real* moral obligation on her. However, what this perspective is obviating is the result of the choice; or the effects that a decision as such can entail for the *character* and the moral *integrity* of the agent. The mother, Williams would say, cannot prevent the sense of loss that her decision will entail.

Having this in mind, we can now expand upon the premises of the example and say that not only does the mother have moral reasons for being a vegetarian, but also that this particular project defines and consumes a great deal of her life. She even belongs, we could say, to a non-profit organization that campaigns against the killing of animals for consumption; she participates in protests against these acts, writes pamphlets and texts that relate to all the harms that eating meat causes and the slaughtering of animals that it entails. In this case, we could hardly say that her *acceptance* of her son's consumption of meat is an easy decision to embrace, and even less so if we were to add the universality principle within the deliberative scenario and add to it the very important notion that 'we are taking about her son.' In that case, Williams would say, the dilemma that is denied by the deontological system should be confirmed.

The last ingredient added a sort of sentimental relationship that binds her to her son, and which can turn the mother's deliberation into a bitter individual controversy that could very well place her in a situation which would be possible to qualify as tragic, in the sense that no matter what she does, or decides, there will be a loss or a moral sacrifice. This, especially because it is difficult to ignore the fact that we are dealing with a relationship that is obviously a part of her *ground* projects and that pertains to her most deeply rooted desires and interests.

Recognizing the seriousness of all these variables—the sincere and profound attachments of the mother and her genuine interest in making a morally justified decision—the deontological perspective places her at a sort of crossroads, especially because in cases of conflict this moral perspective requires us to adopt an impartial perspective.

This means that if we want our decision to be morally justified it necessarily has to be taken in an impartial way. However, Williams has certain reservations as to whether this affirmation is one hundred percent morally correct, especially if we see it from the perspective of the life of the moral agent. Which is why he argues that the requirement made by the principle of impartiality: "cannot necessarily be a reasonable demand on the agent. There can come a point at which it is quite unreasonable for a man to give up, in the name of the impartial good ordering of the world of moral agents, something which is a condition of his having any interest in being around in that world at all." [39]

Of course, what Williams seeks with all of this is to highlight the tension, that according to him exists between the 'moral point of view' and the 'character' or the 'moral integrity' of moral agents. [40] In fact, the claim that this tension exists is one of the central points of the criticism Williams directs against the 'moral systems.' However, his position is not radical, in the sense that the moral agents should *never* make decisions from an impartial point of view.

In his *Persons, Character and Morality*, Williams presents this situation by saying: "[h]owever, once morality is there, and also personal relations to be taken seriously, so is the possibility of conflict. This of course does not mean that if there is some friendship with which his life is much involved, then a man must prefer any possible demand of that over other, impartial, moral demands. That would be absurd." [41]

As I said, this position is not a radical one. This is an important characteristic that we must not foresee, because Williams thinks that taking both ends of the line as categorical would be absurd, this is to say that moral agents should *never* make impartial decisions, as requiring them to *always* make impartial decisions. [42] Both cases will strengthen the tensions between the moral point of view and the character of people.

In *The Architecture of Integrity*, Daniel Markovits explains how the personal point of view (the *first person* perspective) and the external point of view (or the *third person* perspective), enter into a conflict that could prove to be tedious for modern ethics. [43] The first point of view, according to Markovits, elaborates a more intimate approach to ethics which allows us to conclude that an act is ethically justified when it promotes the success of the agent. That happens when its efforts are in accordance with the life plan that a person has chosen to live by and manages to achieve the ends that the agent considers admirable. The second point of view represses and even neglects this characteristic of the moral life. This other perspective according to Markovits "neglects and even suppresses this feature [integrity] of moral life. This suppression has given rise to a new and distinctive form of subjugation, associated with understanding morality solely in terms of sacrificing oneself to satisfy burdensome duties owed to others."[44]

In *Morality: an Introduction to Ethics,* Bernard Williams makes the following reflection:

> [W]hy a man who is concerned about others may not also be reasonably concerned about himself. Under Kantian emphasis, however, this suddenly emerges as a problem, since to act with regard to one's interest, in a straightforward way, is to act from a kind of motive, which has nothing to do with morality at all and is indeed alien to it. Since we are presumably enjoined to maximize moral action, extremes of self-denial would seem to follow, as derived, indeed, from the concept of morality itself. At the best, doing what one simple wants to do will constitute unregulated and probable guilty departures from the moral point of view. To cope with this problem, the Kantian tradition produces a set of 'duties to oneself,' recognition of which licenses one to do for moral reasons some of the things one would be disposed to do anyway.[45]

Considering this it sounds plausible to say that if Williams could formulate an opinion as to whether the mother in our example had to decide, without sacrificing much of what is important in her life, she would surely answer that she must tolerate her son being a hamburger lover, without this implying that she has to either throw her vegetarianism overboard or that she has to adopt a general obligation which requires her to accept all hamburger lovers of the world. In other words, her tolerance would be justified on the mere grounds that she is referring to her *son*.

It would then seem that Williams sustains that in cases of tolerance, such as the one mentioned, the intended ubiquity of the moral point of view falters. The mother's son could be tolerated without causing major damage to the mother's convictions, and this would be far from being justifiable from a deontological point of view. The real justification, Williams would say, has nothing to do with the impersonal and impartial standards of morality and everything to do with the role that the tolerator occupies in the life of the tolerated. For Williams, the standard is what makes a life worth living. He finds this way of seeing morality to be much more genuine and substantive than the Kantian canon of general moral obligations.[46]

I believe it is important to point out the hint of certain particularistic strategies or maneuvers present in the moral perspective adopted by Williams. Although this is something I will address in the next chapter, I just think it is important to consider that the entire discussion presented here and constructed around some of Bernard Williams's thesis and ideas about ethics and morality can be useful as an introductory part of what I am about to present in the last part of this book. This is mainly because a central part of it will be based on the idea that tolerance as a moral ideal has to be backed up by a special type of practical reason. Moreover, I will rely heavily on the ideas and philosophical positions of Williams.

## NOTES

1. Forst, "Toleration, Justice," 75.
2. G. E. M. Anscombe, "Modern Moral Philosophy," *Philosophy*, 33, 124 (Jan., 1958): 5.
3. Williams, *Ethics*, 201–202.
4. Williams, *Ethics*, 174.
5. Sandel, *Liberalism*, 167.
6. Callcut, *Reading*, 4.
7. Most of the theses that I enumerate here can be found in chapter 10 of Bernard Williams *Ethics and the Limits of Philosophy*. Williams dedicates this chapter to a systematic encapsulation of all the theses and critiques which up to that point had been directed against contemporary moral theory. You can also see, Sophie Grace Chappell, "Bernard Williams" *Stanford Philosophy Encyclopedia* (2006) accessed September 2, 2015.
8. W. D. Ross, *The Right*; Shelly Kagan, *The Limits of Morality* (Oxford, Clarendon Press, 1989).
9. Bernard Williams, *Problems of the Self* (Cambridge University Press, 1973), 183–184.
10. Williams, "Moral Luck," 31.
11. Bernard Williams, *Shame and Necessity* (University of California Press, 1993), 69.
12. Chappell, "Bernard Williams."
13. Chappell, "Bernard Williams."
14. Williams, "Toleration, a Political," 128.
15. Williams, "Toleration, a Political," 128, 138.
16. Williams, "Toleration, a Political," 130.
17. Williams, "Toleration, a Political," 128, 138; Williams, "Toleration: an impossible virtue?," 23.
18. Williams, "Toleration: an impossible virtue?," 21.
19. Karl Popper, "Toleration and Intellectual Responsibility," in *On Toleration*, S. Mendus, D. Edwards, 17-34; Mill, *On Liberty*, 37.
20. Bernard Williams, "Tolerating the Intolerable," in *Philosophy as a Humanistic Discipline*, ed. A. W. Moore (Princeton University Press, Princeton and Oxford, 2006), 126.
21. Williams, "Toleration, a Political," 128.
22. Thomas Nagel, *Equality and Partiality* (Oxford University Press, 1991), 156.
23. Thomas Nagel, "Moral Conflict and Political Legitimacy," *Philosophy & Public Affairs*, 16, 3 (1987): 228–229.
24. Williams, "Toleration, a Political," 131.
25. Williams, "Toleration, a Political," 131.
26. Rawls, *Political*, 77; Nagel, *Equality*, 141, 159, 164.
27. Williams, "Toleration: an impossible virtue?," 19.

28. Williams, "Toleration: an impossible virtue?," 19.

29. Rawls, *Political*, 77.

30. Richard Rorty, "The Prioriy of Democracy to Philosophy," in *The Virginia Statute for Religious Freedom*, ed. Merril D. Peterson and Robert V. Vaughan (Cambridge University Press, 1988), 262.

31. Williams, "Toleration, a Political," 132.

32. Williams, "Toleration, a Political," 132.

33. Williams, *Ethics*, 181–182.

34. Williams, *Ethics*, 182–183. (Brackets are mine)

35. Martha C. Nussbaum, *The Fragility of Goodness: Luck and Ethics in Greek Tragedy and Philosophy* (Cambridge University Press, 2001), xxvi–viii; Martha C. Nussbaum, *El Paisaje del Pensamiento: La inteligencia de las emociones* (Barcelona, Paidós, 2008).

36. Immanuel Kant, *Fundamental Principles of the Metaphysics of Morals* (England, Forgotten Books, 2008), 71.

37. Williams, "Persons, character," 12–13.

38. Williams, "Persons, character," 13–15.

39. Williams, "Persons, character," 14.

40. Daniel Markovits, "The Architecture of Integrity," in *Reading*, ed. Daniel Callcut, 126.

41. Williams, "Persons, character," 17.

42. Williams, *Ethics*, 80–81, 197–202.

43. Markovits, "The Architecture," 110–111.

44. Markovits, "The Architecture," 111. (Brackets are mine)

45. Bernard Williams, *Morality: an Introduction to Ethics* (Cambridge University Press, 1993), 68–69.

46. Williams, *Ethics*, 196.

# SIXTEEN

## Tolerance as a Dispositional Property

In chapter 11, two ideas regarding the concept of tolerance were advanced: The first one was taken from Rainer Forst's statement according to which tolerance is a *normatively dependent concept*. What Forst defends with this idea is the substantial vacuity of tolerance which has to be filled by referring to specific conceptions of *justice* which have to be in accordance with a notion of practical reason.

Nevertheless, here I will argue that there is a difference in saying that tolerance depends on a conception of justice or on a specific notion of practical reason and, another, to say that tolerance is compatible with any conception of justice or with any notion of practical reason. The substantial vacuity of tolerance does not make out of it a compatibly open concept. This last statement is reinforced with the second idea: that tolerance is also a *contextual dependent concept*. According to what has been said until now, the idea that tolerance is a normatively dependent concept is due to this second idea. Tolerance is not open to any conception of justice neither to any notion of practical reason due to its strong dependence on specific facts and circumstances. In the pages that follow I will sustain that tolerance is a contextually dependent concept because of its aretaic roots. Both characteristics, its contexts dependency and its aretaic foundations, make it a very hostile ideal for any principle or rule-based theory of practical reason such as the deontologism.

This last statement has been largely discussed in the previous chapters by saying that tolerance is not compatible with moral deontologism, and it has been backed up by Williams's general remarks about the impossibility of tolerance within the structure of the 'moral system' analyzed in the previous chapter. Williams's critiques, as we have seen, are directed towards the 'moral systems' and thought to denounce the failure that formal theories of morality face when dealing with substantive ethical concepts such as the one of 'tolerance.' As we have seen, Williams attributes these failures to the fact that these theories reduce ethical life as a whole into concepts such as 'duty' and 'obligation.' For him, no doubt these concepts play an important role in ethics still they fall short to explain the complexity of moral life as a whole. Ethical concerns, for Williams, are much wider and complex, and they encompass concepts such as friendship, family, society, personal interests and desires and moral theories need to make room for ideals such as social justice, empathy, solidarity, courage, gratitude. These concepts are thicker in nature and because of that they can have difficulties to be developed by principle or rule-based structures of practical reason.

This kind of thought towards contemporary moral philosophy follows the same line of criticism initiated by Elizabeth Anscombe in 1958 when she published her *Modern Moral Philosophy*.[1] Anscombe criticized modern moral philosophy's preoccupations with legal conceptions of ethics. For Anscombe, modern moral theories became blind by encapsulating ethics in the idea of universally applicable principles and by adopting a legalistic idea of morality. Anscombe's scope of analysis considered primarily J. S. Mill's and Henry Sidgwick's utilitarianism next to Kant's deontologism, but her conclusions are general to all kind of consequentialists and deontological theories that are constructed upon the perspective that moral rules impose certain kinds of obligations which should be applicable to any moral situation that we face.

What both perspectives have in common is the idea that modern moral theories, the ones that Williams inscribes into the 'moral system,' cannot deal with a big number of ethical issues because they sustain a very reduced perspective about morality. As Rosalind Hursthouse has put it:

> There are a number of different stories to be told about why an increasing dissatisfaction with deontology and utilitarianism should have resulted in the revival of virtue ethics, but certainly part of any story seems to be that the prevailing literature ignored or sidelined a number of topics that any adequate moral philosophy should address. Two I mentioned above—motives and moral character; others were moral education, moral wisdom or discernment, friendship and family relationships, a deep concept of happiness, the role of emotions in our moral life, and the questions of what sort of person I should be, and how we should live. And where do we find these topics discussed? Lo and behold, in Plato and Aristotle.[2]

In the case of tolerance, the examples offered before as the ones of the 'vegetarian mother' or 'fashion designer' show us that in order to give a full account of an exercise of this disposition we need to use notions such as the 'moral character' of the tolerator, or his/her rational capacities to go beyond the *mere* acceptance of moral principles. It has been argued that if liberals do not want tolerance to become a tyrannical mechanism of morality it must allow the tolerator to pay attention to his/her personal attachments, legitimate deep desires and the means he/she considers worthy for achieving a good life. If this is the case, tolerance as a moral ideal needs a more substantive theoretical base than the deontic account offered by some liberals. In that case, then, we need to change our theoretical and philosophical understanding of the acts of tolerance.

Williams and Anscombe, among other philosophers such as MacIntyre, Murdoch, Foot, Hursthouse and Nussbaum have advanced the influential idea that moral philosophy must turn toward a broader understanding of ethics that can strengthen the emphasis on other types of substantial concepts besides those of 'duty' and 'obligation.' What they propose, in sum, is that moral philosophy must to take an *aretaic turn*.

Taking into consideration the criticisms that have been made of deontological liberalism in previous chapters, mainly those related to the rule-following criteria, defended by deontological authors as the basic structure of morality, leaves us with an open question regarding the exercise of tolerant attitudes: if deontological moral theories (as any other kind of moral theory principle or rule-following centered) cannot give plausible answers to the problems raised by tolerance, mainly understood as a dispositional property, what other options are open?

There is a trademark in the moral conceptualization of tolerance that requires our attention: the idea that tolerance is a *dispositional property*. We must remember that this way of understanding tolerance has also been accepted and embraced by deontological liberal authors. What should we understand when deontologists state that tolerance is not a passing attitude or a one-time conduct but that it is something that can be "tested in diverse and reiterated circumstances,"[3] or when deontologists conceptualize tolerance as a "virtue of justice"[4] or as a virtue that must be practiced by citizens in a well ordered society?[5] What should we understand when deontological philosophers understand tolerance as a virtue, as a dispositional property or as a character trait, and later when they also describe it in terms of isolated acts?

Glen Newey has referred to this last problem as the *dual-predictability* of virtues which was explained in chapter 8. According to Newey, this strategy is recurrent within those theories that reduce virtue-based or *aretaic* concepts such as tolerance into a following rule criterion of moral action.[6] The dual-predictability of tolerance professed by deontologism sustains that the dispositional property allows us to classify some sort of actions as acts of tolerance without assuring that the individual who performs such action is a tolerant person him/herself. This phenomenon, according to Newey, is due to "a neglect of *character* (of modern moral theory) as an independent explanatory notion within ethical theory. Ethical theory establishes a set of prescriptions for theory-approved action, and generates from this a motivation, or set of motivations, which the agent ought to have [. . .] to possess virtue is then understood as having the disposition to be motivated to perform the theory-approved action(s)."[7] But to display a disposition of character adequately is not sufficient to say that we have been only guided by rules, other kind of elements must be present as well. At this point let us recall the words of Philippa Foot on this matter: "the man who is wise does not merely know *how* to do good things such as looking after his children well, or strengthening someone in trouble, but must also want to do them. And then wisdom, in so far as it consists of knowledge which anyone can gain in the course of an ordinary life, is available to anyone who really wants it."[8]

The point raised by Foot and Newey must catch our attention in at least one way: being acquainted with moral rules and principles and being able to follow them in relevant circumstances does not suffice for acting as a virtuous person. This means that not interfering in the acts of someone else that we disapprove of because there is a principle that obliges me to not interfere does not mean that we are actually being tolerant. If we notice, the difference marked by Foot and Newey leads us to consider the possibility that if our conception of tolerance is exclusively related to those acts of not interfering merely guided by the existence of one principle (or several principles) we might be reducing in an unjustified way the moral ideal of tolerance as a whole. As Robert Audi has recently put it:

> the adverbial forms of virtue terms—such as "courageously," "honestly," and "justly" [or "tolerantly"]—can apply to actions not performed from the relevant virtues, and even to actions aimed at pretending to manifest those virtues. Given this *thin use of virtue terms*, the distinction between action merely in conformity with virtue and action from it may be regarded as a special case of a distinction between conduct of a behaviourally specified type e.g. meting out equal shares, and conducts described mainly in terms of how it is to be explained, e.g. as done from a sense of justice.[9]

For aretaic based concepts, such as tolerance, it is not sufficient to say that an action is the morally correct action when it is of the right *type* according to the prescriptions of moral rules. This reductivism, I believe, has been caused by the way which deontological moral theories take moral acts to be the right acts. In Kantian moral theories 'right actions' are defined in terms of their compliance with moral duty. Of course the reductivism I am referring to is related in some ways to the old philosophical quarrel between deontological and virtue ethics regarding the difference between acting *from inclination* and acting *from duty*.[10] Still, the specific point I wish to refer to is one of the sources of this reductivism. We can find these sources in the structure of deontological theories that frames moral conducts into a world of opposite binary concepts: permitted/prohibited. Ronald Dworkin, for example, in *A Matter of Principle* sustains the idea that legal concepts (and moral concepts in general) are 'dispositive concepts' of the sort that if "the concept holds in a particular situation, then judges have the duty, at least prima facie, to decide some legal claim one way; but if the concept does not hold, then judges have the duty, at least *prima facie*, to decide the same claim in the opposite way."[11] Under these terms an action is either right or wrong, therefore, it will be odd to say that two different courses of action under the same circumstances can both be right or can both be wrong. This is the bivalence thesis taken as the regular discourse in modern moral philosophy with the intention to disappear all the different kind of normative gaps. The expression 'right action,' together with its other applications and associations: 'required/obligatory,' 'forbidden/permissible,' is taken to be unique in character and the quintessence of any rational moral discourse.

The point in hand is that aretaic concepts do not rule themselves under these terms. Aretaic concepts, on the contrary, are based on terms of *good, well* and *virtuous*, rather than deontic ones such as *right, duty* or *obligation*. Virtues favor "talking in terms of *good* action (*eupraxia*), of acting *well* (or badly), rather than in terms of *right* action."[12] That is the reason why Hursthouse can imagine a situation where two generous parents act completely different with their children and both act well. Aretaic concepts allow the possibility of two virtuous agents facing the same circumstances to act differently. This possibility marks the difference between two different moral perspectives: one based only on *duty* and another partly based on *inclination*.

It has already been argued on tensions that a morality based on a sense of duty can create with tolerance, but on the top of that, we must also be aware that to tolerate out of duty removes great deal of the essence of a full tolerant agent; to tolerate under a full conviction of being practicing an act of justice. This difference will be made clear once we explore the meaning of tolerance as a dispositional property.

The term 'disposition' has raised several discussions in the history of philosophy which I do not intend to introduce here.[13] Providing a fully adequate account of these discussions is difficult, still, it is important to have at least a basic idea of what is understood under a 'dispositional property' when it is alluded to tolerance. Normally it is accepted that a disposition is a kind of property which is characteristic of a certain object. Properties can be of two kinds: *dispositional* or *categorical*. To explain the difference between these two we can turn to Kevin Timpe's example:

> Compare the solubility of a sugar-cube in water with its volume. The sugar-cube's solubility means that it would dissolve if placed in water. The sugar-cube need not actually be placed in water to be soluble; one simply sees that it is soluble when it is placed in water. In contrast, one need not do anything to the sugar-cube to see that it has the categorical

property of volume, for the sugar-cube always manifest this property
in a way that it does not always manifest solubility in water.[14]

Dispositional properties, such as the solubility of sugar, involve condi-
tionality while categorical properties, such as the volume of the sugar, do
not. Still, if we take dispositional properties in such a simple way they
will not differ much from categorical properties at least in one important
aspect: both, understood in this way, are taken to be something that
objects or individuals do not acquire voluntarily: some people might
have the disposition to blush when embarrassed or to sneeze when it gets
dusty, this without willing to blush or to sneeze, just as some people are
taller and others are shorter. In the case of categorical properties this does
not appear to be a problem. But in the case of dispositional ones it does. If
we think otherwise, then neither tolerance nor virtues in general, can be
understood as something that we cherish and practice voluntarily. In that
case, it would make sense to say that someone has been involuntarily
tolerant or involuntarily generous.

In part, this problem arrives to us when we relate dispositional properties to mere habits of conduct. A habit may be defined as a certain
acquired regularity of acting.[15] Some habits even become involuntary
reactions to some state of affairs. But this is not the notion of 'dispositional property' that deontologists use, nor is it the one that the rest of moral
philosophers have in mind. Reason must be present in any account of
'dispositional property' in order to take it out of that ford of involuntari-
ness where they can be drawn. Stephen Darwall captures this idea nicely:
"Those dispositions which constitute character [. . .] are dispositions to
act for certain reasons, that is, to act, and in acting to have certain reasons
for acting."[16]

When dispositions are not conceived as inherently related to reason,
they cannot become constitutive features of a moral character. This is
something that we have known about moral dispositions since Aristotle:

> none of the moral virtues are present in us by nature, since nothing that
> exists by nature is habituated to be other than it is. For example, a
> stone, because it is borne downward by nature, could not be habituated
> to be borne upward, not even if someone habituates it by throwing it
> upward ten thousand times. Fire too could not be borne downward,
> nor could anything else that is naturally one way be habituated to be
> another. Neither by nature, therefore, nor contrary to nature are the
> virtues present; they are instead present in us who are of such a nature
> as to receive them, and who are completed through habit.[17]

Then moral dispositions differ from mere physical dispositions such as
the solubility of sugar because they also include the idea of reason and
willingness. However they are still being considered conditional, as Aristotle has taught us, because nobody is born with moral dispositions per
se. On the contrary, moral dispositions are acquired through experience

and practical behavior, they rely on habit and trained practical reason. The conjunction between habituation, reason and will is the one that gives meaning to the term 'excellences' or 'virtues.'[18]

Disregarding the substantial differences that we can find between various virtue ethicists (either they defend an eudemonistic perspective of virtues or an agent based account, or an ethics of care), all contemporary developments in the field depart from Aristotle's theoretical structure and this has a reason: Aristotle has set the bases for a full account of ethical virtues, and it is from his account that we can find a real rival moral perspective to deontological theories. In this sense, it is important for us to start by considering some of the basic premises of his account. For the purposes that I have in mind in these last two chapters, I will focus exclusively in the relation between virtues and some sort of particularism.

Aristotle describes ethical virtues in terms of "states," "condition" or "disposition" (*hexis*). Virtues are understood under his terms as tendencies or dispositions, induced by habits, to have appropriate feelings.[19] In the second Book of the *Nicomachean Ethics* Aristotle distinguishes between two different kinds of excellences: those of the *intellect* and those of *character*.[20] The first kind of excellences is defined by Aristotle as excellences of thought, excellences that include epistemic and intellectual virtues such as technical expertise and practical wisdom. We can acquire these excellences through instruction and experience. The second kind of excellences, those of character, is defined by Aristotle as dispositions to act and feel in certain ways. These other excellences are the result of habituation or customs.

Certainly, moral education and personality development are a major part of virtue ethics. Moral development relies on the availability of good role models. Virtue ethicists do not disregard what Hursthouse has called "mother's-knee rules" such as 'Don't lie,' 'Keep promises,' 'Help others,' "although it is a mistake to define a virtuous agent simply as one disposed to act in accordance with deontologist's moral rules."[21] Of course, if virtuosity was to be explained by the idea that individuals know how to follow rules, the whole of virtue ethics would be absorbed by deontology. But "[v]irtue ethicists want to emphasize the fact that if children are to be taught to be honest, they must be taught to love and prize the truth, and that *merely* teaching them not to lie will not achieve this end."[22] If we pay close attention to this understanding of moral dispositions then it becomes difficult to attach the idea of tolerance as a virtue to a simple principle-based theory as deontologists do.

The difference between a *mere* rule-following structure as the deontological one and a virtue perspective is explained in Aristotle's ethics through the intrinsic relationship that according to him exists between the two kinds of excellences: those of the *intellect* and those of *character*. But mainly, this difference is to be found in how Aristotle relates *practical wisdom* (which is considered as an intellectual virtue) and the *excellences of character*. The relation between practical wisdom and the dispositions of a moral character is to be found in Aristotle's idea of "proper proportion," which he describes as a mean between two extremes: "Excellence [of character], then, is a disposition issuing in decisions, depending on intermediacy of the kind relative to us, this being determined by rational prescription and in the way in which a wise person would determine it. And it is intermediacy between two bad states, one involving excess, the other involving deficiency." [23]

In some passages in Book VI of the *Nicomachean Ethics*, Aristotle argues that a right action, the one that finds the intermediate point between two bad states, cannot be achieved without an exercise of practical wisdom (*phronesis*). [24] In that same Book, he argues that practical wisdom makes our deliberations be correctly guided towards the good that has been defined by virtue:

> First, then, let us say that wisdom and prudence are necessarily choice worthy in themselves, since each of them is a virtue of each part [of the soul] even if neither one of them makes or produces anything. Second, they do in fact make or produce something, not as the art of medicine produces health, but, rather, just as health produces health, so wisdom produces happiness. For wisdom, being a part of the whole of virtue, makes one happy by being possessed and by being active. Further, the relevant work is completed in accord with prudence and moral virtue. For virtue makes the target correct, prudence the things conducive to that target. [25]

It should be clear that Aristotle is not offering us a decision procedure; on the contrary, he insists that that this is something that ethical theories cannot do. What must be done in any particular occasion depends on the circumstances, and these vary from one occasion to another. This explains why he thinks that a practically wise person has a special sensitivity to evaluate in every situation the morally relevant features for acting correctly. Here it is important to stress the expressions "in every situation" and "on any particular occasion."

For Aristotle, as for almost all virtue ethicist, an a priori arithmetic method that can elucidate the middle point between two bad states does not exist. The intermediate point between them varies from one situation to another. Virtue lies in means that must arrive at a balanced decision in each situation. Or, the means are to be determined in a way that takes into account the particular circumstances. We must remember that for Aristotle "prudence is not concerned with the universals alone but must also be acquainted with the particulars: it is bound up with action, and action concerns the particulars." [26] A virtuous person knows that sometimes circumstances require a small degree of anger, while others, might call for great anger. To know which the correct reaction is, one needs a careful reading of the particular features presented by each circumstance.

For modern virtue ethicists such as Murdoch, McDowell and Blum, moral sensitivity or moral perception about particulars, in this Aristotelian way of understanding, play a major role in any moral deliberation. As it is known, Murdoch gives a central role to perception in ethics. She calls this perception the "loving attention."[27]

For Murdoch, the moral endeavor takes place in personal relationships such as friendship and family relations. The loving attention to a friend or to our child requires from us to understand their needs and assure that they are met. For Murdoch, "The moral task is not a matter of finding universalizable reasons or principles of action, but of getting oneself to attend to the reality of individual other persons."[28] McDowell follows very closely the conception of Murdoch about moral perception. McDowell speaks about sensitivities to aspects of moral reality as being 'salient' for the agent.[29]

Newey says that for McDowell "the virtues can be regarded as circumstantial sensitivities which are quasi-cognitive in character, but irreducible to the grasp of a set of rules; basically this sensitivity tells the agent in the circumstances what to do. Virtue, qua circumstantial sensitivity, also confers on its possessor an appropriate motive."[30] And Newey is right about this. McDowell following Aristotle's idea of practical wisdom connects the importance of perception to the limitations of an ethic based on rules and procedures arguing that rules cannot capture the full moral sensitivity of a person of good.

For Lawrence Blum, traditional rule (principle)-based accounts of morality lack three distinct moral operations. The first one, according to Blum, is the idea of Perception: "perceiving features of a situation confronting one, including the perceptual individuating of the 'situation' as a morally significant one." The second one that Blum mentions is Recognition: "recognizing those features as morally significant ones, to be taken into account in deliberating about what to do." The third is Discernment: "knowing how to implement the principles one takes to be conclusive in determining what to do."[31]

We can say that all virtue-based accounts of morality share essentially the same philosophical framework and the same concerns regarding contemporary moral theory. All of them share the same Aristotelian roots and the same disenchantment about modern moral theory. The criticisms that they have raised to rule(principle)-based theories is that they cannot give a full account of morality as it is in our lives. Nevertheless, the criticisms have passed the frontiers of expressing what is wrong about those kinds of theories and have advanced concrete proposals.

Regarding the problems that have been pointed out throughout this work, specifically speaking, those related to the universal character of moral norms, their priority over ethics and the impartiality thesis, need a response from some other structure of practical reason which is compatible with the idea of tolerance understood as a moral disposition or as a character trait.

At the end of chapter 14 "Tolerance in the Moral System," I pointed out that moral universalism can be understood from two different perspectives. One of these perspectives is directly derived from Kant's thought, and the other was introduced by Richard Hare. The first type of universalistic thesis, the Kantian one, dictates that a person must act in accordance with the principle that states that the maxim of their acts is to become a universal law.[32] In other words, this principle requires that if someone wants to act in a morally correct manner, one has to ask oneself whether the way in which one is acting is the way in which every single rational agent should act. On the other hand, the moral universalist principle, held by philosophers such as Hare, maintains that if an agent decides $X$ in circumstances $C$, he/she must necessarily also decide $X$ in a case $C'$ that features the same relevant characteristics contained in $C$.[33] In the instances where I have criticized moral universalism I have done so because it does not grant the possibility to tolerate an act $a$ of an agent $X$ and later not tolerating an act $a'$ (that shares the same relevant characteristics than $a$) of an agent $Y$. In this part I will discuss this second way of understanding the universality principle.

I have said that this form of universalism linked to tolerance can be objected in at least two ways. The first one is a critique upon which I have been insisting: in cases of tolerance the thesis of consistency that moral universalism imposed on practical reasoning has, indisputably, important normative repercussions for the basic systems of values. This way of configuring tolerance takes it to a counterintuitive conclusion: each act of tolerance strengthens the realm of intolerances. There is no doubt that the number of convictions that an individual may come to sustain are finite. To moral deontologism every act of tolerance is unrepeatable. Because of reasons of consistency and coherence, the universality principle takes that if an act of the class $A$ has been 'tolerated' once, then any other act of the same class $A$ cannot be tolerated again. This consequence of course is underlined by the deontological thesis of the priority of the 'right' over the 'good' which frames tolerance into a world of opposite binary concepts. According to this perspective, then: if we decide to 'allow' (tolerate) an act or a conduct that injures one of our relevant convictions we are constrained in future cases to keep 'allowing' the same kind of acts and conducts because in the first exercise of tolerance we realize that our conviction cannot be morally enforced upon others. Vice versa, if we decide not to tolerate an act or a conduct that injures one of our relevant convictions it is because, after a balancing procedure, we come to realize that such a conviction was morally justified and therefore it has to be 'moralized' (taken as reasonable using Rawls's terms). In such a case we are morally constrained to not tolerate any future cases that share the same relevant characteristics. Described in that sense, tolerance for logical reasons becomes suicidal.

I emphasize the fact that this happens due to logical reasons because it could be counter-argued that morally speaking tolerance must have limits because otherwise it will lose all of its sense. Definitely, it is not morally acceptable to tolerate everything. Nonetheless, locating tolerance under an aretaic perspective offers a response to the problems of the limits that can be called: *the contextual response*. The contextual response deals with the problems of the limits of tolerance in a completely different way. The context in which the problems of tolerance arise, "including its historical antecedents and the larger social setting in which it arises, will determine its nature, the resources for its solution, and whatever solution the problem admits of."[34] This is the "contextual response." Instead of trying to reach a determined catalogue of conducts and acts that are intolerable beforehand, the contextual response would agree on the fact that not everything is tolerable, yet we need to know what is tolerable and what is not tolerable according to the contextually relevant features that give rise to the conflict in the first place. In this sense, the contextual response proposed here will not abandon the idea that there are things that cannot be tolerated, but still, it abandons the idea of a fixed set of intolerable things as moral deontologism pretends. We could say that according to this perspective the limits of tolerance are to be imposed by the relevance that moral reasons would acquire in relation to the specific circumstances of tolerance. This perspective rejects the deontological thesis "that moral considerations are fixed from eternity in a form that is perfectly precise and consistent."[35] Furthermore, it will favor the possibility of reestablishing tolerance as a dispositional property to be evaluated in terms of *good action* (*eupraxia*), or acting well, rather than in terms of 'right/wrong' actions.

## NOTES

1. Anscombe, "Modern Moral Philosophy."
2. Rosalind Hursthouse, *On Virtue Ethics* (Oxford University Press, 1999), 2–3.
3. Garzón, "No pongas," 182.
4. Forst, "Toleration, Justice," 71.
5. Rawls, *Political*, 194.
6. Newey, *Virtue*, 5, 87–94.
7. Newey, *Virtue*, 5–6. (Parentheses are mine)
8. Phillippa Foot, *Virtues and Vices and Other Essays in Moral Philosophy* (Los Angeles, University of California Press, 1978), 6.
9. Robert Audi, "Acting from Virtue," *Mind*, 104, 415 (1995): 451. (Brackets and emphasis added)
10. Robert C. Bartlett and Susan D. Collins, trans., *Aristotle's Nicomachean Ethics: A new translation* (University of Chicago Press, 2011), Book 1, Ch 8, 16, (1099a12); Kant, *Groundwork*, 13–15; Hursthouse, *On Virtue*, 92–94.
11. Dworkin, *A Matter*, 119.

12. Hursthouse, *On Virtue*, 69.

13. For example, Gilbert Ryle, *Concept of Mind* (London & New York, Routledge, 2009), chapter 5; D.M. Armstrong, *A Materialist Theory of Mind* (London & New York, Routledge, 1993); J. L. Mackie, *Truth, Probability and Paradox: Studies in Philosophical Logic* (Oxford University Press, 1973); D. H. Mellor, "In Defense of Dispositions," *The Philosophical Review*, 83 (1974): 158–181; A. D. Smith, "Dispositional Properties," *Mind*, 86, 343 (1977): 439–445, among many others, that have discussed the conceptual features of the term 'disposition'.

14. Kevin Timpe, "Moral Character," *Internet Encyclopedia of Philosophy* (2008), accessed September 2, 2015.

15. Georg Henrik von Wright, *The Varieties of Goodness* (New York, Routledge & Kegan Paul, 1963), 143.

16. Stephen L. Darwall, "Two Kinds of Respect," *Ethics*, 88, 1 (1977): 43.

17. Aristotle, Book 2, Ch 1, p. 26, (1103a18).

18. Foot, *Virtues and Vices*, 6.

19. Aristotle, Book 2, Ch 2.

20. Aristotle, Book 2, Ch 1, p. 26, (1103a15).

21. Hursthouse, *On Virtue*, 19.

22. Hursthouse, *On Virtue*, 19.

23. Aristotle, Book 2, Ch 6, (1106b36–1107a4). (Brackets are mine)

24. Aristotle, Book 6, Ch. 2, pp. 116–ss, (1139a20).

25. Aristotle, Book 6, Ch. 12, p. 131, (1144a).

26. Aristotle, Book 6, Ch 7, p. 124, (1141b15).

27. Murdoch, *The Sovereignty*, 64–65.

28. Lawrence A. Blum, "Iris Murdoch and the Domain of the Moral," *Philosophical Studies*, 50 (1986): 343.

29. John McDowell, "Virtue and Reason," *The Monist*, 62 (1979): 345.

30. Newey, *Virtue*, 112.

31. Lawrence Blum, "Moral Perception and Particularity," *Ethics*, 101, 4 (1991): 714.

32. Kant, *Fundamental Principles*, 71; Nino, *Ética*, 110–111.

33. Hare, *Freedom*, 30–31.

34. James D. Wallace, *Moral Relevance and Moral Conflict* (New York, Cornell University Press, 1988), 53.

35. Wallace, *Moral Relevance*, 53.

# SEVENTEEN

# The Contextual Response

Until now I have argued that tolerance by being a virtue (as a disposition-al property) is not compatible with a scheme of practical reason that is exclusively based on the idea that following rules or principles which only respond to a 'right/wrong' criterion is the essence of morality. If tolerance is a virtue, it requires what other virtues do: a perspective of practical reason sensitive enough to contexts and emotions. This perspective is the one I have called the contextual response to deontological theories. The contextual response tends to uphold an aretaic understanding of tolerance by providing a perspective of practical reason more committed to the particular features of moral problems than to the mere idea of following universal binding rules.

The contextual response is related in some points to the moral particularism defended by Jonathan Dancy; though, not to his entire theory. I agree mainly with his objections against universal ("generalist" in his terms) and impartial moral criteria and with his constant concern about the deontological negligence towards contextual salient features. However the contextual response that I am advancing will not agree with his proposal as a whole. For example I do not agree with his rejection of moral principles and rules. It is important to clarify that accepting the existence of rules and principles does not contradict the idea of an aretai-cally centred practical reason. Rosalind Hursthouse has argued that virtue ethics is also based in rules just that they are different in the way they work in our reasoning: "not only does each virtue generate a prescription—do what is honest, charitable, generous- but each vice a prohition—do not do what is dishonest, uncharitable, mean." In the case of Hursthouse these rules are called *V-Rules*.[1]

In this sense, the contextual response to the conflicts of tolerance accepts the existence of many different moral considerations, including the existence of rules and principles that in a way reflect the complexity of human life and the variety of problems faced living such a life, but it also defends the idea that "generally, acting reasonable and intelligently in practical matters consists in more than just doing what rules say, more, that just passively and blindly following the rules."[2] Wallace has summed up this as follows:

> Unless we are to remain morons, practically speaking, we must at the same time learn to adapt the ways we learn to circumstances that vary in indefinitely many ways from the circumstances in which we were taught.[3]
> [. . .]
> The intelligent individual actively applies rules to the matter at hand.[4]

To make this clear, I will first refer to Dancy's arguments with which the contextual response agrees, and later I will explain the kind of particularism that is adopted by the contextual response.

One aspect in which this response deeply agrees with Dancy is that the quality that deontological philosophers claim to be their strongest resource is in fact their worst vice. Dancy says that:

> [The] technical virtue of the account is that it gives a good sense to the idea that moral principles, if true, are necessarily true. Traditionally, this idea amounts to one of three things. The first is the useless idea that if this action is right, then any action similar to it in all non-moral respects is right. [. . .] The second thought is not uselessly true, but grotesquely false. This is that if this action is right because of its F-ness, then any action that is F is necessarily right. [. . .] The third thought is that if a property is morally relevant in one case, it necessarily has the same relevance wherever it recurs.[5]

As stated by Dancy, it seems that the universalistic weakness lies in its rigid logical scheme. This characteristic of moral universalism is the one that, in section IV, made us wonder about its moral qualities. Some of the reasons that have been previously proposed refer to the idea that deontologism is logically impaired when it comes to speak reiteratively about tolerance within situations that have the same relevant characteristics. Regarding this point Dancy proposes two ways of criticizing moral universalism. One refers to the *internal* problems that we can find within its structure, the other refers to the kind of *motivation* that is offered by moral universalism.

According to Dancy, one of the central problems of the notion of universalism begins with its contention that "a person who makes a moral judgment is committed to making the same judgment of any relevantly similar situation."[6] There are two kinds of arguments that follow from this stance. The first one, to which Dancy pays most of his attention, is directed at the internal structure of universalism. The second one, which has been developed with great precision by John McDowell, attempts to mine the motivational criteria that this proposal may have.[7] It is true that, even though they are presented as two different arguments, both of them overlap to a certain degree. They manage to be consistent. However, since I have explained before, McDowell's idea of the moral sensitivities to the reality of the individual, for the purposes of supporting the contextual response, now I will only focus on Dancy's argument concerning the *internal* problems.

Dancy begins his argument with a devastating affirmation: "the doctrine of universalizability is clearly false."[8] Of course, these sorts of affirmations require strong support; it is not enough to declare it false as for us to accept his argument. Especially when in Western moral philosophy this doctrine has governed moral philosophy for quite a long time. Dancy grounds his affirmation saying that, in first place, "I cannot possibly be obliged to make the same judgment wherever that same set of limited properties recurs. For there may in a new case be a strong reason against the judgment which was not present in the first case [. . .]."[9] Dancy calls these types of reasons "*defeaters.*"

We do not require necessarily that the "defeaters" be absent in the first case. On the contrary, they could also have been present in that case, but they may have acted with far less intensity than the one in the second case. Dancy explains this by using the following example which is quite enlightening:

> For instance, the first action is kind and generous but a bit thoughtless. We approve of it for its kindness and generosity, not for its thoughtlessness. The second action is just as kind and generous, but grossly thoughtless. We many now wish to disapprove of this action, but the doctrine of universalizability, as formulated, prevents us from doing so unless we revise our opinion of the first action.[10]

It is certain that universalists at this point could argue that instead of paying attention to the reasons in favor of the first action (its kindness and generosity) we should pay attention to the entire group of reasons, those that are in favor as well as those that go against our acceptance (kindness, generosity and thoughtlessness). However, Dancy replies to this universalistic strategy with this other counter-example:

> [. . .] suppose a man knocks a woman down with his car and puts her into the hospital. When he pays for special care for her, visits her and so on, we approve of his (subsequent) actions. They are expressions of regret and an attempt to make amends so far as possible, and these facts are our reasons for approval. We are not therefore committed to approving of any other person who behaves in exactly the same way, but whose ultimate purpose is to seduce the woman away from her husband. And we cannot escape this point by saying that the fact that the first person had no ultimate purpose of seduction was among our reasons for approval.[11]

Faced with this, the advocates of universalism would be tempted to further broaden the universalistic base. They would now require the similarities to extend past all the factors operating in favor of and against the original judgments, all the way through to the presence or absence of certain factors that might have, to some extent, affected the original moral judgment. Of course, what would happen at this point is that the basis for the doctrine of moral universality would begin to expand in a way that it has never done it before. This would entail that eventually, at any given time, universalizability would falter by having to include within its base of similar relevant criteria all the natural properties included under each individual case, therefore losing the structure that it had maintained so far.

I find this situation, presented by Dancy's arguments, to be highly enlightening. On the one hand, because one of the most important problems presented by the agents of tolerance is assuming the commitment to logical consistency that universalism imposes on them. At the same time however, the agents of tolerance that remained entrenched within universalism's moral perspectives suffered from a sort of moral *vertigo* each time they were faced with the idea of not assuming the thesis of universal consistency and began to think that it could be right for them to tolerate an action $X$ today and tomorrow not tolerate an action $X'$, that shares the same relevant characteristics. This situation, as I have previously argued, cornered them into having to eliminate (or to moralize) one of their moral convictions from their basic normative systems.

According to the practical consequences of the theory of universalism, this situation meant that the elimination of a conviction did not entail a moral loss or regret. On the contrary, it implied that the elimination was the result of a practical deliberation that concluded the falsity of said conviction. I will not dwell in particular on the situation of the feelings of loss or regret that acts of tolerance may generate, because in the following paragraph I will say something in this respect. For the time being, I will address the tension that is generated between the doctrine of moral universality and the virtue of tolerance.

It seems that if we pay close attention to Dancy's critiques, they should free us from the theoretical perplexity we encountered with the examples of the liberal vegetarian mother and the fashion designer presented in the previous chapters. Within the theoretical perspective of moral universality, these problems appeared to be much more tragic than they do now. The difference between the university professor and the fashion designer was, precisely, the presence of a group of reasons that defeated the professor's tolerance of his wife's ruffled shirt, and which in turn granted the designer the opportunity not to tolerate it.

Before delving into the central point of this situation, I must mention that the moral particularism defended by Dancy is not only dedicated to attack universalism through the use of counterexamples. Dancy's defense of moral particularism is more profound than the simple exercise of finding ingenious examples that serve to place universalism in a bind. Dancy's critique of universalism covers three routes. Dancy criticizes the three main figures that subscribe to theories of moral universalism: the *atomist* conception of moral reasons, the *supervenience* relationship and the *subsumptive* model. In what follows, I will only focus on the critiques of the *atomist* conception and the *subsumptive* model because these are the two characteristics that generate most of the problems for the moral ideal of tolerance.

Dancy criticizes the atomist conception of the theories of universalizability (generalists) by saying that one of the problems of universalism is found in the way it conceives moral reasons within practical reason. Universalists think that every situation can be described in terms of a combination of independent (atomic) and irreducible elements. For example, a moral norm or principle may stipulate 'a,' 'b,' 'c' and 'd' as relevant properties that serve to determine the moral wrongness (or immorality) of a given action. Now let us suppose that, within a particular action, the properties present are 'a' and 'd,' and that their presence is enough for that behavior to be considered as morally incorrect according to universalism's logical criteria.

Instead, Dancy's particularism sustains a *holistic* conception of moral reasons.[12] The moral relevance of each one of the properties that appear within a case is granted by the specific circumstances and context within which the stated properties have occurred. Martínez Zorrilla explains this as follows:

> Let us suppose that "a" means "communicating false information" (lying). Under a universalist conception, the notion that an individual action can be subsumptive in "a" always constitutes (for logical reasons) a moral reason (a morally relevant element), precisely because it is taken into account by a norm of the system. Instead, for particularism, the notion that lying may have moral relevance (irrespective as to whether it favors or goes against the correction of the behavior) depends on the context within which it is situated and, therefore on the many other elements that are also present in each concrete situation.[13]

Accepting that the moral relevance of the properties is granted by the circumstances and the context from where they emerge is highly relevant for the idea of tolerance as I have defended. The other criticism that Dancy makes refers to the subsumptive model. Of course, the criticism he directs against the atomist conception is closely related to it. This model of rationality understands moral reasoning as the practice of subsuming facts into norms. Any fact that is contained within the normative presumptions of a rule or principle must entail the consequences foreseen by such rule or principle. If the moral norm prohibits lying, any act in which we find the property of "not telling the truth" will be morally incorrect.

Under this form of moral reasoning we tend to overlook properties or *"salient features"* that *"shape"* the concrete situation.[14]

Dancy's critique is directed from what he calls a "narrative rationality" that enters into contrast with the "subsumptive rationality." Dancy explains this difference with an aesthetic example: he compares this situation with one in which someone attempts to describe a building from an artistic point of view as opposed to a purely architectural point of view. The latter way of describing the building would only focus on matters relating to the materials used, the dimensions, proportions and technical shapes of the construction, while the former one would take other striking factors into account, such as certain contrasts between the geometric shapes, the shadows they generate, particular details, etc., which are ultimately those that help us to issue a judgment on the beauty or ugliness of the building.[15]

The aesthetic analogy is not purely artificial for Dancy. Actually, Dancy thinks that moral discourse is, to a greater or lesser extent, a *perception* more than deductive reasoning; understanding the situation has more to do with *examining* the case and *seeing* what elements stand out and configuring an evaluation, than it does with elaborating syllogisms.

These two criticisms made to universalism and the way in which Dancy configures moral thought help us to see the "dilemma of tolerance" and the problem of the "limits" from quite a different perspective. Let us bear in mind that we have accepted the notion which states that an act of tolerance is configured by three circumstances. All of them require, using Dancy's terminology, that we take into account the *salient* features of the circumstances of the case. That is to say, first of all the tolerator has to assess whether the injured conviction is morally relevant in the face of the concrete circumstances, then he/she has to evaluate his/her hierarchical quality in the face of the individual who harmed his/her conviction, and later has to balance the concrete situation as to decide if it is morally permissible to tolerate something that he/she believes is wrong.

Then, from the perspective of the subsumptive rationality the cases of tolerance initiate with a form of: X is doing *a*, in accordance with the norm N: *a* is morally incorrect, therefore, I must condemn conduct X. According to the structure of subsumptive rationality, the moral reasoning would come there to an end. For acts of tolerance, the model is complicated by several variants.

The reasoning in these cases could be presented as follows: X is doing *a*, in accordance with my relevant conviction (norm) N: *a* is morally incorrect, and I have the necessary competence (or power) to stop the conduct of X, *however. . .* And it is at this point where the normative conflicts are generated by tolerance. The agent of tolerance reflects upon the existence of another norm contained within his/her system that prohibits him/her from applying the consequence contemplated. In the previous chapters it was said, precisely, that the dilemma of tolerance must be understood as a dilemma in concreto. The two norms in conflict can consistently coexist within a normative system in abstracto. Nonetheless, there are factors foreign to the subsumptive reasoning that make that moral agents have to face normative incompatibility or inconsistency to which makes reference the 'however' referred to above.

Before I have explained that the conceptual requirement of having competence to tolerate something was not as simple as the fact of subsuming our position under the content of certain rule (legal, moral, social, convivial, etc.); rather we also had to take into account the 'role' that was being played at the time being. It is because of this that a friend can suffer from the smoke of my cigarette when we meet in my office for a chat, but can refrain from tolerating my smoking when we meet at his place, or that my boss can tolerate my chatter during an office meeting and suffer it when we are in the theater. According to what has been defended, the factors that define the competence we have to tolerate certain conduct are contextually dependent.

Something similar happens with the normative force of my moral convictions. It is possible for a father to tolerate his son drinking coca-cola at a party and not tolerate it when they are at home. The circumstances can change the normative force of the injured conviction. This is, broadly speaking, what I meant under the 'however.'

The case of the liberal vegetarian mother can also be reconstructed in these terms. It is possible that, up until this moment, she has allowed other people to eat red meat in front of her. We could say that this conduct has been guided, among other things, by the firm conviction that she does not have the necessary competence to change or interfere with the preferences of other people on the one hand, or the lack of moral sensitivity of some individuals on the other. In those cases, she did not have the necessary competence to speak of tolerance, and hence we would not say that she tolerated these situations. What we could say is that she was indifferent—although given the moral relevance of her conviction, this is unlikely. Another possibility is that she was being patient. However, in the case of her son, first and foremost, she does believe that she has the necessary competence (being his mother) to prohibit him from eating red meat.

Nonetheless, it should be remembered that the problem she finds herself facing is that she also sustains a conviction according to which it is morally required to allow the free development of her son's personality. This situation undoubtedly intensifies her situation, because she knows that if she were to intervene in (i.e. not tolerate) her son's substantive decisions, she could, to a certain degree, infringe upon her liberal ideals. The fact that we are dealing with her *son* can no doubt be considered as one of the reasons that 'triggers' the mechanism of tolerance and increases the normative strength of her conviction. That is to say, the liberal mother had not been cornered into thinking about tolerance when another person from outside the scope of her intimate relationships ate red meat. Therefore, the matter could be considered as the first case, in a series of cases of tolerance. In this sense, if the vegetarian mother were to adopt a moral deontological perspective she would have to opt between one of the two convictions at stake: the moral reasons that she has for being vegetarian and for objecting the slaughter of animals for human consumption or allowing people to autonomously develop their own plans of life.

Nonetheless, it is not necessary to commit to this type of criterion in order to sustain the possibility of a morally justified decision. In the case that haunts the vegetarian mother, she can argue that tolerating her son's inclinations as a hamburger lover does not necessarily imply that her conviction will have to be eliminated.

Certainly, deontologists would say that this decision cannot be taken as morally justified because the mother is conditioning a moral judgment and, also, that she has changed her 'attitude' towards that norm. Also they could say that in fact she is adapting the norm depending on the circumstances in an arbitrary way. But the reasons that sustain this moral judgment relate to her role as a mother and, therefore, cannot be extended to any other cases that may present similar general characteristics. However, her status as mother also doubles up as the reason for tolerance, playing also the role of a relevant characteristic that is absent in the rest of possible cases.

Until now I have presented the part of Dancy's moral particularism that supports the idea of the contextual response. The general idea has been that in situations of tolerance, circumstances and particular contexts define the weight that each set of reasons have for deciding whether to tolerate or not. This situation relates concretely to the tension referred above between the in concreto conflicts of tolerance and the thesis of moral universalism, a tension that I have thus far been attempting to denounce.

However, the contextual response based on aretaic concepts such as *good, well,* or *virtuous* does not walk all the way down the road accompanied by Dancy's theory. Doing otherwise would suggest that the contextual response also denies the existence of moral principles and rules; as Dancy's moral particularism does. By doing this it will appear that the contextual response abdicates any possibility of moral objectivity that is harnessed by the mere idea of tolerance (and to virtues in general). This, in consequence, would link this position to a certain kind of relativism: the kind that sustains that an act has concrete and unrepeatable circumstances; therefore, the idea of norms ruling conduct is impossible.

As it has been said before, the contextual response does not fully accept Dancy's particularism. In this sense, it is important to clarify which kind of particularism guides the idea of the contextual response to tolerance. Cullity and Holton point out the existence of two theses held by moral particularism: (1) on the one hand, we find the thesis that states that there are no moral principles in the sense that they are usually conceived by universalistic thought, and (2) on the other hand, we have the thesis that states that at least some of the empirical circumstances of a case lack a "fixed" moral relevance (always in favor of or always against its correction), rather that these may vary depending on the context.[16]

Dancy's particularism defends both theses jointly. The contextual response only defends the second one. This would qualify the contextual response as a *particularism of reasons*, in contrast with Dancy's theory that defends a particularism of rules and a particularism of reasons at the same time. In this way, the contextual response defends the importance of rules and principles. However, it links their normative weight to the context within which they are being invoked. The central thesis of this posture is that, even though rules and principles might have certain specific contents, they acquire different relevance and normative strength depending on the individual circumstances of each and every case in point.

An act of tolerance is always trapped between something that is *important* and valuable for our life and something that is morally required by an ideal of how we should behave with others. Taken in that way, any decision has the probability to come accompanied by a sense of loss or regret. The objection raised by the contextual dependence thesis is that tolerance, when guided by a deontological perspective of practical reason, obviates the value that ethical beliefs and other kind of values have for the *character* and for the *integrity* of individuals. In this way, the sense of loss or regret, that is taken as consubstantial to tolerance, becomes stronger or recalcitrant. Instead, the contextual response defends the idea that a structure of practical reason that gives a closer look to the contextual features and circumstances will also take into consideration the importance that ethical and other values have in the life of individuals, softening, in that way the sense of loss that is consubstantial of tolerance.

Deontological liberalism pays little attention to the ontological nature of tolerance by not conceiving it as the representation of a conflict between two moral requirements that seem important. On the contrary, for deontologism the priority of the 'right' over the 'good' seems to be the referential tool to disentangle the conflicts of tolerance without making any effort of *perceiving* the value of our ethical and other type of values.

The contextual response here considered, takes very seriously the idea of having a sense of loss or regret. According to this perspective the sense of loss or regret is far from being a mere feeling or a sentiment. It must be considered as a rational attitude that appears to be present in every case of tolerance, and that cannot be removed by making reference to the priority principle.

As we have seen in chapter 15, Bernard Williams says that the feeling of regret is due to the results that go beyond intention. In Williams's sense, we do not experience moral regret during our deliberation but after we decide what to do. Thus, regret is the outcome of a decision.

Dancy refines this idea by saying that:

> [Regret] is an attitude rather to a feature that *explains* the creation of residual duties—that is the source of those duties. As such an attitude, it would not be feeling involved (which there sometimes isn't), the nature of the feeling (its phenomenology) is not what we are after here, since that explains nothing. What we have in mind rather is the sense that though one indeed made the right choice, still either there was something of value which this choice lacked and another alternative did not lack, or there was something of disvalue which this choice had and another alternative lack. [17]

Taken in this sense, Dancy continues, "regret has two aspects, regret for an element of value which our choice lacks, and regret for an element of disvalue which our choice has. The second of these is shown to be rational, within the constraints of our approach, by the fact that the reasons against remain in the picture as salient features of the situation. The first is shown to be rational by the adoption of a form of pluralism which is committed [to an] intermediate form of incommensurability." [18]

Understood in this way, the idea of regret contains the one of 'lacking.' Any decision that we take will lack something of value that the other choice had. This is what other philosophers have called the moral residue. Lariguet, for example, distinguishes between two types of moral residue that can be generated when solving conflicts such as the ones of tolerance: one is a psychological residue, and the other is a normative residue. [19] Psychological residue relates to mental states such as 'guilt,' 'shame,' 'remorse,' 'sadness,' etc., whereas, normative residue refers to the existence of a norm, principle or value that has been set aside.

The distinction drawn by Lariguet is not idle from an analytical point of view. However, in general terms, both types of residues overlap. The loss that is experienced from not choosing a value (moral or ethical) that we consider as relevant has psychological expressions such as remorse or the feeling of guilt: in other words, abandoning a decision that we consider also as having something of value is the source of these psychological expressions. It is possible that exactly because of this, philosophers such as Bernard Williams or Martha Nussbaum always refer to this moral residue as a psychological matter rather than a normative consequence, since they presume that the former presupposes the latter. [20]

What I am interested in highlighting beyond this discussion, is something very brief: theoretical indifference in the face of a moral residue can also be seen as a mistake made by the deontological moral theories in order to account for acts of tolerance.

Typically, tolerance has been seen as the lesser of two evils. However, this conception of tolerance has been interpreted in different ways. One of them presents the two evils considering them as two instrumental costs; a conflict between an action that might entail greater consequences than those incurred by taking a different course of action (tolerating the Huguenots can bring economic benefits, whereas not tolerating them can bring benefits of social peace).[21] Under the scheme of tolerance as a moral ideal, we can also see tolerance as the decision between two evils. But in this case, the two evils faced by the tolerator are brought about by the fatal non-compliance with one of two values that are at stake (if I tolerate my son eating hamburgers I am allowing the continuing slaughter of animals for consumption, whereas if I do not tolerate him eating hamburgers, then I am violating his freedom and his autonomy). Deontological theories deny the possibility of a moral loss or sacrifice that can produce a sense of regret. This means that deontological theories deny the ontological status of an act of tolerance. It is due to this ontological perspective that tolerance traditionally has been understood as the lesser of two evils.

The central problem of all of this has been denounced by Bernard Williams in a text entitled *Ethical Consistency*. Williams explains the problem that even led Socrates himself to think, on one occasion, that some gods sustained false beliefs or unjustified claims precisely because men sometimes found themselves cornered by two moral claims.[22] Williams argues that the problem is found in equating the conflicts between moral convictions with conflicts between beliefs. In a conflict between beliefs, the most rational thing to do is to try to find out which one of the two conflicting beliefs is true. If one of them turns out to be true, then, by way of logical reasoning, the other one must be false and the individual will find that he/she needs to set it aside. Even in cases that involve believes, setting aside one of them that was thought to be true after discovering that it is not, can also generate a sense of loss. Consider a scientist or a historian who, because of this, loses a theory they thought to be correct and in which he had invested a great deal.[23]

Nevertheless, this is not the case for moral conflicts and it is because of this that they bear a greater resemblance to conflicts between desires. If, after the deliberation, one of them turns out to be victorious, the other one does not necessarily has to be considered false and, therefore, abandoned.[24]

At the end of his *Justice and the Limits of Liberalism* Michael Sandel makes a remarkable reflection related to the importance that liberal deontological theory gives to the 'good':

> for deontological doctrine such as Rawls' it might be thought that viewing the good as wholly mired in contingency, despite its implausibility generally, would have at least the redeeming advantage of making the primacy of right all the more compelling. If the good is nothing more than the indiscriminate satisfaction of arbitrarily given preferences, regardless of worth, it is not difficult to imagine that the right must overweight it.[25]

Deontological liberal theory as a theory of practical reason puts all the stress on the idea of the 'right' as a product of the 'Reasonable' for assessing the correctness of our actions. In this way, one of the main things that has been widely criticized, by Sandel and by many others[26] is that deontological structures of practical reason neglect the value that the conceptions of the good and ethical values have in the life of individuals.

Modern liberal deontologism, as we have seen, solves the problems of tolerance by primarily making reference to the priority of the 'right' over the 'good.' Nevertheless, this mechanism has been the target of most of our criticism. First, because with this principle the limits of tolerance become so rigid that they make out of this concept a suicidal concept. Second, because it does not provide a plausible way out from the 'dilemma of tolerance,' either because it rejects the existence of such kind of conflict or because it considers them as an epistemic deficiency of individuals who find themselves within a dilemmatic situation. And third, because deontologism as a structure of practical reason fails to provide a plausible explanation about the idea that in a conflict of tolerance our ethical values should be outweighed indisputably by moral norms without considering the facts and the circumstances that surround a case that calls for tolerance.

One of the problems that liberal deontological moral theories have to face is that *via* the priority principles they take conflicts of values as conflicts of beliefs: in conflict of values if one of the values is not reasonable, then it must be abandoned. This obviates the sense of regret that a rational choice between two important values can generate.

Now then, denying the practical relevance of the sense of regret makes deontological theories blind to a great deal of practical consequences that surround tolerance. Let us say that, if the tolerator can, by any means, forecast what loss or sacrifice he/she will produce with his/her decision this will put at odds the mere idea of tolerance. Here the question that has to be asked is: how rational it is to be tolerant under a structure of practical reason that does not pay attention to the significance that ethical values can (and in fact do) have in the life plans of individuals?

## NOTES

1. Hursthouse, *On Virtue*, 36.
2. Wallace, *Moral Relevance*, 65.
3. Wallace, *Moral Relevance*, 55.
4. Wallace, *Moral Relevance*, 65.
5. Jonathan Dancy, *Moral Reasons* (Oxford UK & Cambridge USA, Blackwell, 1993), 69.
6. Dancy, *Moral Reasons*, 80.
7. John McDowell, "Non-cognitivism and Rule-following," in *The New Wittgenstein*, ed. Alice Crary and Rupert Read (London/New York, Routledge, 2001), 42.

8. Dancy, *Moral Reasons*, 80.

9. Dancy, *Moral Reasons*, 80.

10. Dancy, *Moral Reasons*, 80.

11. Dancy, *Moral Reasons*, 81.

12. Jonathan Dancy, *Ethics without Principles* (Oxford, Clarendon Press, 2006), 71–89.

13. David Martínez Zorrilla, *Conflictos constitucionales, ponderación e indeterminación normativa* (España, Marcial Pons, Colección Filosofía y Derecho, 2007), 169.

14. Dancy, *Moral Reasons*, 112.

15. Dancy, *Moral Reasons*, 113.

16. Garrett Cullity and Richard Holton, "Particularism and Moral Theory," *Proceedings of the Aristotelian Society*, 76 (2002): 169-209; Garrett Cullity, "Particularism and Presumptive Reasons," *Proceedings of the Aristotelian Society*, 76 (2002): 169–190.

17. Dancy, *Moral Reasons*, 120. (Brackets are mine)

18. Dancy, *Moral Reasons*, 123.

19. Lariguet, *Encrucijadas*, 100–101.

20. Williams, *Shame*, 69-70; Nussbaum, *El Paisaje*, 21.

21. Maurice Cranston, "John Locke and the Case for Toleration," in *On Toleration*, ed. Mendus and Edwards, 102–103.

22. Nussbaum, *The Fragility*, 30.

23. Williams, "Ethical Consistency," in *Moral Dilemmas*, ed. Ch. Gowans, 120.

24. Williams, "Ehical Consistency," 117–118.

25. Sandel, *Liberalism*, 167.

26. MacIntyre, *After Virtue*; Taylor, *The Sources*; John Finnis, *Reason in Action: Collected Essays* (Oxford University Press, 2011), Vol. I, 128; Williams, *Ethics*, 16–17.

# Bibliography

Ackerman, Bruce. *Social Justice in the Liberal State*, Yale University Press, 1980.

Alchourrón, Carlos and Bulygin, Eugenio. *Análisis Lógico y Derecho*, Centro de Estudios Constitucionales, Madrid, 1991.

———. *Introducción a la Metodología de las Ciencias Jurídicas y Sociales*, Astrea, Buenos Áires, 1987.

Alexy, Robert. *Teoría de la Argumentación Jurídica*, Centro de Estudios Constitucionales, Madrid, 2008. (Robert Alexy, *Theorie der Juristischen Argumentation. Die Theorie des rationale Diskurses als Theorie der juristischen Begründung*, Suhrkamp Verlag, Frankfurt am Main, 1983).

———. *Teoría del discurso y derechos constitucionales*, Cátedra Ernesto Garzón Valdés, ITAM/UAM/ ELD/ INACIPE, Fontamara, México, 2004, pp. 47–70.

———. *Teoría de los derechos fundamentales*, Centro de Estudios Constitucionales, Madrid, 1993. (Robert Alexy, *Theorie der Grundrechte*, Suhrkamp-Verlag, 1986.)

Anscombe, G. E. M. "Modern Moral Philosophy," *Philosophy*, Vol. 33, No. 124, (Jan., 1958), pp. 1–19.

Aristotle. *Aristotle's Nicomachean Ethics. A new translation*, trans. Robert C. Barlett and Susan D. Collins, University of Chicago Press, 2011.

———. *The Nicomachean Ethics*, trans., F.H. Peters, M.A. 5th edition (London: Kegan Paul, Trench, Truebner & Co. 1893), Available at: http://oll.libertyfund.org/title/903on2013–07–10.

Armstrong, D.M. *A Materialist Theory of Mind*, Routledge, London & New York, 1993.

Arteta, Aurelio. "La tolerancia como barbarie," in Manuel Cruz (comp.) *Tolerancia o barbarie*, Gedisa, Barcelona, 1998, pp. 51–76.

Atienza, Manuel and Ruiz Manero, Juan. *Ilícitos Atípicos*, Trotta, Madrid, 2000.

———. *Marx y los derechos humanos*, Editorial Mezquita, Madrid, 1983.

Athanassoulis, Nafsika. "Virtue Ethics," *Internet Encyclopedia of Philosophy*, July, 2010.

Audard, Catherine. *John Rawls*, Acumen, England, 2007.

Audi, Robert. "Acting from Virtue," *Mind*, Vol. 104, No. 415, 1995, pp. 449–471.

Barry, Brian. *Theories of Justice*, University of California Press, 1989.

Berlin, Isaiah. *The Proper Study of Mankind. An Anthology of Essays*, Farrar, Straus and Giroux, New York, 2000.

Blum, Lawrence A. "Moral Perception and Particularity," *Ethics*, Vol. 101, No. 4, 1991, pp. 701–725.

———. "Iris Murdoch and the Domain of the Moral," *Philosophical Studies*, No. 50, Reidel Publishing Company, 1986, pp. 343–367.

Bobbio, Norberto. *Thomas Hobbes*, FCE, México, 1995.

Callcut, Daniel (ed.). *Reading Bernard Williams*, Routledge, London/New York, 2009.

Chappell, Sophie Grace. "Bernard Williams," *Stanford Philosophy Encyclopedia*, 2006.

Cohen, Andrew Jason. "What Toleration Is," *Ethics*, No. 115, 2004, pp. 68–95.

Comanducci, Paolo. "Sobre el problema de la tolerancia," Vázquez, Rodolfo (comp.), *Tolerancia y pluralismo*, Ediciones Coyoacán, México, 2005.

Constant, Benjamin. *Principles of Politics. Applicable to All Representative Governments*, Liberty Fund, Indianapolis, 2003.

Cranston, Maurice. "John Locke and the Case for Toleration," Mendus, Susan and Edwards, David (eds.), *On Toleration*, Clarendon Press, Oxford, 1987, pp. 101–121.

Crary, Alice and Read, Rupert (eds.). *The New Wittgenstein*, Routledge, London/New York, 2001.

Cruz, Manuel (comp.). *Tolerancia o barbarie*, Gedisa, Barcelona, 1998.

Cullity, Garrett, and Holton, Richard. "Particularism and Moral Theory," *Proceedings of the Aristotelian Society*, Supplementary Volumnes, Vol. 76, 2002, pp. 169–209; Part I, Cullity, Garrett, "Particularism and Presumptive Reasons," pp. 169–190.

Dancy, Jonathan. *Ethics without Principles*, Clarendon Press, Oxford, 2006.

———. *Moral Reasons*, Blackwell, Oxford-Cambridge, 1993.

———. "Ethical Particularism and Morally Relevant Properties," *Mind*, New Series, Vol. 92, N0. 368, 1983, pp. 530–547.

Darwall, Stephen L. "Two Kinds of Respect," *Ethics*, Vol. 88, No. 1, 1977, pp. 36–49.

De Lucas, Javier. "¿Para dejar de hablar de la tolerancia?," *Doxa. Cuadernos de filosofía del derecho*, No. 11, Alicante, España, 1992, pp. 117–126.

Dworkin, Gerald. *The Theory and Practice of Autonomy*, Cambridge University Press, 1997.

Dworkin, Ronald. *Justice for Hedgehogs*, The Belknap Press of Harvard University Press, 2011.

———. "Do Liberal Values Conflict?," Lilla, Mark, Dworkin, Ronald and Silvers, Robert B. (ed.), *The Legacy of Isaiah Berlin*, New York Review of Books, 2001, pp. 73–90.

———. *A Matter of Principle*, Harvard University Press, 1985.

———. *Taking Rights Seriously*, Harvard University Press, 1978.

Elster, Jon. *Taming Chance: Randomization in Individual and Social Decisions*, The Tanner Lectures on Human Rights, Utah University Press, IX, 1988.

Farrell, Martín Diego. *Utilitarismo, Liberalismo y Democracia*, Fontamara, BEFDP, México, 2007.

———. *Privacidad, autonomía y tolerancia. Ruidos disonantes en ética*, Hammurabi, Buenos Aires, Argentina, 2000.

Ferrajoli, Luigi. *Derechos y Garantías. La Ley del más fuerte*, Trotta, Madrid, 1999.

Finnis, John. *Natural Law and Natural Rights*, Oxford University Press, 2011.

———. *Reason in Action. Collected Essays*, Vol. I, Oxford University Press, 2011.

Firth, Roderick. "Ethical Absolutism and the Ideal Observer," *Philosophy and Phenomenological Research*, 12, 3 (Mar, 1952): 317–345.

Forst, Rainer. *The Right to Justification. Elements of a Constructivist Theory of Justice*, Columbia University Press, 2012.

———. "Toleration," *Stanford Encyclopedia of Philosophy*, 2007.

———. "Toleration, Justice and Reason," McKinnon, Catriona and Castiglione, Dario (ed.), *The Culture of Toleration in Diverse Societies. Reasonable Tolerance*, Manchester University Press, 2003, pp. 71–85.

———. *Toleranz im Konflikt*, Francfort del Meno: Suhrkamp, 2003.

———. *Contexts of Justice. Political Philosophy beyond Liberalism and Communitarianism*, University of California Press, 2002.

Foot, Philippa. *Virtues and Vices and Other Essays in Moral Philosophy*, University of California Press, 1978.

Freeman, Samuel (ed.). *John Rawls. Collected Papers*, Harvard University Press, 2001.

Fried, Charles. *Right and Wrong*, Harvard University Press, 1978.

Garzón Valdés, Ernesto. "¿Cuál es la relevancia moral del concepto de dignidad humana?," in Eugenio Bulygin, *El Positivism Jurídico*, Cátedra Ernesto Garzón Valdés, Fontamara, México, 2005, pp. 13–58.

———. "El sentido actual de la tolerancia," in Robert Alexy, *Teoría del discurso y derechos constitucionales*, Cátedra Ernesto Garzón Valdés, ITAM/UAM/ ELD/ INACIPE, Fontamara, México, 2004, pp. 13–43.

———. *Instituciones Suicidas. Ensayos de Ética y Política*, Paidós-UNAM, México, 2000.

———. "Algunas reflexiones más acerca del concepto de tolerancia. Comentarios a los comentarios de Pablo Navarro," *Doxa. Cuadernos de filosofía del derecho*, Alicante, España, No. 14, 1993, pp. 423–428.

———. *Derecho, Ética y Política*, Centro de Estudios Constitucionales, Madrid, 1993.

Gauthier, David. *Morals by Agreement*, Oxford University Press, 1986,

Gerard, Philippe. *Droit et Démocratie. Réflexions sur la Légitimité du Droit dan la Société Démocratique*, Publications des Facultés Universitaires Saint-Louis, Bruxells, 1995.

Gowans, Christopher W. (ed.). *Moral Dilemmas*, Oxford University Press, 1987.

———. "Introduction: The Debate on Moral Dilemmas," Christopher W. Gowans (ed.), *Moral Dilemmas*, Oxford University Press, 1987, pp. 3–33.

Graham, Gordon. "Tolerance, Pluralism, and Relativism," Heyd, David (ed.), *Toleration. An elusive virtue*, Princeton University Press, 1996, pp. 44–59.

Gray, John and Smith, G. W. (ed.). *On Liberty in Focus*, Routledge, London/New York, 1996.

Green, Leslie. "On Being Tolerated," paper delivered at "The Legacy of HLA Hart" Seminar, *Cambridge Forum for Legal and Political Philosophy*, July 28, 2007.

Guariglia, Osvaldo. *Moralidad. Ética Universalista y Sujeto Moral*, FCE, México, 1996.

Halberstam, Joshua. "The Paradox of Tolerance," in *The Philosophical Forum*, 1982–83, Vol. 190, pp. 190–206.

Hare, Richard Mervin. *Moral Thinking*, Oxford University Press, 1989.

———. "Moral Conflicts," *The Tanner Lectures on Human Values*, The Utah State University, October 1978.

———. "Wrongness and harm," in R. M. Hare, *Essays on Moral Concepts*, London, 1972.

———. *Freedom and Reason*, Clarendon Press, Oxford, 1964.

Harrison, Geoffrey. "Relativism and Tolerance," *Ethics*, Vol. 86, No. 2, 1976, pp. 122–135.

Hart, H. L. A. *The Concept of Law*, Clarendon Law Series, Oxford, 1997.

Hawthorn, Geoffrey (ed.). *In the Beginning was the Deed. Realism and Moralism in Political Argument*, Princeton University Press, 2005.

Heyd, David (ed.). *Toleration. An elusive virtue*, Princeton University Press, 1996.

Heysse, Tim. Toleration and Political Conflict. A Comment on Rainer Forst's Analysis of Toleration," *Bijdragen. International Journal in Philosophy and Theology*, Vol. 7. No. 4, 2010, pp. 391–406.

———. and Segaert, Barbara, "Perplexities of Tolerance. Introduction," *Bijdragen. International Journal in Philosophy and Theology*, Vol. 71, No. 4, 2010, pp. 351–357.

Hobbes, Thomas. *Leviathan*, Penguin Classics, 1985.

Horton, John and Mendus, Susan (ed.). *Aspects of Toleration. Philosophical Studies*, Methuen, London/New York, 1985.

———. "Toleration as a Virtue," Heyd, David (ed.), *Toleration. An elusive virtue*, Princeton University Press, 1996, pp. 28–43.

Hurka, Thomas. *Perfectionism*, Oxford University Press, 1993

———. "Why Value Autonomy?," *Social Theory and Practice*, Vol. 13, No. 3, 1987, pp. 361–382.

Hursthouse, Rosalind. *On Virtue Ethics*, Oxford University Press, 1999.

Kagan, Shelly. *The Limits of Morality*, Clarendon Press, Oxford, 1989.

Kant, Immanuel. *Fundamental Principles of the Metaphysics of Morals*, Forgotten Books, 2008.

———. *Groundwork of the Metaphysics of Morals*, Cambridge University Press, 1997.

Kelsen, Hans. *Teoría Pura del Derecho*, Universidad Autónoma de México, 1976. (Hans Kelsen, *Reine Rechtslehre*, Auflage, Wein, 1960)

Kekes, John. *The Morality of Pluralism*, Princeton University Press, 1993.

Kraut, Richard. "Aristotle's Ethics," *Stanford Encyclopedia of Philosophy*, 2010.

Kymlicka, Will. "Liberal Individualism and Liberal Neutrality," *Ethics*, Vol. 99, No. 4, 1989, pp. 883–905.

Lariguet, Guillermo. *Encrucijadas Morales. Una aproximación a los Dilemas y su Impacto en el razonamiento Práctico*, Theoria cum Praxi, Madrid/México, 2011.

———. *Dilemas y Conflictos Trágicos. Una Investigación Conceptual*, Temis-Palestra, Lima-Bogota, 2008.

———. "Conflictos trágicos genuinos, ponderación y límites de la racionalidad jurídica. En torno a algunas ideas de Manuel Atienza," *Isonomía. Revista de Teoría y Filosofía del Derecho*, No. 24, ITAM, México, 2006, pp. 93–114.

———. "Conflictos trágicos y Derecho. Posibles Desafíos," *Doxa*, No. 27, Alicante, 2004, pp. 317–348.

Larmore, Charles. "Political Liberalism," *Political Theory*, Vol. 18, No. 3, 1990, pp. 339–360.

———. *Patterns of Moral Complexity*, Cambridge University Press, 1987.

Lemmon, E. J. "Moral Dilemmas," *The Philosophical Review*, Vol. 71, No. 2, 1962, pp. 139–158.

Lilla, Mark, Dworkin, Ronald and Silvers, Robert B. (ed.). *The Legacy of Isaiah Berlin*, New York Review of Books, 2001.

Locke, John. "A Letter Concerning Toleration, being a Translation of the Epistola de Tolerantia, *On line Library of Liberty, The Works of John Locke*, Vol. 5, 2010.

MacCormik, Neil. *Legal Reasoning and Legal Theory*, Clarendon Law Series, Oxford, 1994.

MacIntyre, Alasdair. *Whose Justice? Which Rationality?*, Duckworth, London, 1988.

———. *After Virtue*, University of Notre Dame Press, 2007.

Mackie, J. L. *Truth, Probability and Paradox. Studies in Philosophical Logic*, Oxford University Press, 1973.

Marcus, Ruth Barcan. "Moral Dilemmas and Consistency," *The Journal of Philosophy*, Vol. 77, No. 3, 1980, pp. 121–136.

Marcuse, Herbert. "Repressive Tolerance," Wolff, Robert Paul, Moore Jr., Barrington, Marcuse, Herbert, *A Critique of Pure Tolerance*, Beacon Press, Boston, 1969, pp. 81–123.

Martínez Zorrilla, David. *Conflictos constitucionales, ponderación e indeterminación normativa*, Marcial Pons, Colección Filosofía y Derecho, España, 2007.

Markovits, Daniel. "The Architecture of Integrity," Callcut, Daniel (ed.), *Reading Bernard Williams*, Routledge, London/New York, 2009, pp. 110–138.

McDowell, John. "Non-cognitivism and Rule-following," Crary, Alice and Read, Rupert (ed.), *The New Wittgenstein*, Routledge, London/New York, 2001, pp. 38–52.

———. "Virtue and Reason," *The Monist*, No. 62, 1979, pp. 331–350.

McKinnon, Catriona. *Toleration: A Critical Introduction*, Routledge Press, 2006.

———, and Castiglione, Dario (ed.). *The Culture of Toleration in Diverse Societies. Reasonable Tolerance*, Manchester University Press, 2003.

Mellor, D. H. "In Defense of Dispositions," *The Philosophical Review*, No. 83, 1974, pp. 158–181.

Mendus, Susan. *Toleration and the Limits of Liberalism*, MacMillan, London, 1989.

———, (ed.). *Justifying Toleration. Conceptual and Historical Perspectives*, Cambridge University Press, 1988.

———, and Edwards, David. *On Toleration*, Clarendon Press, Oxford, 1987.

Meyerson, Denis. "Three Versions of Liberal Tolerance: Dworkin, Rawls and Raz," *Jurisprudence*, Vol. 3, No. 1, 2012, pp. 37–70.

Mill, John Stuart. *On Liberty*, in John Gray and G. W. Smith (ed.), *On Liberty in Focus*, Routledge, New York, 1996, pp. 23–128.

Mohino, Juan Carlos Bayón. *La normatividad del Derecho: deber jurídico y razones para la acción* (Madrid, Centro de Estudios Constitucionales, 1991).

Moore, A.W. (ed.). *Philosophy as a Humanistic Discipline*, Princeton University Press, Princeton and Oxford, 2006.

Mosteller, Timothy. *Relativism. A Guide for the Perplexed*, Continuum, New York, 2008.

Muguerza, Javier. *Desde la perplejidad*, Fondo de Cultura Económica, México, 1990.

Mulhall, Stephen and Swift, Adam. *Liberals & Communitarians*, Blackwell Publishing, 1996.

Murdoch, Iris. *The Sovereignty of Good*, Routledge Classics, 2002.

Nagel, Thomas. *Equality and Partiality*, Oxford University Press, 1991.

———. "Moral Conflict and Political Legitimacy," *Philosophy & Public Affairs*, Vol. 16, No. 3, 1987, pp. 215–240.

Nancy Fraser. "Recognition without ethics?," McKinnon, Catriona and Castiglione, Dario (ed.), *The Culture of Toleration in Diverse Societies. Reasonable Tolerance*, Manchester University Press, 2003, pp. 86–108.

Navarro, Pablo. "Reflexiones acerca del concepto de tolerancia," *Doxa. Cuadernos de Filosofía del Derecho*, No. 13, Alicante, España, 1993, pp. 277–284.

Newey, Glen. *Virtue, Reason and Toleration. The Place of Toleration in Ethical and Political Philosophy*, Edinburgh University Press, 1999.

Nicholson, Peter. "Toleration as a Moral Ideal," in John Horton, Susan Mendus (ed.), *Aspects of Toleration. Philosophical Studies*, Methuen, London/New York, 1985, pp. 158–173.

Nino, Carlos S. *Ética y Derechos Humanos. Un Ensayo de Fundamentación*, Astrea, Argentina, 2005.

Nussbaum, Martha C. *The Fragility of Goodness. Luck and Ethics in Greek Tragedy and Philosophy*, Cambridge University Press, 2001.

———. *El Paisaje del Pensamiento. La inteligencia de las emociones*, Paidós, Barcelona, 2008.

Ohlsson, Ragnar. "Who Can Accept Moral Dilemmas?," *The Journal of Philosophy*, Vol. 90, No. 8, 1993, pp. 405–415.

Ovejero, Félix. *Incluso un Pueblo de Demonios: Democracia, Liberalismo, Republicanismo*, Katz, Madrid, 2008.

Plato. *The Republic*, Penguin Classics, 2003.

Pogge, Thomas. *John Rawls. His Life and Theory of Justice*, Oxford University Press, 2007.

Popper, Karl. *The Open Society and Its Enemies*, Routledge Classics, Two Volumes, London/New York, 2005.

———. "Toleration and Intellectual Responsibility," in S. Mendus, D. Edwards, *On Toleration*, Clarendon Press, Oxford, 1987, pp. 17–34.

Raphael, D. D. "The Intolerable," Mendus, Susan (ed.), *Justifying Toleration. Conceptual and Historical Perspectives*, Cambridge University Press, 1988, pp. 137–153.

Rawls, John. "The Idea of Public Reason Revisited" (1997), Samuel Freeman (ed.), *John Rawls. Collected Papers*, Harvard University Press, 2001.

———. "The Priority of Right and Ideas of the Good" (1988), Samuel Freeman (ed.), *John Rawls. Collected Papers*, Harvard University Press, 2001, pp. 449–472.

———. "The idea of an Overlapping Consensus" (1987), Samuel Freeman (ed.), *John Rawls. Collected Papers*, Harvard University Press, 2001, pp. 421–448.

———. "Justice as Fairness: Political not Metaphysical" (1985), Samuel Freeman (ed.), *John Rawls. Collected Papers*, Harvard University Press, 2001, pp. 388–414.

———. "Kantian Constructivism in Moral Theory" (1980), Samuel Freeman (ed.), *John Rawls. Collected Papers*, Harvard University Press, 2001, pp. 303–358.

———. "Fairness to Goodness" (1975), Samuel Freeman (ed.), *John Rawls. Collected Papers*, Harvard University Press, 2001, pp. 267–284.

———. "Outline of a Decision Procedure of Ethics" (1951), Samuel Freeman (ed.), *John Rawls. Collected Papers*, Harvard University Press, 2001, pp. 1–19.

———. *A Theory of Justice*, Oxford University Press, 1999.

———. *Political Liberalism*, Columbia University Press, 1996.

———. "Constitutional Liberty and the Concept of Justice," *Nomos*, vol. VI, *Justice*, 1963.

Raz, Joseph. *Ethics in the Public Domain. Essays in the Morality of Law and Politics*, Clarendon Press, Oxford, 1995.

———. *Practical Reason and Norms*, Princeton University Press, 1990.

———. "Autonomy, Toleration, and the Harm Principle," in Susan Mendus (ed.), *Justifying Toleration. Conceptual and Historical Perspectives*, Cambridge University Press, 1988, pp. 155–175.

———. *The Morality of Freedom*, Clarendon Press, Oxford, 1985.

———. *The Concept of a Legal System. An Introduction to the Theory of Legal System*, 2° ed., Clarendon Press, Oxford, 1980.

Rees, J. C. "A Re-Reading of Mill on Liberty," *Political Studies*, Vol. 8, No. 2, 1960, pp. 113–129.

Rivera, Fabiola. "Rawls, Filosofía y Tolerancia," Vázquez, Rodolfo (comp.), *Tolerancia y Pluralismo* Ediciones Coyoacán, México, 2005, pp. 135–165.

Rivera López, Eduardo. *Ensayos sobre Liberalismo y Comunitarismo*, Fontamara, BEFDP, No. 58, México, 1999.

Rorty, Richard. "The Prioriy of Democracy to Philosophy," in Merril D. Peterson and Robert V. Vaughan (eds.), *The Virginia Statute for Religious Freedom*, Cambridge University Press, 1988, pp. 257–282.

Rosenblum, Nancy L. (ed.). *Liberalism and the Moral Life*, Harvard University Press, 1989.

Ross, W. D. *The Right and the Good*, Oxford University Press, 2003.

Ryan, Alan. "Mr. McCloskey on Mill's Liberalism," *The Philosophical Quarterly*, Vol. 14, No. 56, 1964, pp. 253–260.

Ryle, Gilbert. *Concept of Mind*, Routledge, London & New York, 2009.

Sandel, Michael J. "Morality and the Liberal Ideal," in *Public Philosophy. Essays on Morality in Politics*, Harvard University Press, 2006.

———. *Public Philosophy. Essays on Morality in Politics*, Harvard University Press, 2005.

———. *Liberalism and the Limits of Justice*, Cambridge University Press, Second Edition, 1998.

———. *Democracy's Discontent. America in Search of Public Philosophy*, The Belknap Press of Harvard University Press, 1998.

———. "Moral Argument and Liberal Toleration: Abortion and Homosexuality," *California Law Review*, Vol. 77, No. 3, 1989, pp. 521–538.

Scanlon, T. M. "The Difficulty of Tolerance," Heyd, David (ed.), *Toleration. An elusive virtue*, Princeton University Press, 1996, pp. 226–239.

Schmitt, Annette. "Las circunstancias de la tolerancia," *Doxa. Cuadernos de filosofía del derecho*, No. 11, Alicante, Spain, 1992, pp. 71–85.

Silva-Herzog, Jesús. "Razones para la Tolerancia," Vázquez, Rodolfo (Comp.), *Tolerancia y Pluralismo*, Ediciones Coyoacán, México, 2005, pp. 83–95.

Smart, J. J. C. and Williams, Bernard. *Utilitarianism. For and against*, Cambridge University Press, 1973.

Smith, A. D. "Dispositional Properties," *Mind*, New Series, Vol. 86, No. 343, 1977, pp. 439–445.

Smith, Steven D. "The Restoration of Tolerance," *California Law Review*, Vol. 78. No. 2 (Mar., 1990), pp. 305–356.

Sher, George. *Beyond Neutrality. Perfectionism and Politics*, Cambridge University Press, 1997.

Shklar, Judith N. "The Liberalism of Fear," Rosenblum, Nancy L. (ed.), *Liberalism and the Moral Life*, Harvard University Press, 1989, pp. 21–38.

Taylor, Charles. *Sources of the Self. The Making of Modern Identity*, Cambridge University Press, 1992.

———. *Hegel and Modern Society*, Cambridge University Press, 1979.

Ten, C. L. "Mill on Self-Regarding Actions," *Philosophy*, Vol. 43, No. 163, 1968, pp. 29–37.

Timpe, Kevin. "Moral Character," *Internet Encyclopedia of Philosophy*, 2008.

Trujillo, Isabell. *Imparcialidad*, Instituto de Investigaciones Jurídicas de la UNAM, México, 2007.

Vázquez, Rodolfo. *Las Fronteras Morales del Derecho*, Fontamara, BEFDP, No. 112, México, 2010.

———. *Entre la Libertad y la Igualdad. Introducción a la Filosofía del Derecho*, ed. Trotta, Madrid, 2006.

———, (comp.). *Tolerancia y pluralismo*, Ediciones Coyoacán, México, 2005.

———. *Liberalismo, Estado de Derecho y minorías*, Paidos-UNAM, México, 2001.

Vernon, Richard and LaSelva, Samuel V. "Justifying Tolerance," *Canadian Journal of Political Science, Revue canadienne de science politique*, Vol. 17, No. 1, 1984, pp. 3–23.

Vicent, Manuel. *No pongas tus sucias manos sobre Mozart,* Madrid, Debate, 1983.

Villoro, Luis. *Creer, saber, conocer*, Siglo Veintiuno ed., México, 1982.

von Wright, Georg Henrik. *An Essay in Deontic Logic and the General Theory of Action* (Amsterdam, North-Holland, 1968) 80.

von Wright, Georg Henrik. *The Varieties of Goodness,* Routledge & Kegan Paul, New York, 1963.

Waldron, Jeremy. *Law and Disagreement* (Oxford University Press, 1999), 1.

Wallace, James D. *Moral Relevance and Moral Conflict*, Cornell University Press, 1988.

Wall, Steven. *Liberalism, Perfectionism and Restraint,* Cambridge University Press, 1998.

Warnock, Mary. "The Limits of Toleration," in Susan Mendus and David Edwards (eds.), *On Toleration,* Clarendon Press, Oxford, 1987,pp. 123–139.

Williams, Bernard. "Toleration: An Impossible Virtue?," David Heyd (ed.), *Toleration. An elusive virtue,* Princeton University Press, 1996, pp. 18–27.

———. "Tolerating the Intolerable" (1999), Moore, A.W. (ed.), *Philosophy as a Humanistic Discipline*, Princeton University Press, Princeton and Oxford, 2006, pp. 126–152.

———. "The Liberalism of Fear," Hawthorn, Geoffrey (ed.), *In the Beginning was the Deed. Realism and Moralism in Political Argument*, Princeton University Press, 2005, pp. 52–61.

———. "Toleration, a Political or Moral Question?," Hawthorn, Geoffrey (ed.), *In the Beginning was the Deed. Realism and Moralism in Political Argument*, Princeton University Press, 2005, pp. 128–138.

———. *Shame and Necessity,* University of California Press, 1993.

———. *Morality: an Introduction to Ethics,* Cambridge University Press, 1993.

———. *Moral Luck. Philosophical Papers 1973–1980,* Cambridge University Press, 1981.

———. *Ethics and the Limits of Philosophy,* Harvard University Press, 1985.

———. *Problems of the Self,* Cambridge University Press, 1973.

Wintgens, Luc J. *Droit, Principes et Théories. Pour un Positivisme Critique*, Bruylant, Bruxelles, 2000.

———. "Les Possibilités et les Limits du Langage Libéral," *Archives de Philosophie du Droit*, Droit et Économie, 1992, pp. 205–226.

Wolff, Robert Paul, Moore Jr., Barrington, Marcuse, Herbert. *A Critique of Pure Tolerance*, Beacon Press, Boston, 1969.

Zimmerling, Ruth. *El Concepto de Influencia y otros Ensayos*, Fontamara, BEFDP, No. 33, México, 1993.

Zizek, Slavoj. *Defensa de la intolerancia*, Sequitur, Madrid, 2007.

# Index

# About the Author

René González de la Vega is professor of political and moral philosophy at the National Autonomous University of Mexico. He is the author of *La Filosofía del Derecho de Ernesto Garzón Valdés: Una Biografía Intelectual sobre la primera parte de su obra*, and with Guillermo Lariguet, he published the book *Problemas de Filosofía del Derecho: Nuevas Perspectivas*. Currently he is in charge of the research department of the Federal Judiciary Institute and he has been Mexico's representative in the Organization of American States.

CPSIA information can be obtained at www.ICGtesting.com
Printed in the USA
BVOW04*0033131016

464871BV00002B/3/P